... FAREWELL TO OLD ENGLAND FOREVER...

the story of those who emigrated to the Australian colonies by sailing ship in the nineteenth century.

Doug Limbrick

Published in Australia by Doug Limbrick

First published in Australia by Doug Limbrick 2017
Copyright © Doug Limbrick 2017

This work is copyright. No part of this publication may be reproduced, stored in a retrieval system or transmitted in any form or by any means electronic, mechanical, photocopying, recording or otherwise, without the prior consent of the publisher.

Cataloguing-in-Publication detail available from the National Library of Australia.

Author: Limbrick/ Doug
Title: Farewell to Old England Forever
ISBN: 978-0-646-96826-1 (paperback)

Interior design and typesetting by Publicious
Book cover design by Jeremy Limbrick

Published with the assistance of
Publicious Book Publishing
www.publicious.com.au

Other nonfiction books by the author:

    From the Wars of the Roses to Colonial Victoria

    The *Stag* Diary – Passage to Colonial Adelaide 1850

    Running the Marathon With Cancer

For more details see: www.douglimbrick.com

Comments/enquiries to: info@douglimbrick.com

Front cover:

Tom Roberts
Coming South 1886
oil on canvas
63.5 x 52.2 cm
National Gallery of Victoria, Melbourne
Gift of Colonel Aubrey H. L. Gibson (Rtd)
in memory of John and Anne Gibson,
settlers (1887), 1967 (1738-5).

This book is dedicated to those individuals and families who journeyed half way around the world on small sailing vessels during the nineteenth century seeking a better life in the Australian colonies.

Acknowledgements

A number of people provided invaluable assistance during the course of my writing this book. I am particularly grateful for the resources that are available through the vast collection of material at the National Library of Australia (NLA). The considerable holdings on microfilm, available as a consequence of the Australian Joint Copying Project, were heavily drawn upon. Original documents and old manuscripts were readily available through the various library-reading rooms. My thanks go to the staff of the NLA for their assistance and patience. The Woden Valley Branch of the Canberra Library has also been of considerable assistance in locating many publications for me to borrow while researching this project. I would also like to acknowledge the assistance provided by the State Library of Victoria and the State Library of New South Wales with pictorial material and the assistance provided by the staff of the Mortlock Reading Room of the State Library of South Australia. I would also like to thank the National Gallery of Victoria for approving the use of a gallery painting by Tom Roberts (*Coming South* 1886) for the book cover. My editor Dr Pam Faulks (Clarity Proofreading & Editing) made valuable suggestions during the final drafting process for which I am grateful. A considerable amount of design and graphics assistance has been provided by Jeremy Limbrick, which has considerably enhanced this publication. My thanks also to family and friends who showed interest in this project and offered encouragement and advice.

Author's Note for readers:

Measures of distance and weight and type of currency have been maintained, as they were in nineteenth century Britain and the Australian colonies. Hence metric and decimal terms are not used. Thus to assist readers who may want to convert terms used in this book the following may be of use:

- 1 mile is approximately equivalent to 1.6 kilometres;

- 1 yard is approximately equivalent to 0.9 metres;

- 1 foot is approximately equivalent to 0.3 metres;

- 1 ton is approximately equivalent to 1.02 tonnes;

- 1 ounce is approximately equivalent to 28.4 grams;

- 1 gallon is approximately equivalent to 4.5 litres;

- 70° Fahrenheit is approximately equivalent to 21° Celsius.

It should be noted that the currency used in this book comprises pounds (£), shillings (s) and pence (d).

This book contains many quotations from historic sources including letters, diaries, pamphlets and newspapers. In using these quotations I have left any misspellings intact and avoided the use of commonly used terms to identify misspellings (such as the Latin word: *sic*).

Contents

List of Illustrations x

Preface xiii

Chapter 1 - Early Arrivals. 1

Chapter 2 - The Emigration Debate 15

Chapter 3 - Deciding to Emigrate 24

Chapter 4 - Those Who Came 84

Chapter 5 - The Emigrant Vessels and their Crews 104

Chapter 6 - Preparation and Embarkation 141

Chapter 7 - Passage to the Colonies 181

Chapter 8 - Arriving 216

Appendices

     A. Calendar of Key Nineteenth-Century Events. . . . 248

     B. Glossary of Terms. 261

Bibliography 265

Index 272

List of Illustrations

Chapter 1
1. Sketch of a Macassan Prau
2. First Fleet Anchored in Sydney Cove 27 January 1788 – painting by John Allcot.
3. Hobart Town on the River Derwent 1830 – painting by W J Huggins.

Chapter 2
4. Rubbish is not to be shot here – The Bulletin, 11 August 1883.

Chapter 3
5. Female Emigration to Australia – Poster for encouraging female emigration 1834.
6. Montage of Life on the Diggings

Chapter 5
7. Sail Plan – ***Lady Ebrington.***
8. Diagram of Sail Rigging comparing a Ship & a Barque.
9. ***Thermopylae*** duelling with the ***Cutty Sark.***
10. The ***Cutty Sark*** – watercolour by F Brown.
11. The ***Schromberg.***
12. The ***Great Britain*** Among the Icebergs – wood engraving Illustrated Sydney News, 21 January 1871.
13. The ***Great Britain*** on display Bristol – photographs by author 2009.
14. The Steamer ***Croesus*** on her maiden voyage to Sydney 1854.
15. The ***Marco Polo*** - painting by Thomas Robertson.
16. American Clipper ***Red Jacket*** 1853 – watercolour by D M Little.
17. The ***Lightening*** – watercolour by D M Little.

18 Below Decks Sketch of ship ***Bourneuf.***
19 The ***Preussen*** – watercolour by C Dickson Gregory.
20 The ***Dover Castle***, 1033 tons built 1858.
21 Montage of seven "boats past & present" – published Melbourne 1890.

Chapter 6

22 Irish Emigrants Leaving Home Priest's Blessing. – Illustrated London News, 1851
23 Government Emigration Depot Birkenhead – Illustrated London News, 10 July 1852.
24 The Embarkation, Waterloo Docks, Liverpool - Illustrated London News, 6 July 1850
25 Emigrants Embarking – Australian Sketcher 18 December 1880.
26 Emigrant Ship ***St Vincent*** Being Towed Out –Illustrated London News, 13 April 1844.
27 The ***Prince of Wale***s – old East Indiaman.
28 Cross Section of a Square Rigged Vessel – by Jeremy Limbrick.
29 Emigrant Ship Between Decks – Illustrated London News 17 August 1850.

Chapter 7

30 Sketches on Board an Emigrant Ship – Illustrated Australian News, 24 March 1875 (engraver Samuel Calvert).
31 Map Showing the Two Routes Used to Sail to the Australian Colonies.
32 Vessel in Big Seas.
33 Photograph of the ***Torrens*** damaged after striking an iceberg.
34 The ***Constance*** on Her Passage from Plymouth to Adelaide 1849 – artist T G Dutton.
35 Furling the Sails, ship ***Discovery***.
36 Emigrants at Dinner: typical scene of steerage class emigrants beneath decks – Illustrated London News, 13 April 1844.
37 A Burial at Sea, 1880 – illustrated Australian News, November 1880.
38 Montage of Emigrants Going to Australia.

Chapter 8

39   The Emigrants – Illustrated London News, 19 June 1852.
40   The ***Dunbar***, Lost at the Gap Sydney 1857.
41   The ***Loch Ard*** Breaking Up – Australian Sketcher, 13 June 1878.
42   Landing Passengers from Immigrant Ship ***Jerusalem***.
43   Emigrants Landing at Queen's Wharf, Melbourne by Nicholas Chevalier.
44   Queen's Wharf, Melbourne 1850's – artist S T Gill.

Preface

"O ye that sleep in lonely graves by distant ridge and plain,
We drink to you in silence now as Christmas comes again,
To you who fought the wilderness through rough unsettled years –
The founders of our nation's life, the brave old pioneers."[1]

A considerable number of years ago, at 3 pm on a very hot January afternoon, I was baptised Douglas Norton Limbrick in a small timber church in rural Gillenbah, New South Wales, a short distance from the farm of my maternal grandparents, Jeremiah and Anne Norton. Jeremiah and Anne were both the children of emigrants. They had met and married in country Victoria and gradually moved north in wagons seeking a better life. Like many other pioneers they eventually established their own farm on which they managed to raise nine children.

The small church where I was baptised and the nearby one-room school were the meeting places of this farming community. They served well the families that pioneered that area, but like similar buildings in many other small rural communities, they have been the victims of progress and development and, consequently no longer exist.

I am sure that many readers will be able to relate to the story of disappearing rural communities like Gillenbah through their own family histories and personal experiences. The pioneering families who selected land and who established those small rural communities represent part of the nineteenth-century Australian emigration story. I suspect that in some small way my curiosity about family pioneers contributed to the development of my long-term interest and, later, passion,

---

1. Patterson, A.B. *Pioneers.* The Collected Verse of A.B.Patterson, Angus & Robertson, 1964, p236.

about nineteenth-century emigration, and to my decision to spend an enormous amount of time researching the emigration process and subsequently writing this book.

In researching nineteenth-century emigration I quickly developed a fascination for the stories of those individuals who emigrated and settled in the colonies. After delving into this subject for several years it became clear to me that the full story about nineteenth- century emigration (the reasons why people decided to emigrate, the processes involved, the difficult decisions to be made, the assistance given, the emigration vessels, the journey and the arrival process) was not readily available within the one publication (at least not in a form that satisfied my curiosity about the operation of the emigration process and how it came together to enable the nineteenth-century emigrants to embark on the longest sea passage of that period). Of course I don't deny the existence of many wonderful and informative publications dealing with the history of the Australian colonies and about immigration/emigration, including excellent insights into the happenings of the nineteenth century. In fact, during my research for this book I consulted many publications and other material dealing with ships, shipping and immigration/emigration in the nineteenth century (they are referenced in this book). However, there seemed to be a dearth of publications that provided the comprehensive overview of nineteenth-century emigration to Australia, from start to finish, that I was particularly searching for. The process of nineteenth-century emigration to the colonies under sail I feel is a vital part of Australian history. My aim was thus to tell this story in a way that would be easily readable by a wide cross section of people interested in the story of nineteenth-century emigration, the old sailing vessels and the shaping of the colonies.

Undertaking the research for this book has taken me on an excursion through many fascinating old documents, including many originals. I have spent many hours reading a large number of manuscripts, diaries, letters, ships logs, etc. One of my dilemmas was in deciding what to use and what to discard in order to achieve a balance of views and insights (particularly from the viewpoint of the nineteenth-century emigrant). I trust that I have made the right choices and I hope that I have done them justice in my attempt to distil from them the feelings of the writers within a nineteenth-century context and to utilise them in a way that would be meaningful and interesting to contemporary readers. My aim has been to make a broad cross-section of this enormous amount of material accessible to people of all ages interested in Australian history.

I hope that readers get as much enjoyment from reading about the story of those who emigrated to the colonies in the nineteenth century as I did in researching and writing it. I thus wish you happy reading.

Doug Limbrick

CHAPTER 1

Early Arrivals

From distant climes o'er wide spread seas we come,
Though not with much eclat or beat of drum,
True patriots all, for be it understood,
We left our country for our country's good.[2]

During the course of the nineteenth century large numbers of men, women and children left their homes and came by sailing vessel as emigrants to the Australian colonies. They faced many difficult decisions, often based on little or conflicting information. Having decided to emigrate they still faced many uncertainties, had to contend with a long and hazardous sea passage and reconcile themselves to the knowledge that they would probably never see friends and relatives again. Those who emigrated to North America in large numbers faced similar decisions, but the length of their journey was relatively short compared to a journey to the Australian colonies. Surely the first journey to the moon in the twentieth century was undertaken with a much greater certainty of arrival and return, and a greater feeling of support and communication, than that which prevailed on the nineteenth-century passages to the Australian colonies. I thus have profound respect for those nineteenth-century emigrants and find it difficult not to conclude that they were very special people. While they came to the colonies for a variety of reasons, with different hopes and aspirations, they were undoubtedly possessed of those illusive and intangible qualities, which together produced the pioneer.

---

2. Excerpt from 'The Prologue by a Gentleman of Leicester'. Opening of the Theatre of Sydney, Botany Bay, 1796.

Early Arrivals

The earliest inhabitants of Australia were of course the Aboriginal people. In a sense they also emigrated to Australia. No one is able to give us an exact date of their arrival. However, archaeologists have uncovered evidence indicating that human beings have been on the continent for at least 50,000 years. There seems to have been a sea gap between Australia and Asia for a very long time (certainly during the Pleistocene period – 3 million to 10,000 years ago). Like those that arrived in the nineteenth century these first arrivals must have been special people, also possessed of a pioneering spirit. One imagines that they were some of the more adventurous stone-age people moving south from their northern homes, using their primitive sailing craft (probably rafts made of bamboo). It seems that they probably landed in the northern-most part of the large landmass (now known as Papua New Guinea) and gradually moved south over the continent. This was possible because Papua New Guinea was at that time still joined to the Australian mainland. When Captain James Cook first sighted the eastern coast of Australia in 1770 there were probably about 300,000 Aboriginal people widely dispersed throughout the continent, living in some 600 tribes. They had learnt over the years how to skilfully manage the environment and how to manage and maintain the resources of the country.

People had visited Australia regularly over many years from countries that lie to the north. For example the Macassans, from the Indonesian trading centre of Macassar, had for centuries been regular visitors to northern Australia to fish mainly for trepang (a marine animal commonly known as the sea cucumber). Remains of Macassan campsites have been found on Australia's north coast and date back at least eight hundred years. They came in large numbers in boats called praus (a small sailing vessel). It seems that they fished in dugout canoes and that some of these canoes were traded with the Indigenous people. Other objects were also traded, including knives, axes, smoking pipes and fishhooks, in exchange for tortoiseshell and pearl shells. Not all contact between the Macassans and the Indigenous people was peaceful. Sometimes there was violent conflict.

There is an area in Eastern Arnhem Land, Northern Territory, close to Yirrkala, which contains artefacts depicting Macassan and Aboriginal objects. The area is known as the stone pictures of Wurrwurrwuy. The stone pictures depict a range of subjects including Aboriginal camps, fish traps, and images relating to the Macassan trepang industry including praus, canoes, the stone fire places where trepang were boiled and Macassan houses. The depictions of praus show internal arrangements of these vessels. Clearly the Aboriginal people of that area were familiar with the workings of the Macassan praus. There are also rock painting of praus. While the Macassans may have been visiting the northern Australian coast before 1650 it appears from Dutch East India Company documents that intensive catching and processing of trepang for the Chinese market probably began in about 1750.[3]

Matthew Flinders during his epic voyage around Australia recorded meeting a fleet of Macassan praus in the Arnhem Land region and of ascertaining from the captain of the fleet that Macassan praus came to the coast of northern Australia every year on the north-west monsoons to collect and dry trepang which they sold to the Chinese. Phillip Parker King, travelling in the **Mermaid** also recorded meeting large numbers of Macassans several times during April 1818 while charting the north-west coast of Australia. On the first occasion King counted fifteen vessels and estimated that the combined crew was about three hundred. In King's case he reported that the Macassan's were not very friendly and that on several occasions he ordered his men to action stations, had the guns loaded and ran out and ran up the English ensign.

Sketch of a Macassan Prau

---

3. Macknight, C.C. Macassans in the Aboriginal Past. Archaeology in Oceania 21:69-75, pp.133-4.

The Papuan people regularly travelled to Cape York Peninsula and Arnhem Land across the Torres Strait. Papuan culture and language had an influence on Indigenous culture in the Cape York area. Dugout canoes, ornamental masks and grave posts were introduced to the Indigenous peoples. In return the Papuans acquired spears, ornaments and other weapons.

It's also possible that Chinese traders and explorers may have made the journey to Australia centuries before European explorers.

It seems that as European thinkers became increasingly sure in the belief that the world was a sphere, they also felt that there must be a large landmass on the other side of the globe to balance the known world of Europe, northern Africa and west Asia. This landmass was increasingly referred to as 'Terra Incognita' (unknown land). Matthew Flinders is given the credit for applying the name 'Australia' to the continent in 1804, although the word in several forms had been used for centuries. It seems that the first use of the word in a publication appeared in an astronomical diagram published in Frankfurt by Cyriaco Jacob zum Barth in 1545. The word used in this publication is derived from 'australis', Latin for 'southern'. Despite the name 'Australia' appearing in 1545, maps after that time frequently used the term 'Terra Australis'.

The Portuguese-born explorer Pedro Fernandes Queiros believed he had discovered the long sought-after southern continent, and for many years petitioned the king of Spain to permit colonisation. After returning from a 1595-96 expedition from Peru, where he was chief pilot, he was convinced that the southern continent extended from New Guinea towards the Strait of Magellan, and that it equalled Europe and Asia in size. In December 1605 he sailed again from Peru in command of two vessels with the aim of finding and colonising the southern continent. In May 1606 the expedition reached Vanuatu and Queiros believed he had reached his goal. He named the largest island 'La Australia del Espiritu Santo'. His attempt to form a settlement failed and he was forced to sail for Mexico arriving in November 1606. In the following few years he continued to assert that he had found the great southern continent. He died on his way to Peru in 1615, his quest unaccomplished.

In the early part of the seventeenth century the new Dutch republic created a vast trading empire that involved much of Asia. This trade primarily occurred through the Dutch United East India Company (Verenigde Oost-Indische Compagnie or VOC). As a result of the markets developed by the VOC Europeans became increasingly interested in India and the Pacific Ocean. This led to a revolution in mapping of these areas.

Given the size of the Dutch trading empire it's not surprising that the first records of European mariners sailing into Australian waters involved Dutch vessels. This occurred around 1606 and the records contain their observations of this unknown southern land, which the Dutch called 'New Holland'. The first vessel to chart the coast and meet with Aboriginal people was the ***Duyfken*** captained by Dutchman, Willem Janszoon. Between 1606 and 1770 (when Captain James Cook sailed along the east coast of Australia), an estimated 54 European vessels from a range of nations made contact. Many of these were merchant vessels from the Dutch United East India Company and included the ships of Abel Tasman who chartered parts of the north, west and south coasts of Australia (New Holland). The first European to leave behind a record of his visit was Dirk Hartog. Hartog set off from the Cape of Good Hope in the ***Eendracht*** across the Indian Ocean for Batavia (present day Jakarta) and was probably blown off course by strong westerly winds (the Roaring Forties). As a consequence, in October 1616 he came upon the west coast and spent three days examining the coast and nearby islands. When he departed he left a pewter plate affixed to a post (now known as the Hartog Plate) containing a record of his visit. The plate is now in the Rijksmuseum in Amsterdam.

The first Englishman to explore the west coast was William Dampier. The publication of his book, *A New Voyage Round the World,* in 1697 was a popular sensation, creating interest at the Admiralty. In 1699, Dampier was given command of the 26-gun warship **HMS Roebuck**, with a commission from King William III. His mission was to explore the east coast of New Holland. Following the Dutch route to the Indies Dampier arrived at Dirk Hartog Island on the west coast of New Holland in August 1699. He anchored southeast of Cape Inscription, at a place now called Dampier's Landing. Dampier explored the island and surrounding waters, noting Bernier and Dorre Islands and the northern end of Peron Peninsula, which he thought was an island. During this time his cook, Mr. Goodwin, died, becoming the first European known to have been buried on Australian soil.

Dampier made many detailed observations of local wildlife and named the area "Shark's Bay" in recognition of the large number of sharks in the area. He also made the first scientific collection of Australian plants, marking the beginning of scientific interest in Australia. The collection is still preserved at the Oxford University and includes Dampiera, a blue-flowering genus that now bears his name. By December 1699 Dampier had chartered areas around New Guinea as he moved towards his goal of examining the east coast of New Holland. However by this time his vessel was in such bad shape he had to abandon his plans for examining the east coast.

James Cook was the first European to chart the east coast. Sailing in the barque **HMS Endeavour** he claimed the east coast, under instruction from King George III, on 22 August 1770, naming it New South Wales. The coast of Australia, featuring Tasmania as a separate island was mapped in detail by English mariners and navigators, George Bass and Matthew Flinders, and French mariner, Nicolas Baudin. A nearly complete map of the coastline was published by Flinders in 1814. This early period of European exploration is reflected in the current names of landmarks such as Torres Strait, Arnhem Land, Dampier Sound, Tasmania, the Furneaux Islands, Cape Frecinyet and La Perouse.

While European explorers had periodically charted and landed on various parts of the vast Australian coast, dating from the early seventeenth century, the first European settlers did not arrive until towards the end of the eighteenth century. These first white settlers came mainly from England and Ireland. They came with Captain Phillip and his fleet of eleven ships, which sailed into Botany Bay on 18 January 1788, after a journey of more than 15,000 miles that took over eight months. Phillip relocated to Port Jackson and hoisted the British flag on 26 January 1788.

First Fleet Anchored in Sydney Cove 27 January 1788[4]
(National Library of Australia, Bib ID: 624123)

These first white settlers, numbering about 1000, had not come as emigrants. They comprised about 750 convicts and over 200 officials and soldiers. It would be safe to conclude that none of those arrivals wanted to make Australia their home. The convicts had been banished from their homeland and separated from friends and relatives as punishment for crimes that they had committed. Given a choice, the convicts and the gaolers alike would have returned home as quickly as possible.

The settlement was founded as a matter of expediency to replace the arrangements, which had existed with plantations in the American colonies to accept convicts as a source of cheap labour (plantations had been accepting about 700 convicts each year). By 1783 English gaols and prison hulks were filled with prisoners whose sentences of transportation could not be carried into effect. Various experiments were tried by the British Government; the West Coast of Africa had proved a death trap for the unfortunates who were sent there. The remaining colonies in America made quite clear their determination not to accept convicts, and returned to England shiploads that were sent out. It was thus imperative

---

4. From a painting by John Allcot, published in the Sydney Mail, 26 January 1938.

that a solution be found. In 1784 the suggestion was made in the House of Commons that New Zealand should be opened up as a penal colony; but nothing was done. It was not until the opening of Parliament in January 1787 that the King informed both Houses that "a plan had been found for transporting a number of convicts, in order to remove the inconvenience which arose from the crowded state of the gaols".[5] By that date New South Wales had been decided upon as the location.

The decision to send this expedition to Australia under Phillip had not been without opposition and, in fact, New South Wales was founded under an atmosphere of distrust and suspicion. There were many who felt that sending prisoners to Botany Bay was a waste of money. One ardent and ongoing critic of transportation was Jeremy Bentham. Throughout his career he described transportation as a poor punishment claiming that it did not inflict enough pain on the offenders. After transportation had commenced he argued that there weren't enough gaolers to supervise the convicts and to impose discipline and he contended that there was no evidence that the process reformed those who were transported. Others felt that the place was too remote and too uncivilised for any European people to live permanently. Only a few years earlier England had been forced out of her American colonies and had to grant them independence. As a consequence some felt that establishing further colonies was a waste of money and they were determined to spend as little as possible on New South Wales.

However, there were others who viewed Australia as a good location for a prison settlement. Despite the pessimism and ambivalence of some, there were those who had great hopes for the new colony. Governor Phillip was one of these and he was optimistic about the possibility of establishing a flourishing settlement. He tried to encourage convicts to take up farming to support themselves and he offered some of them free grants of land. However, most of the convicts were city or town people who knew nothing of farming, and there were no farmers in the colony to guide them in this activity, so this was not a great success.

The local authorities in New South Wales soon realised that the colony would need free settlers if it was to move beyond being purely a remote

---

5. Hansard. Parliamentary History of England, Vol. XXVI. p.211.

gaol and become self-supporting. Phillip recognised the worthlessness of most of the convicts and the unreliability of the military. Free men were essential to supervise the work of the convicts, take charge of the stores, see to the issue of provisions, and above all, to produce the foodstuffs, which the convicts were unable or unwilling to produce. This led to the implementation of the first of many schemes to encourage people to migrate to Australia.

The experience gained in the first few years taught Phillip that immigrants would have to be carefully chosen if they were to benefit the colony. They would need to be practical farmers with enough property to give them an interest in the success of their endeavours. He believed that such people as these, if "intelligent and industrious" could not fail. But he warned the Government against people who were lacking both in "property and industry", for they would inevitably become a burden and an expense on the colony.[6]

By November 1791, there were only eighty free settlers in New South Wales and its dependency, Norfolk Island. The settlers included thirty-one men who had been discharged from the marines, eleven seamen, forty-four convicts whose sentences had expired, and only one man who had not come either as convict, soldier or sailor. Twenty-eight of the men were married and the total population was about 3500.[7] Phillip had quickly recognised that the material he had to work with was not good and the tasks to be performed were substantial.

Against this background the first assisted free migrants embarked in 1792, when nine adults and four children were given free passage to Sydney. The men included three farmers, one gardener, one millwright, one blacksmith and one baker. When they arrived on 16 January 1793 they were given grants of land of 50 to 100 acres in size and sufficient food, stores and clothing to last them for two years. They also had convict servants assigned to help them with the farms. This venture was not a great success because the land close to Sydney was not particularly suitable for agriculture. Phillip was not present to witness the arrival

---

6. Phillip to Grenville, No. 3, 17 June 1790. Historical Records of Australia. Series I, Volume 1. pp. 180-1.
7. Madgwick, R.B. Immigration into Eastern Australia 1788-1851. Sydney, 1969. p.11.

of this group, to oversee their settlement and to see the results of their work as he had resigned his post during 1792 and sailed for England in December that year.

Captain John Hunter arrived to assume the Governorship of the colony in September 1795. He pointed out almost at once that the colony could never attain any degree of social stability unless industrious and respectable people were sent out by the home Government. He maintained that many of the people who had been allowed to settle were "truly worthless characters" and he included in this category the majority of settlers previously sent out from England.[8]

While the early attempts by Phillip and Hunter to attract particular types of migrants were not particularly successful, Bligh, who governed from 1806 to 1810, also tried to bring farmers out from England. Unfortunately emigrant qualifications were not checked prior to embarkation and a number of those who arrived were unqualified for the task and quite ineffective as farmers. There was little support or enthusiasm in England for these early attempts by successive Governors to attract free settlers.

In fact during the early years of settlement emigration was either forbidden or discouraged because the idea still prevailed that Britain was under populated; and that mercantilist wealth depended on population. The War of American Independence and the French Revolution and Napoleonic War caused the English ruling classes to regard democratic and liberal ideals with disfavour. Accordingly new colonies were treated less liberally than the old. Thus colonies like New South Wales were viewed with toleration rather than encouragement and little was done in the early years to accelerate growth, either economically or politically. As a consequence of the outcome of the American War, Britain ignored the accepted principles of the time normally applied to overseas development when establishing New South Wales. Because of the war with France, New South Wales was almost entirely disregarded for some twenty years, except as a convenient dumping ground for convicts.

---

8. Hunter to King, 30 April, 1796. Historical Records of Australia. Series I, Volume 1. p.565.

However, even though New South Wales was largely ignored during this period it would be false to assume that Britain was no longer imperialistic. Not even the strongest opponents of colonial expansion condemned all colonies irrespective of their nature and relation to the mother country. The chief characteristics of the post-war period were a movement away from America and towards India; and a return to the policy of safeguarding and extending British mercantile and maritime rights in the West Indies. Thus, while largely ignoring the remote colony of New South Wales, colonial policy was on the one hand still mercantilist while on the other hand it was still actively expansionist. British trade interests were very important; for example the British Parliament expressed its intention of going to war with Spain in 1790 rather than accept the proposed Spanish restrictions on trade in the North Pacific.

Britain strove to consolidate its Eastern interests by securing for Britain those ports which had a strategic importance for the Eastern trade. It took possession of the Dutch colony of the Cape of Good Hope in 1795, and again permanently in 1806, not because of any idea of making the Cape a starting point for an African Empire but because of the danger of French power in India. The Cape was a key position in the defence of the Indian trade, and an important port of call for the East India Company's ships. Enthusiasm for the Eastern Empire also led to the occupation of Ceylon in 1795, Mauritius in 1810, Singapore in 1811, and Hong Kong in 1841. In short, Great Britain was still prepared to go to almost any lengths to develop and protect her trade. However, it was world trade, and particularly Indian and Far-Eastern trade, that she had in view, rather than a far-flung Colonial Empire.

Australia's first two settlements, Sydney and Hobart Town (established in 1804), had begun life as urban gaols. They remained small port settlements for a number of years. Sydney's population rose from about 1000 in 1788 to 2500 by 1799. However, by 1828 Sydney had grown to 10,800 while Hobart Town stood at 5000. Much of this early growth was due to the arrival of convicts. By this time the Aboriginal people in both regions had been dispersed, as the European arrivals took the land that had been occupied by Aboriginal groups for thousands of years.

By the 1830s Sydney's population had begun to expand rapidly because of a combination of increasing numbers of convicts and emigrants arriving in the colony. The increases were partly in response to Sydney's role as a port for the export of the produce from its hinterland. This role was enhanced with the development of a growing railroad network from the middle of the nineteenth century. Thus Sydney continued to grow steadily throughout the nineteenth century, even through the depression of the 1890s, so that by the early 1900s it became Australia's first city with a population of more than half a million.

Hobart, on the other hand, grew much more slowly, partly because the settlers became more dispersed as they sought their livelihood in other parts of the island. A population of 19,000 in 1861 had only increased to 35,000 by 1900.

Hobart Town on the River Derwent 1830 (painting by W J Huggins)
(State Library of Victoria)

The first settlement in Queensland, comprising some eighty-five people (29 convicts, 22 sailors plus wives and children) who arrived from Sydney on the *Amity,* was established in September 1824 at Redcliffe on Morton Bay. This was moved in May 1825 up the Brisbane River to what is now the site of Brisbane city centre. Brisbane began to grow as the rich agricultural hinterland was exploited. It became the capital of the new colony of Queensland in 1859 and its population reached 6000 in 1861. From this time the population grew steadily, doubling in size every decade until the 1890s and reaching 119,000 by 1901.

A colony was established on the Swan River (Western Australia) in June 1829 as Australia's first convict-free colony. The poor soil did not induce many settlers to stay. By 1832 Perth only had 360 people. Labour shortages led to a demand for convicts in the 1840s. The first convicts arrived in 1850 and transportation continued until 1868. By 1901 Perth and Fremantle had a combined population of some 60,000.

A series of navigators and explorers from Sydney explored the southeast coast of the continent from about 1797, including Port Phillip (up to the mouth of the Yarra River). However there wasn't much interest in settling in Victoria until the early 1830s. The first settlement was at Portland Bay in 1834. Pastoralists from Van Diemen's Land (including John Batman and John Faulkner) began to take a keen interest in settling the area around the Yarra River, which is now the site of Melbourne. Expeditions formed by Faulkner and Batman left Launceston around the same time arriving in the Yarra in August and September 1835 respectively. After an initial disagreement Faulkner and Batman decided that there was plenty of land for both groups. John Bateman claimed to have purchased the land in the area from the Aborigines on an earlier visit to the area in1835. Governor Bourke authorised that a site for a township on the banks of the Yarra estuary be surveyed in March 1837 and the new town was officially named Melbourne in honour of the British Prime Minister, Lord Melbourne. Until 1850 the Port Phillip district was part of New South Wales. The discovery of gold in Victoria in 1852 led to large numbers of people arriving in Melbourne on their way to the goldfields. The city's population increased from 29,000 in 1851 to 125,000 in 1861. At this time it was larger than Sydney. Melbourne underwent a spectacular boom in the 1880s during which time many grand houses and public buildings were erected. However, the economy suffered badly with the depression of the 1890s and Sydney again became the largest city.

Kangaroo Island was the site for the first South Australian settlement with the first people arriving in July 1836. Adelaide was subsequently selected by Colonel Light as the site for a new colony and it grew slowly to a population of only 15,000 by 1851. However, the development of the wheat and wool industries saw a doubling of the population in the 1860s and 1880s. South Australia claimed the land now known as the Northern Territory in 1863 and, after a failed attempt to establish a settlement at Escape Cliffs, the Darwin site was settled in 1869. By 1890 its population had reached 5000.

Thus the colonies in Australia were settled at first tentatively, with emigration activities progressively developing as the century progressed. The quest for immigrants commenced in earnest in the 1820s, at first from Sydney and Hobart Town, but later from the other colonies. Although limited immigration had commenced soon after settlement it was from the outset a controversial matter, both in England and in the colonies, throughout the nineteenth century. The matter was debated, at times hotly, by a wide variety of people, including colonists, officials, members of the British Parliament, capitalists, explorers, writers, and many others.

The debate occurred because of the conflicting views that were held by various groups and individuals. It was often based on, or led to, misinformation and confusion about what conditions were really like in the colonies. Despite the debate and the often poor publicity it attracted for the colonies, many men, women and children sold their belongings, packed their bags, said goodbye to relatives and friends and embarked on a very long, uncomfortable and difficult voyage to the Australian colonies throughout the nineteenth century. The story told in this book is the story of those who made that decision to emigrate to Australia.

CHAPTER 2

The Emigration Debate

There a waste of noble lands
Teems with good ungathered bread;
Here a waste of noble hands
Longs to work, and to be fed;
Turn the hands upon the land-
Nothing more do I demand.[9]

As indicated in the previous chapter the matter of emigration from the United Kingdom to the Australian colonies was controversial from the start of colonisation and continued to be so throughout the nineteenth century. Although free settlers began to arrive in the colony of New South Wales from the late 1790s their numbers were relatively small until the mass immigration schemes of the 1830s took effect. This can be seen from the General Muster of October 1821, which recorded 31,072 Europeans in New South Wales and 7735 in Van Diemen's Land. The following table shows the composition of the population:

Colonial Population – 1821 Muster[10]

Composition	New South Wales	Van Diemen's Land
Convicts, including ticket of leave	13,841	3939
Emancipists	5312	935

---

9. Foy, Charles. Emigration or No Emigration, Facts for Emigrants. Pamphlet. Belfast, 1874. p.6.
10. Historical Records of Australia, 1821 Muster, I, X, p. 575, Sydney 1917-1922.

Born in the colony	1884	}1118
Arrived free	1489	
Officials/ Military	1262	551
Children	7224	1192
Unknown	60	-
	31,072	7735

Note: The Muster did not distinguish between children born in the colony of New South Wales and those who arrived as immigrants (it is clear from other data that the majority of children in 1821 were born in the colony). The Muster also recorded 240 persons on vessels in Sydney harbour who are not included in the above table. The Muster did not separate those born in the colony and those arriving free in Van Diemen's Land.

At this point in the history of the colonies the emancipists and native-born children far outnumbered the free immigrants. Many of those living in the colonies saw free immigrants as interlopers and were resentful of the favourable treatment given to them by way of land grants and other privileges. After all, they had cleared the land, grown the crops and built the settlements and towns, and therefore felt they had an investment in the colony. Those born in the colonies had of course known no other home.

On the other hand there were some colonists who were of the view that if the colonies were to become self-sufficient they would need to develop and exploit the resources of the country. This would require a considerably expanded labour force, which the colonies were incapable of providing from within.

In the early years of the century, government opposition to emigration persisted despite the rapid increase in Britain's population, and in spite of the publication of Malthus' 'Essay on Population' in 1798 indicating that the continued growth in population would lead to an over supply of labour that would inevitably lower wages resulting in poverty. Malthus' work led to the passage of legislation for the conduct of a national population census the first of which in 1801 provided evidence that the population was growing rapidly. Up until about 1815 opposition to emigration rested mainly on the need for men to swell the ranks of the army and navy, and produce war supplies. In addition, the exigencies of the war allowed the Secretary for the Colonies little time to consider anything outside Europe, except the problem of checking French aggression in India, the West Indies and Africa. New colonies and colonial populations might have involved the government in expenditure, which it could not afford to incur. There was only deviation from this policy where the aspirations of Napoleon seemed to demand the annexation of new territory, such as Malta, Egypt, India, the Cape and West Indies.

While government in the early years was against emigration, there was nonetheless in Britain mixed views about the wisdom of encouraging emigration to the Australian colonies. Some saw no profit in it and also remembered the losses, which had occurred as a result of Britain being forced to grant independence to the American colonies. There were also those who claimed that the colony of New South Wales was a financial cost without any return to the mother country. For example, Joseph Banks complained that Britain had "possessed the country of New South Wales more than ten years and not one article has hitherto been discovered by the importation of which the mother country can receive any degree of return for the cost of founding and maintaining the colony".[11] However, there were others who believed the colonies had considerable potential and would make a significant contribution to the enhancement of the British Empire. Within the pro-emigration 'group' there existed a variety of views about the purpose of emigration to the colonies, and about a number of matters including how it should be financed, the conditions under which it should occur, and the type of emigrant the colonies needed. These and other matters shaped the various emigration schemes and activities that prevailed during the course of the nineteenth century.

However, while this debate was occurring within Britain, matters were also progressing within the colonies, which helped to force the issue. By the 1820s Sydney and Hobart Town had become important ports in their own right. This occurred in part because of their recognition as an important part of the China and India trade routes. New industries were also developing in the colonies. For example they were developing in the areas of whaling and sealing, which helped consolidate their importance as ports. The developments occurring in the pastoral and agricultural areas also added to the importance of Sydney and Hobart Town as ports.

---

11. Day, David. Claiming a Continent: A New History of Australia. Harper Collins, 2001, p.49.

These and other developments made it difficult for those in Britain to ignore the demand that this created for labour, which directly impacted upon the emigration debate in Britain.

The Blue Mountains was crossed in 1813 thus opening up vast areas of new grazing land in New South Wales. John McArthur demonstrated how well-suited merino sheep were to conditions in New South Wales and other English landowners soon realised they could make a good profit by raising sheep and exporting wool to England.

However, until about 1820 the number of free settlers remained very small. This was largely the result of England's involvement in a war with France and hence the colonies were largely left to their own devices. Then between 1820 and 1830, a period when settlers were largely obliged to pay their own fares, over 7000 wealthy immigrants arrived in the colonies forming a new 'upper class' - labelled for some considerable time the 'pure merinos'.

At home many pamphlets were written and published during the nineteenth century on the subject of emigration to the colonies and many people toured England speaking on the subject. One pamphleteer argued in 1848 that England would benefit from emigration in three interrelated ways:

- emigration would diminish pauperism in England;
- emigration would reduce colonial expenditure by the country; and
- emigration would increase the Imperial revenue and diminish taxation in general.[12]

These three themes were picked up by a variety of writers and speakers during the nineteenth century in order to argue the case for or against supporting emigration to the colonies.

On the question of pauperism it was argued that there were simply too many people in England for the present system of government to support. The result was poverty and deprivation for many. The answer was felt to lie in disposing of the excess population through an emigration program. This it was said would be the quickest way to remedy such 'evils'.

---

12. McDonald, P M. Emigration: Its Advantages to Great Britain and Her Colonies. Pamphlet, London 1848.

In keeping with this line of argument there were those who contended that it was therefore important to ship all the paupers to other countries and keep in Great Britain those who could support themselves. Others felt this approach to be flawed because the relief it would provide to Britain would only be temporary.

However, the supporters of this argument were convinced that there were simply too many people in Britain for the country to support. There was concern that this excess of population was increasing every year and that the existing system of government was incapable of dealing with the problem. This line of argument was then extended to suggest that the departure of "any number of our population under a system that would ensure success in the colonies could tend to diminish pauperism in England".[13]

Thus some thought was given to what was needed to ensure success in the colonies and this led to consideration of who should emigrate and under what circumstances. There was of course disagreement about these matters. Some felt that the simplest and most efficient system would be one that concentrated on emigration of the paupers. One writer argued that for a mere 4 pounds 12 shillings and 6 pence (the difference between the passage cost and the annual cost of maintaining a pauper) Her Majesty's Emigration Commissioners could send a pauper to Australia, which would 'disburden the country' of a pauper and convert a consumer into a good customer.[14] The writer added a further observation about the total cost of supporting the poor in the home country:

> "Seven million sterling – which is near about the present annual amount of our national poor rate – it should be recollected, represents so much waste of capital, so long as it continues employed in maintaining some hundreds of thousands of our people in conditions of permanent poverty.
> Would it not be better for those thousands of people if it were largely applied locating them in some positions of productive industry; transferring them from a land groaning thus under

---
13. ibid. p. 8
14. Hodgson, Arthur. Emigration to the Australian Settlements - being the substance of lectures delivered in the spring of 1849. Second Ed. London 1849, p.23.

the pressure of a superabundant population, to lands which are indigent for the waste of them?"[15]

Others argued that it did not really matter who emigrated because the departure of those in the labour force would leave jobs for paupers to take up. A third opinion argued for a balanced group to be sent to the colonies, which should include a wide range of skills and thus enhance the chances of the colonies prospering.

The colonies were predictably critical of any suggestion of using Australia as a dumping ground for the mother country's poor. Harsh language was used at times to describe those people who were unwanted in Britain but yet thought suitable for the colonies. The illustration below is an example of the more graphic type of opposition coming from the colonies.

Rubbish is not to be shot here![16]
(National Library of Australia, Drawer A100)

---

15. ibid. p. 23.
16. *The Bulletin.* 11 August, 1883. p. 13.

On the matter of using emigration as a means of reducing colonial expenditure it was thought that a system of colonisation of sufficient scale was needed to ensure success of the new colonists and ensure prosperity in the colonies. As a consequence this process would progressively release the British exchequer of the burden involved in supporting the colonies.

This line of thinking was taken further by others who felt that, not only would the burden of supporting the colonies be reduced, but that emigration would in fact increase Imperial revenue and lead to reduced taxation in Britain, and that the substantial supply of crown land in the colonies was important to achievement of this end. The sale of this land, it was argued, would attract both labour and capital to the colonies. The labour would arrive mainly from Britain as emigrants and the capital would arrive via British investment. The result of this would be increased profits with the overall effect of Britain becoming more prosperous and taxes being more easily paid. This notion had been put forward by Edward Gibbon Wakefield in his book: *A Letter from Sydney*. Although he had never been to Sydney this did not concern him or the large number of people who read the book. In the book Wakefield suggested a plan he called 'systematic colonisation'. The colony of South Australia was in fact settled largely on the basis of the Wakefield plan. Some of his supporters had formed the South Australian Association. The British Government had agreed to the settlement on the basis that the sale of land would cover the costs of administering the colony.

The Wakefield approach was not without its critics. By the middle of the nineteenth century there were a number of critics that were convinced that this system was working against emigration and the future of the colonies. One of these critics, John Sidney, wrote widely in an attempt to persuade and guide the British to emigrate to the colonies. He was adamant that the Wakefield system was an obstacle to populating and civilising the colonies because the system:

> *"...makes land scarce and dear instead of cheap and plentiful. Until this system has been reduced to its proper level, all attempts at systematic imperial Colonisation will fail."*[17]

---

17. Sidney, John. Sidney's Australian Hand-Book. How to Settle and Succeed in Australia. London, 1848. p. 20.

Hence there was an emerging feeling that emigration could be useful to both the Old World and the New. In the Old World it would help address the problem of pauperism, provide a new market for British manufacturers and generally lead to improved domestic prosperity and conditions. It was further felt by some that emigration could direct attention away from new theories and philosophies, such as socialism and Chartism (a working men's movement for social and political reform) that were thought to be threatening the very foundations of British society. The benefits of emigration to the New World would include the alleviation of the chronic labour shortage and an improved colonial society through provision of a more 'wholesome' and industrious class of people to replace the convict labour.

In summary, the proponents of emigration argued that the "sons of Britain would rot in their native land if they did not carry the steam-engine, the ploughshare, the halleluiahs of Christianity and all the other achievements of British civilisation into the remotest parts of the Australian wilderness".[18]

There were of course those who were sceptical of this position. They felt that the active support of emigration would drive from Britain the cream of the young. Others were suspicious that emigration was being used as a smoke screen, having been perpetrated to prevent workers from seeing that the only remedy for their misery lay in a radical change to the way wealth was distributed in Britain.

As stated earlier in this chapter, the colonists also participated in the debate – at times actively advocating increased immigration to satisfy colonial needs, and at other times being less than enthusiastic about emigration and periodically expressing hostility towards new arrivals.

One writer chastised others for not seeing a future in the colonies and expressed in passionate terms his feelings that the colonies would become the centre of a new empire in the southern hemisphere:

---

18. Clarke, C M H. A History of Australia Part III. Melbourne 1979. p. 227.

> *"...I have no hesitation in adding that New South Wales is one of the proudest monuments of Christian civilisation of our country - founded with the refuse of gaols and prisons; peopled originally by the lowest class of emigrants, planted at the antipodes as if we were ashamed of the outcasts and afraid of their moral pestilence; yet has this extraordinary colony become the centre of a new empire in the southern hemisphere, from which all blessings of Britain will radiate to millions yet unborn..."*[19]

From the viewpoint of the British Government it took the growing strength of English industrialisation and the demand for wider overseas markets to finally break the influence which mercantilism had on international and colonial trade. With foreign trade freed, colonial policy broadened from an outpost system to a system of settlement. Rapidly increasing industrialisation provided a population surplus as well as a surplus of produce for export. This gave rise to a demand in Britain for commodities such as wool, wheat and cotton, which the colonies might be expected to produce.

Although the debate subsided somewhat in Britain and Ireland from the middle of the nineteenth century, the colonies showed continuing signs of resistance at various times as the century passed on (the cry: 'Australia for the Australians' was often heard).

Thus, while the debate continued in various forms throughout the nineteenth century, the people continued to come to this new potential empire in the south. Against this backdrop of controversy and in all probability oblivious to it, men, women and children made their own assessment of the advantages and disadvantages of emigrating to the Australian colonies and acted accordingly. Some were sponsored to join relatives and friends, some paid their own way and many were assisted through various emigration schemes. However, in the longer term, unplanned events, like the discovery of gold, were often far more influential than government attitudes or any scheme of government intervention, in bringing large numbers of emigrants to the colonies.

---

19. Hodgson, Arthur. Emigration to the Australian Settlements. London, Second Ed. 1849. p. 43.

CHAPTER 3

Deciding to Emigrate

Who would true valour see, let him come hither;
one here will constant be, come wind, come weather.
There's no discouragement shall make him once relent his vowed intent
to be a pilgrim...[20]

Those who chose to emigrate to the Australian colonies in the nineteenth century possibly had much in common with the pilgrims that John Bunyan wrote about in the seventeenth century; people prepared to face all manner of difficulty.

However, for many the extent of the difficulties involved in emigrating to Australia was largely a mystery. Thus it's evident that for most people the immediate problems associated with emigrating to the colonies in the nineteenth century were not at all clear.

The decision to emigrate can be influenced significantly by the economic, social and political conditions of the homeland compared with those of the country to which emigration is contemplated. These factors were important to varying degrees in influencing people in England to emigrate to the Australian colonies in the nineteenth century. They are explored in this chapter.

For the average nineteenth-century emigrant the decision to emigrate to Australia would have been the most difficult decision that person would have ever made. Clearly prospective emigrants would have been aware that

---
20. Bunyan, John. The Australian Hymn Book. Hymn 467. Sydney, 1977.

emigrating to the colonies would have most likely meant saying goodbye to relatives and friends forever (the words of the ballad, '...farewell to old England forever....', although written about the convicts were equally applicable to significant numbers of emigrants). One early nineteenth-century writer commented on the distress involved in emigration as follows:

> "…..a repugnance to emigration which is only overcome generally by the pressure of extreme distress. There is the separation of families and connections and the final danger of separation of the colony from the mother country".[21]

Thus the majority of emigrants would have made the decision knowing that they would have been unlikely to ever have the return fare. They also understood the isolation, which resulted from the vast distance, the long passage time and the communication difficulties. At the very best they could have looked forward to communications from relatives and friends no more than twice per year. Despite the ongoing debate during the nineteenth century about emigration, including the views expressed by public speakers and pamphleteers, there was a considerable deficiency in suitable unbiased and accurate information about life in the colonies, particularly for the labouring classes (many of who were illiterate). Many viewed the colonies with suspicion, as places for criminals. Why then did they come, and in such relatively large numbers? It is clear that those people who emigrated to the Australian colonies in the nineteenth century did so for a wide variety of reasons.

It would be reasonable to conclude that some may have decided to emigrate as a result of a sudden impulse or possibly encouragement to leave quickly, but for most it would have been a deliberate and very carefully considered decision. Reaching the decision would have involved the interplay of a combination of factors. These factors included the impact of the changing social and economic conditions in the United Kingdom, the perceived opportunities in the colonies, encouragement by the government and possibly relatives that had already emigrated and simply the opportunity for a new start with the hope of a better life and future for self and family. For many people weighing these factors up would have been confusing, difficult and probably very agonising.

---

21. Bacon, Richard. The Distresses of the Agricultural Labourer and Its Remedy. London, 182?, p.63.

For most of the emigrants there was a push-pull effect — they were pushed from their homes and land by adversity and changing conditions and pulled by the promise of new opportunities and horizons and probably for many, the offer of assisted passage. It is clear that some were 'encouraged' to emigrate by being offered very little choice (poverty, destitution, the workhouse or emigration).

Conditions in the United Kingdom

By the end of the eighteenth century a number of changes were occurring to manufacturing, mining and agriculture that, taken together, were having an impact on British life. One consequence was a significant move of population from the countryside to the towns and cities. During the eighteenth century the population had also expanded rapidly. This growth in population combined with increasing urbanisation was causing concern for British authorities. These two factors were also having an adverse impact on the lives of many people in Britain.

While much of the population growth resulted in migration to London in the eighteenth century, the growth in the early nineteenth century was most rapid in the north and north-west counties. For example, the population in the Lancashire County expanded by twenty-three per cent in the decade from 1801 to 1811.[22]

The population growth in the eighteenth century and leading up to the start of the nineteenth century in the British Isles is illustrated in the table below.[23]

Population of British Isles

Year	England and Wales	Scotland	Ireland	Total
1701	5,826,000	1,040,000	2,540,000	9,406,000
1751	6,140,000	1,250,000	3,125,000	10,515,000
1801	9,156,000	1,599,000	5,216,000	14,972,000

---

22. Mathias, Peter. The First Industrial Nation. London, 1969, p. 198.
23. Deane, Phillis and Cole, W.A. British Economic Growth 1688-1959. Cambridge, 1969. p. 6.

Much of the movement from the country was the direct result of 'enclosure'. This was causing the emptying of villages and rural communities, which had traditionally characterised the British landscape. Before this shift, farming, the occupation that employed the great majority, had been run on an open-field basis. Each member of an agricultural community had his own piece of land. For the wealthy the piece would be large. Even the poor labourers had a strip of land that was theirs. However, this system was not particularly efficient or productive.

The landed gentry, being aware of the problems of the open-system, started to buy up land and to enclose it by fencing it. Thus the centuries-old system was progressively replaced with tenant farmers responsible to a landlord. Whenever landowners met any opposition, they appealed to parliament, which was always willing to assist with legislation. By 1815 most of the British countryside was enclosed. While enclosure did increase the quantity of food for the growing population, it also created a huge number of landless labourers who had nothing and nowhere to go. Employment, when it did come, was largely seasonal and the introduction of the threshing machine proved to be an incentive for rural disorder, including arson and increased tension. Many moved around in search of other land, but finally most were forced to leave the countryside and move into urban areas in search of work.

Those who remained in the south as agricultural labourers were affected by a decline in demand for English Southdown wool. This was caused by competition in the market from wool from German sheep that had been crossed with Spanish merinos. Hence unemployment amongst agricultural labourers rose further. A further problem for those in rural areas associated with enclosure was caused by the Game Laws of 1816, which limited the hunting of game to landowners. The penalty for poaching, or even being found in possession of a net at night, was transportation for seven years. The enclosure movement had enabled landowners to extend their parks and warrens, but had deprived villagers of common land from which to net or trap extra meat, to supplement the poor diet they could afford on low wages. Landowners began to protect estates with spring guns and mantraps, which also injured gamekeepers. Casualties among gamekeepers increased from attacks by poachers too. If a poacher was about to be caught by a gamekeeper and only the two of them were around, it was probably in the poacher's best interests to kill the gamekeeper to avoid transportation.

Increasing food prices exacerbated these problems for the working classes. The Corn Laws, which were a series of statutes enacted between 1815 and 1846, kept corn prices at a high level. These measures were intended to protect English farmers from cheap foreign imports of grain following the end of the Napoleonic Wars. Under these statutes 'corn' meant grain of all kinds, not simply the vegetable corn. During the Napoleonic Wars, the British blockaded the European continent, hoping to isolate the Napoleonic Empire and bring economic hardship to the French. One result of this blockade was that goods within the British Isles were protected against competition from outside sources. Farming became extremely lucrative, and farming land was traded at very profitable rates. When the wars ended in 1815 the first of the Corn Laws was introduced. This law stated that no foreign 'corn' would be allowed into Britain until domestic 'corn' reached a price of 80 shillings per quarter. The beneficiaries of the Corn Laws were the nobility and other large landholders who owned the majority of profitable farmland. Landowners had a vested interest in seeing the Corn Laws remain in force. And since the right to vote was not universal, but rather depended on land ownership, voting members of Parliament had no interest in repealing the Corn Laws. The artificially high grain prices encouraged by the Corn Laws meant that the working class had to spend the bulk of their income on grain and grain products just to survive. This meant that for much of the population they could not afford to purchase manufactured goods. So manufacturers suffered and had to lay off workers. Further, because Britain would not import European grain, European countries were unable or unwilling to import British manufactured goods. The unemployed workers from the manufacturing sector, like those from the countryside, had difficulty finding employment, so this increased the economic downturn in the country. After constant and considerable agitation, the government under Sir Robert Peel was persuaded to repeal the Corn Laws in 1846.

During the first quarter of the nineteenth century, with increasing prices, business failures, high unemployment and rural distress, there was serious social unrest and increased agitation for change. This created an environment conducive to the emergence of people with radical ideas. From 1811 to 1820 there were a series of events, which demonstrated the frustration and discontent of the working class:

- 1811-16 – Luddite (textile artisans) attacks on mills (leading to the hanging of 17 at York);
- 2 December 1816 – Spa Field riots (seeking electoral reform);
- 28 January 1817 – attack on the Prince Regent's carriage;
- March 1817 – march of the Blanketeers (a march where blankets were carried to draw attention to the plight of unemployed spinners and weavers);
- June 1817 – the Pentrich Rising (a riot related to unemployment caused by increased industrialisation, where several were killed and a large number injured);
- 16 August 1819 – (where cavalry charged a gathering that demanded reforms);
- February 1820 – Cato Street conspiracy which was an extreme example of discontent by the people (with the death of King George III there was a government crisis and a group of radicals decided this provided an opportunity to exploit the situation and kill all cabinet ministers and the Prime Minister);
- June/July 1820 – the Queen Caroline 'affair' (where King George IV attempted to get rid of his estranged wife using accusations of adultery which were easily proven false by the queen's advocate; leading to further instability and increased distrust of the ruling classes).

In rural areas where large numbers of farm labourers had been displaced by changing economic and social conditions, including being replaced by farm machinery, riots and protests were common. The arrival of the hated threshing machine in agricultural society provided the impetus for agrarian disturbances in 1816, 1822 and later in 1830. These outbreaks of machine breaking, riotous assemblies and incendiarism were an ugly symptom of the destruction of traditional social structures in agrarian society. The following newspaper reports in 1815 and 1816 are typical:

> *"Yesterday se'nnight about 20 people of the labouring class collected in a riotous manner in Gosbeck near Ipswich and destroyed two threshing machines and threatened to destroy many others. The magistrates took steps to support these proceedings. Eight men were conveyed to Ipswich gaol, two of these were allowed bail. When the magistrate left the gaol he was surrounded by the populace who hooted and pelted him till he took refuge*

> in the Great White Horse Inn, the street was filled with people standing about discussing the Corn Bill. Sir William Middleton the magistrate was unable to return to Shrubland Park until 10 pm at night when the crowd dispersed."[24]

> Extract from a letter from Finchingfield in Essex. " I have just returned from the place where the rioters have assembled to the amount of 200 people armed with implements of agriculture as weapons. Last night they destroyed Mr John Smith's threshing machines then this morning they visited Mr Robert Smith's farm at Byton Hall and destroyed a plough on a new construction. On Friday last there was a crowd of nearly 200, armed with axes, saws, spades etc, when they entered the village of Gt Bardfield with the intention of destroying threshing machines, mole ploughs etc, they made their attack on the premises of Mr Philip Spicer who had the spirit and resolution to defend his property with the assistance of 20 of his neighbours who were unarmed and by the Waterloo movement got between the rioters and the barn where the machines were and they wisely retreated".[25]

Solving the problems of the British countryside became a matter requiring urgent attention.

During this period of crisis petitions were made to Lord Sidmouth, the Home Secretary, seeking some address to social problems especially those being faced by the labouring poor.

> "The state of the labouring poor is truly miserable. Such is the want of employment that stout young men are employed by overseers, at three or four shillings a week, merely to prevent them from starving…..The labouring poor in husbandry (including disabled men from the army and navy) are not four fifths employed. The poor rates …are higher than at any period in the last forty years."[26]

---

24. Bury & Norwich Post, 1 March 1815.
25. Bury & Norwich Post, 28 May 1816
26. Letter from W. Sproule to Lord Sidmouth 27 May 1816 cited in Richardson, T.L. Agricultural Labourer's Wages & the Cost of Living in Essex 1790-1840, London, Hambledon,1991, p.83.

Sidmouth maintained that it was not the role of the government to intervene in such problems and so did nothing to alleviate the problems. In fact, rather that investigate the causes of so much discontent the government resorted to a policy of repression. To prevent the outbreak of revolution, which was the government's greatest fear, Lord Sidmouth increased the summary powers of magistrates and under the so-called 'Gag Acts' of 1817, *Habeas Corpus* (prevents unlawful detention of a person) was suspended and 'seditious' meetings prohibited.

It was clear that the economic and social changes occurring in Britain were having greatest impact on the labouring class who had been so important to British agriculture and other parts of the economy for so long. Many of these workers and their families felt they no longer had a place in British society and that the ruling elite and government had deserted them.

> *"The lowers orders of people are, in the altered and novel state of this country, presented only with the gloomy prospect of being, for their long tired unshaken loyalty... speedily reduced, by a restless force of absolute authority, to a wretched state of subjugation to the ruling powers."*[27]

The changes in population size and distribution brought with them associated social problems. There was concern over rising crime in the cities. The focus of this activity was firstly in London, where the largest growth in population had occurred in the eighteenth century, but as the population growth moved north, Manchester came to rival London as the major centre for crime. It appears that the overall crime rate did not increase, but the rise in population meant that more people in the cities were involved in crime. For the poor, crime was often a necessary means of survival. There was little protection from fluctuating food prices and the sixteenth-century Poor Law, being designed to operate on a parish basis, was not able to adapt to changing social and economic circumstances. For those people with few or no skills employment was at best infrequent and haphazard.

A nineteenth century writer commented:

---

27. Small, Robert. Ipswich Journal, 11 February, 1815.

> *"Honest, industrious men, numbering many thousands, are daily enduring privations, suffering hardships and passing through scenes of painful affliction, all of which would be removed could they but find constant and remunerating employment"*[28]

Much of the crime was committed against property. This is interesting when one considers that property was a key principle in the British constitution at that time. The possession of property was the most obvious form of social distinction in British society. An eighteenth-century Scottish philosopher observed that property was "the great source of distinction among individuals".[29] The law dealt harshly with those who committed crimes against property, with sentences provided to offenders including hanging. Many of those who committed such crimes were transported to the Australian colonies.

These changes were occurring at a time when Britain was also struggling financially because of the enormous cost of two wars. The American War of Independence ended in 1783 and was followed by the French Revolution and the War with France (1793-1815). The conclusion of the wars meant that there were now many ex-servicemen seeking employment at a time when unemployment and underemployment were rising and structural changes were occurring in the labour market.

While the middle and upper classes in British society may have been prosperous, the majority of the population was not so fortunate. By contemporary standards the labourer, regardless of location, lived extremely poorly. For example, housing was of a very low standard: small, damp, dark and leaking were often words used to describe housing used by the labouring class and their families. While it is clear that there was an infinite variety of housing and housing conditions for workers, it is nevertheless the case that housing was generally of a very poor standard. A Bath architect wrote: "The greater part of the cottages that fall within my observation, I found to be shattered, dirty, inconvenient, miserable hovels, scarcely affording a shelter for beasts of the forest, much less were

---

28. Russom, J. Australia; A Refuge for the Destitite. London c 1849. p.1.
29. Millar, J. The Origin of the Distinction of Ranks. 178, p.4, cited in Sherington, Geffrey. Australia's Immigrants. Sydney, 1990. p.3.

they proper habitation for the human species..."[30]. It seems that housing grew worse as one moved northwards.

It is also apparent that urban areas were dirty and unhygienic, with smells and smoke-laden air that were particularly offensive. Everywhere sanitation was primitive, there was no pure water (one commentator observed that this is probably why so many looked upon beer as their normal drink)[31], toilets were emptied into the streams and rubbish tipped out the front door. It is hardly surprising that disease was rampant in such confined and dirty conditions. Cholera was a permanent threat. A letter in *The Times* in 1849, signed by 54 people, gives a graphic insight into mid-century urban living conditions:

> *"May we beg beseech your proteckshion and power. We are, Sur, as it may be, living in a Wilderniss, so far as the rest of London knows anything of us, or as the rich and the great people care about. We live in muck and filth. We aint got no privez, dust bins, no drains, no water splies, and no drain or suer in the whole place....The stench of a gully-hole is disgustin. We al of us suffur, and numbers are ill, and if the colera comes Lord help us..."*

The mode of living common to the lower classes was described by two London doctors:

> *"It will scarcely appear credible though it is precisely true, that persons of the lowest class do not put clean sheets on their beds three times a year; that even where no sheets are used, they never wash or scour their blankets .... that from three to eight individuals of different ages often sleep in the same bed, there being in general but one room and one bed for each family.... The room occupied is either a deep cellar, almost inaccessible to light and admitting no change of air, or a garret with low roof and small windows, the passage to which is close, kept dark and filled with bad air..."*[32]

---

30. Cited in Shaw, A G L. Modern World History. Book 1. Melbourne, 1959. p. 12.
31. Shaw, A.G.L. .Modern World History. Book 1. Melbourne, 1959, p. 13.
32. ibid. p. 13.

Rural villages were also plagued by illness and disease, reports of which can readily be found in county and village newspapers. The following report in the *Bury & Norwich Post* on 25 April 1812 is typical:

> *"The small-pox has not been prevalent in the county but Lavenham has been afflicted with this disorder for the last two months to the injury of trade and the terror of the inhabitants and neighbourhood."*

The plight of the average Irish labourer was worse than that of those in other parts of the British Isles. The potato famine is often viewed as the reason for the emigration of large numbers of Irish people in the first half of the nineteenth century. However, for many the failure of the potato crops was simply the last straw.

The economic power of the British factories had a considerable adverse effect on the Irish handicraft industry. This was a cause of stress for many town workers and those engaged in cottage industry. However, the plight of the agricultural workers and the small tenant farmers who were concentrated in the south and west parts of Ireland was by far the worst. Their agricultural methods were primitive and their lifestyle was in many instances barely subsistence farming. Many of them lived in one-room cottages and slept on straw beds. A Dublin barrister giving evidence to the Commission on the Poor in Ireland in 1830, commented that their condition was "the most destitute and miserable that I have ever witnessed, more destitute than I have seen in foreign countries, and more miserable than I could possibly conceive human being could sustain."[33] The absentee landlords in Ireland compounded the problems for the agricultural labourers and small farmers. They were unaware of the difficulties of their tenants and of the degree of difficulty and the level of distress being caused. Most were content to leave management in the hands of land agents. As indicated previously, the population in the British Isles had grown rapidly. In the case of Ireland this resulted in a doubling of the population in the period 1780 to 1840. This rapid growth was accompanied by a process of land subdivision. Thus by 1841 about half of the landholdings of Ireland were under five acres and many were under one acre.

---

33. Cited in Broom, Richard. The Victorians, Arriving. Fairfax, Weldon & Broom Associates, Sydney, 1984. p. 43.

Those who lived on these small plots of land eked out a subsistence life style that relied on potato growing. The potatoes were generally eaten with milk and this combination provided a diet that enabled very basic subsistence living.

The combined effect of potato crop failure and the spread of typhus in the early part of the nineteenth century proved lethal for many Irish families. Potato crops failed periodically for many in the period 1815 to 1845 and each year from 1845 for the following five years, due to the wet weather and the potato blight, which it brought. The continual rains also brought the typhus fever and also resulted in a shortage of turf to fuel the fires. Unable to have fires many shut up their cottages and huddled together for warmth. This aided the spread of the louse, which carried the typhus. A large number of people became sick and many died. Famine, fever, death and misery occurred on an unprecedented scale in the five years following 1845. Many Irish fled in this period leaving behind the famine and disease that claimed the lives of so many relatives and friends.

Conditions in Ireland for the working class family continued to be extremely difficult into the second half of the century. The spread of disease, commonly referred to as pestilence, was common during this time. For example the outbreak of cholera was a cause of much misery and death. The *London Times* carried the following story in 1854:

> *"Despite snow and frost this terrible malady still lingers in some of its old haunts in the northern counties. Lately, according to the Banner of Ulster, it made its appearance for the first time, in Comber, and the fatality has been very great, though as yet the number of cases has been small. The disease still lingers in Newtownards, Ballymena, and Aghadoey, and the neighbouring country districts, though with a gradual diminution, both as to the number and the virulence of the cases. Respecting the progress of the pestilence in Comber the local physician wrote:*
>
> *'On the 15th a woman died after a short attack. On the 16th I was requested by a woman in great distress to go and visit her husband in the Cowvenel. I found this man had been labouring under cholera all night, and was then in collapse; there was no*

fire in the room where he lay, no furniture, save the bed, and that very scantily provided with bedclothes. On this person was the vestige of a shirt. From such hopeless antecedents little was to be expected - he died that night. On the 19th my services were sought some doors above this. On some straw in the corner lay a woman in collapse, in the agonies of cramps, and under the influence of too plentiful supply of spirits. There was neither fire or fireplace. By the application of hot bricks, a tub of hot water, and a little medicine, her situation was rendered somewhat more comfortable. Below were two children - one with glazy eyes and in a state of all but nudity was stretched on a sister's knee beside a fire of 'shows'; the other sitting her side, with its feet in a pool formed by the ejections of its stomach. Some hours after the husband informed me that his wife had some heat restored, and that he had given her a noggin of malt whiskey. The mother and one child died that night. In the same house were another mother and child, laid on a bed of 'shows'; both have since fallen victims to the distemper, as have likewise several others in the same street.[34]

It seems that the conditions in Ireland, including the spreading of cholera, were not only having an impact on the working classes but also others of more substantial means. The *London Times* commented on this on 29 April 1850 as follows:

> *".... Comparatively substantial farmers and their families are making their escape as from a house fire."*

There was also deterioration in the conditions of labourers and small tenant farmers (crofters) in Scotland in the thirty years after the Napoleonic Wars. The Highland Clearances (late eighteenth century to early nineteenth century) saw many crofters and their families evicted from their farms, sometimes by brute force, to make way for large-scale sheep farming. The eviction of highlanders from their homes reached a peak in the 1840s through to the early 1850s. The decision by landlords to evict was made for economic reasons. The highland economy had collapsed, while the population was still rising. Income from black cattle

---

34. *London Times*. 28 December, 1854.

had significantly declined and landlords saw sheep farming as a more profitable alternative. The introduction of sheep meant that people had to be removed. The policy of landlords was to clear the poorest highlanders from the land and to maintain only those crofters who were capable of paying rent. Those crofters who did stay to farm the few remaining small plots, experienced further financial and emotional hardship when a fungus caused potato crops to fail. Since potatoes were one of the only crops that would grow on the small plots the crofters had been allowed to access, the fungus led to widespread starvation and disease. The period between 1846 and 1857 in Scotland became known as the Highland Potato Famine (during this period many people were assisted to emigrate, particularly young men from poor families).

The subdivision of land in Scotland meant that a piece of land that had previously supported only one family had come to support three or four families. Rural industries that had supplemented the incomes of many tenant farmers, such as kelp farming (for fertilizer) and herring fishing were also in decline during this period. Housing was also of an extremely poor standard and the diet of many farming families consisted of potatoes, oatmeal and herrings. The clearances of the 1840s and 1850s and the famine and further clearances later in the century left many highland Scots in poverty and many also felt betrayed. There was a sense that landlord and state had betrayed a generation after their heroic actions at war. This was reflected in a sense of highland military prowess that the highlander felt ought to engender a greater gratitude from landlord and government.

However it's clear that the British Whig government of the 1850s saw emigration as a solution to the problems in the highlands. This view was clearly put in a review report of 1851 conducted by Sir John McNeill, who was responsible for the organisation established to oversee the reformed Scottish Poor Law. McNeill believed, as did many from his background, that charitable relief exacerbated poverty and that permanent solutions came from individuals accepting responsibility for their own fate. His report offered a very definite view that only emigration of a substantial number could prevent future occurrences of famine. It seems that this view continued to prevail throughout most of the nineteenth century.

Highlanders became organised in the second part of the century and attempted to put a counter view. A clear sense of bitterness prevailed during the century at how crofters were treated. Their cause was taken up by a number of people, including poets. The following is an example by a poet who took a strong stand against highland clearances and who in this poem employed the words of an elitist and greedy landowner to protest:

> *"The common people I do not like to see, like to see.*
> *A vulgar village is a blot on propertie, propertie.*
> *Although they say their homes are dear,*
> *I'll have no vulgar peasants here;*
> *I'll keep my land for sheep and deer;*
> *All for me, all for me."*[35]

The lot of the Scottish town labourer was generally better than that of the agricultural worker. Between 1832 and 1836 Scotland was swept by a surge of commercial and industrial activity. These developments had arrived later in Scotland than in England and hence they were accompanied by improved techniques, which had a greater impact on every aspect of Scottish life and in every district. The increasing mechanisation in factories led to replacement of people with machines. For example, the weavers of Paisley were replaced with machine looms in the early 1840s. The combination of changes in the towns and the highlands together with periods of economic downturn forced mass migration upon many Scottish people.

It is clear that throughout the United Kingdom the lot of the labourer and his family and the tenant farmers was not a happy one in the first part of the nineteenth century. For the urban dweller conditions may have been marginally better, but were still extremely difficult and at times very distressing. Thus it seems reasonable to conclude that the impact of urbanisation, the pressures of population increases, unemployment or underemployment, crop failures, disease, illness, and death, would have contributed significantly to the decision by many to emigrate from the British Isles. It's also clear that those who were adversely affected by these changing conditions were frequently

---

35. Bernstein, Marion (1846-1906). The Highland Laird's Song.

targeted for emigration by government and private organisations. This was particularly so as relief for the poor became urgent and the new Poor Laws of 1834 led to a rise in the number of workhouses. Parishes were often keen to encourage, and sometimes financially assist, destitute people to emigrate as this would reduce the welfare burden on the parish. The poor were also very vulnerable and sometimes exploited. Children were particularly vulnerable to exploitation. The following newspaper report is as example:

> *"At Ipswich sessions a bill of indictment was found against the church wardens and overseer of St Margaret Stoke for conspiracy in sending an orphan pauper boy aged 8 years to a chimney sweep and nightman in London after the magistrate had refused consent."* [36]

Pauperism and the Poor Laws

The impact of the Poor Laws on emigration was more complex than might be thought on an initial investigation. The group most affected by the operation of the Poor Laws was the agricultural labourer. The predicament of the agricultural labourer in the 1820s and 1830s was desperate, a fact demonstrated by the composition of his diet, which included little meat and bread and potatoes and often the only drink was water. The system of employing labourers on a daily or hourly basis made it easy for farmers to employ on a short-term basis to cut expenses. At the same time the increasing development of mechanisation meant that less men were required. A contemporary writer noted:

> *"The labourer is now in general, the mere servant of the day, or of the season; and is cast off, when the task is done, to seek a precarious subsistence from other work, if he can find it; if not from the parish rates."* [37]

Contrary to popular belief (including by those who formulated the new Poor Law of 1834) the cost of poor relief was not growing faster than the population nor faster than the national product in the 1820s. The problem

---

36. *Bury & Norwich Post*, 7 August 1811.
37. Thirsk, J. Suffolk Farming in the Nineteenth Century. Suffolk Records Society, 1958, p.22.

was that the cost of poor relief fell unequally on parishes. Impoverished parishes frequently had higher numbers of unemployed and underemployed labour and thus had to bear a far higher burden than wealthier parishes. Assisted emigration was consequently a useful method of saving money on poor relief in the short term. The search by parishes for such extreme solutions is an indication of the magnitude of the problem and reflected the concerns of farmers who had to pay the rates (local taxes).

Rural poverty and the burden that it imposed on the rates was the subject of many passionate political tracts, which almost universally condemned the abject state of 'pauperism' amongst the unemployed and underemployed rural poor. Thus the enemy was not seen as poverty (which was merely lack of money and a feature of a stratified society) but pauperism, which was seen as a character defect involving idleness, unreliability, drunkenness, etc. These character traits caused paupers to fall into desperate financial problems and their increasing numbers it was argued threatened the fabric of society. The difficult economic conditions of the 1830s fostered this attitude of condemnation towards those who were perceived as a type of subclass of undeserving people. A contemporary writer encapsulates this as follows:

> *"The whole life of a pauper is a lie – his whole study imposition; he lives by appearing not to be able to live; he will throw himself out of work, aggravate disease, get into debt, live in wretchedness, persevere in the most irksome applications, may bring upon himself the encumbrance of a family, for no other purpose than to get his share from the parish"*[38]

Pamphleteers of that time produced stories of instances where unscrupulous members of the poor had manipulated the system to which they owed their very subsistence and survival. This antipathy amongst the landowning classes had been bolstered by decades of rural disturbances. This was coupled with bitterness by landowners to the tendency of the unemployed to indulge in poaching. Another prevailing belief of the 1830s, which emerged from the influential writing of Malthus was the notion that paupers had been encouraged to make improper marriages and breed as a result of the support that

---

38. Walker, Thomas. Observations on the Nature, Extent and Effects of Pauperism and on the Means of Reducing It. London, J Hatcher & Sons, 1826, p.18.

had been given in relief during the previous half century. Many of the rural poor were therefore widely assumed to be cynically exploiting the parish relief system.

The Poor Law system proved unpopular, was badly run and subject to manipulation (not only by recipients of relief but by farmers). Many farmers were content to shift the labourers back and forward between farm and the parish. Because the demands for manpower in corn growing regions were seasonal, there was a good degree of employment at harvest time. In winter the workhouses were filled, mainly with single men as married men were generally favoured by farmers due to the high cost of supporting their families in the workhouse. In summer months, when employment was high, the workhouses were used as a kind of labour exchange.

The operation of the Poor Law progressively changed the attitude of farmers to emigration. They were the administrators of the Poor Law at the local level and initially enthusiastically supported assisting recipients of relief to emigrate. However, in the latter part of the 1830s their attitude to emigration changed. It seemed that the financial burden of having a surplus labour force was preferable to losing a flexible labour force. This dilemma for farmers was summarised by one proprietor:

> "The labourers except during harvest, becomes during the greater part of the year a dead weight upon us."[39]

A large surplus of labour was required because different numbers of labourers were required every year depending on the state of the harvest. Resident full-time workers provided farmers with only about half of the labour force needed during harvest. As a consequence farmers intervened to cause the collapse of some schemes to assist the emigration of agricultural workers to the colonies.

Many agricultural labourers became trapped in poverty. They were reluctant to move and hoped that conditions might change. Because a number were uneducated they were easily exploited and persuaded that emigration was not in their interest by rumours of being forced to

---

39. Lee-Warner, H. to Parry, Sir P, 8 August 1835, in Digby, A. The Labour Market and the Continuity of Social Policy After 1834, Economic History Review, No.28, 1975, p.82.

emigrate to unknown undesirable places or by anti-poor law propaganda about being sent to workhouses (after 1834 parishes were grouped into unions and each union had to build a workhouse). Many of the negative perceptions circulating about workhouses had a basis in fact. Conditions in them were kept harsh, so that only those who desperately needed help would ask for it. Although for most people it was not compulsory to go to a workhouse, forced admission was always possible if a worker became unemployed, sick or old. Increasingly workhouses contained only orphans, the old, the sick and the insane. The threat of being sent to a workhouse was ever present in the minds of unemployed agricultural workers. This fear is illustrated in the following letter to the *Bury and Norwich Post* on 14 September 1831 from a man who had emigrated to Canada:

> *"my spirits are good and health much better than when we left England, I have no fear of going to the workhouse, tell my friends in Cratfield from this I was a great fool not to have come 5 years ago."*

The odds were clearly stacked against the unemployed agricultural labourer and thus, as the nineteenth century progressed, more were willing to abandon their birthplace when given the opportunity. The agricultural depression of the 1840s saw more unemployment and placed increased pressure on the parish to provide relief. Renewed efforts were thus made by the parish to assist unemployed labourers to emigrate. During the 1850s and 1860s farm outputs rose, imports were low and prices rose. This marked a revival in farming fortunes known as the 'golden age of farming'. However the countryside was still characterised by disharmony and disruption. Although the wages of farm workers rose they did not increase as fast as food prices. Farm workers, particularly in the south, were among the most poorly paid in the country (receiving about two-thirds the wage of their town counterparts).[40] By this stage positive stories were emerging from those that had emigrated to add some substance to the rumours that had previously circulated about the colonies, which were often viewed with suspicion. These new accounts of conditions in the colonies assisted agricultural labourers in their decision to emigrate. The conditions of rural workers continued to be appalling, as shown in an 1871 report on the conditions of agricultural families:

---

40. Wormell, Peter. The Countryside in the Golden Age of Farming. Abberton Books, 2000, p.69.

> "The average dietary of labouring population in rural areas in Southern England may be described as following – beef and mutton was rarely tasted so that they do not form part of their diet…Bread and cheese forms the main part of their diet for adults, the poor mans cow being a blessing of the past as milk does not or rarely forms much part of the diet in village children, even in infancy …I know a large parish in Suffolk mainly dependent on ditch water in certain seasons the administration of vermifuge would expel from the bowels of perhaps half the children, worms many inches long". [41]

From the 1840s it became increasingly clear to rural labourers and their families that emigration offered a way to escape the poverty of rural England, including the circumstances imposed by the operation of the Poor Law. This process was assisted through the Poor Law Amendment Act of 1834, which empowered the ratepayers of any parish to raise or borrow funds to defray the expenses of the emigration of poor persons willing to emigrate. The usual practice was for the parish to bear the expenses of conveying the emigrants to the port of embarkation and to provide them with money for their immediate needs on arriving in the colony. Frequently the parish was also required to supply an outfit of clothing for the passage. The cost of the passage was borne entirely by the colony. The Poor Law Commissioners saw these provisions in the legislation as not only a way of moving poor people from rural areas but also those in urban areas, particularly from the workhouses.

Conditions in the Colonies

Prevailing conditions in the colonies also had an impact on the flow of emigrants. While economic and social conditions at home continued to present difficulties for many individuals and families this situation contrasted with enthusiastic reports of progress in the colonies with agriculture, commerce and the pastoral industry. The 1820s and 1830s were fairly prosperous years in the colonies and wages were generally good (particularly as compared to wages in the home country). There was a high demand for skilled labour in the building trade, and for pastoral

---

41. *Bury and Norwich Post*, 14th March 1871.

and agricultural workers. The newly-settled Port Phillip District attracted high wages for workers because of the very severe labour shortage. Throughout the whole period from 1820 to 1850 emigration rose and fell as economic and social conditions at home grew worse or better. For most of this period the colonies continued to progress at an encouraging rate. Hence the conditions at home and in the colonies combined to produce the push-pull effect.

Information about favourable conditions in the colonies was distributed in a number of ways in the United Kingdom. There was often an emphasis in the information circulating in the United Kingdom on the much higher wages and better working conditions in the colonies compared to the home country. An example of this is contained in the information provided in a series of lectures given in a number of counties by colonist Arthur Hodgson in the spring of 1849:

> *"The wages in Australia are high; shepherds at this moment are earning from £20 to £30 per annum, and those men who are employed to look after cattle are earning a still greater sum; carpenters are obtaining from £30 to £40 per annum, and even more; married couples, as house servants, £30 to £35 annually; and all these payments are exclusive of food, which is given in every case – namely, a weekly ration to each person of 10lbs. of flour, 10lbs. of meat, 1/4lb. of tea, and 2lb. of sugar; which in England would be worth 8s.4d. per week, or nearly £22 per annum."*[42]

It's interesting that those writing about conditions in the colonies often mentioned the superior climate. This was clearly seen as a factor that may influence prospective emigrants. It's likely that for some people, for example those with certain types of health problems, this could be a significant factor while for others it may simply have been a bonus.

As the century went by there emerged an expanding number of publications extolling the increasing number of services, amenities and sophistication to be found in the colonies, particularly in the cities. They

---

42. Hodgson, Arthur. Emigration to the Australian Settlements (second edition). Trelawney Saunders, Charring Cross, London, 1848, p.24.

frequently spoke in glowing terms of the development that had taken place. The following two examples are typical.

Samuel Sidney wrote extensively about the colonies and in 1852 described Adelaide as follows (when it was in fact still largely a frontier town with a population slightly less than 15,000):

> "...the city of Adelaide appears in the midst of trees, often full of the most rare and curious birds.....Adelaide, although very unlike a city according to European notions, presents a much more pleasing appearance than Melbourne, which is crowded into a narrow valley... South Adelaide is considered the commercial quarter of the town, and contains the principal streets, one of which is 130 feet wide and Government House, in the centre of a domain of ten acres. Hindley-street is the Regent –street of Adelaide..........In the surrounding suburbs many pretty villages have been founded, both inland and on the shore ...Many pretty cottages are to be found in the suburbs as neat and highly finished as in England."[43]

Alexander Sutherland wrote about Melbourne and Victoria and in his largest work there is a 'modest' description of Melbourne:

> "Let us show our visitor the finer aspects ......guide him, some fine spring morning to see the streets of this our Melbourne, the city of many a fond affection; associated with none of the pride of an heroic past, but lovable in the bright, the cheerful, the exhilarating hopefulness of the future she spreads out for her four hundred thousand inhabitants."[44]

While conditions in the colonies may have been superior to those prevailing in the United Kingdom it's not clear to what extent this influenced people to emigrate. Information about conditions in the colonies was increasingly available through newspaper reports, letters to the editor, pamphlets and other printed material, and through lectures

---

43. Sidney, Samuel. The Three Colonies of Australia: New South Wales, Victoria and South Australia. London, 1852, p.365.
44. Sutherland, Alexander. Victoria and its Metropolis, past and present. Volume 2. McCarron, Bird & Co., Melbourne, 1888, p.542.

and public forums. It appears that the volume of this information increased as time went by. However, for many of the working class, particularly those who were illiterate, these sources of information may not have been accessible (although it's clear that information about the colonies was passed about by word of mouth).

During the early part of the nineteenth century Australia failed to benefit from emigration to the same extent as America, not because of less progress or inferior conditions, but probably because of the distance and associated additional cost. However, with the advent of assisted emigration this situation changed. The British government, the colonies and other groups, individuals and private organisations, provided various types of assistance, including free passage, loans, bounty schemes, and subsidised or part-payment of passage. These arrangements were sometimes one time in nature (e.g. a single vessel financed by an individual or society) while other arrangements were more comprehensive, but were often subject to changes in the terms and conditions over time and were frequently different from colony to colony.

Government Assistance

The costs of emigrating to the Australian colonies were high when viewed in the context of the low incomes of many of those who decided to emigrate and the much cheaper cost of sailing to North America. Most of those who emigrated under sail travelled as steerage passengers. This was the cheapest way of travelling to the colonies and, of course, the most uncomfortable. It appears that during the first three quarters of the century only about six per cent were able to afford the luxury of travelling by first, second or intermediate class cabin.[45] This proportion did increase in the last quarter of the century. An agricultural labourer's wage in the mid-nineteenth century was around 10/- per week and steerage passage cost about £10. The passage cost increased significantly during the gold rush and was over two and a half times higher at one point before settling back marginally to around £23 in 1853. The cost of a first-class cabin was around three times the cost of travelling by steerage.

---

45. Hassam, A. Sailing to Australia. Manchester, 1994. p. 9.

The passage to North America was obviously a more attractive option for many. Particularly as a number of prospective emigrants would have had relatives and friends already in North America and the cost of the passage to Australia was some five times more than to North America, and the journey four times as long. Australia also had something of a poor reputation as the home of convicts. Thus the matter of cost had to be overcome.

While some single men were able to obtain free passage by working their way to the colonies as a ship hand, for the majority of emigrants the full costs had to be found or assisted passage obtained.

By 1800 the settlement in the Colony of New South Wales was no longer at immediate risk of starvation. There were still concerns, however, about having enough skilled-labourers to sustain the growing population. In addition to this, the British Government was eager to colonise other areas of the continent before their French enemies were able to. There was also a desire to make money from agricultural exports. These factors contributed to the need for more free settlers, particularly skilled workers, to migrate to Australia.

However, given the debate about the value of emigration, the provision of financial assistance to emigrants required a change in attitude by some significant people in authority in Britain. The changes to British society, described previously in this chapter, particularly the resulting pressure on available resources and increasing crime against property, began to worry some. Likewise the growing costs associated with caring for poor and destitute people, through the Poor Law, was a cause for concern. Thus the changes that were having such an impact on the way individuals and families viewed emigration were also instrumental in changing the mind of many in authority towards emigration and towards the provision of government support and assistance to promote emigration.

In order to overcome the problem of finding funds to finance assisted passage to the colonies it was decided that, rather than give Australian land away to ex-soldiers (whose period of service had finished) and emancipists (convicts who had finished serving a sentence or been granted a pardon before their sentence had expired), colonial land would be sold. The proceeds from land sales would then be used to pay for or subsidise the passage of poorer migrants to Australia. The British Government had been under pressure from Wakefield and his followers to fund emigration by sale of land. Wakefield believed that emigration was an important function of government. It was also clear that by the 1830s the demand for free labour in the colonies was acute, while it was felt that the disproportion of sexes caused immorality and social evils of the most serious kind.[46]

Still cautious about providing financial assistance to encourage emigration the government began with a modest scheme in 1831 to assist female emigration to New South Wales and Van Diemen's Land, financed by the sale of colonial land. It was felt that this scheme would redress the male-female imbalance in the colonies and meet a colonial demand for domestic servants. Two ships sailed in 1832; one for each colony laden with single women, 14 more had sailed by 1836.

At the same time it was decided that part of the funds raised through the land sales would be used for a fairly large scheme of emigration of artisans and agricultural labourers. However, for the time being, the scheme would be restricted to assisting the emigration of mechanics.

The scheme provided a grant of £8, or approximately half the cost of a passage, for selected women (this was an unconditional grant). In 1833 the amount of the grant was increased to cover full fare. In the case of the male emigrants an amount of £20 was advanced but they were required to eventually repay the £20 from their wages. It was planned that both of these arrangements would operate side by side, and they were both placed under the supervision of the Commissioners for Emigration. The Commissioners duly issued regulations to cover the operation of the assisted passage arrangements. The Commissioners were inundated with letters largely from organisations, such as the London Female Penitentiary and the Refuge for the Destitute, and other similar institutions in England and Ireland seeking access to the scheme. The government welcomed the involvement of these organisations as it meant that a ready source of potential emigrants was at hand and this made administration simpler and less costly.

---

46. Madgwick, R.B. Immigration Into Eastern Australia 1788-1851. Sydney University Press, 1969, pp.94-5.

The Commissioners for Emigration were purely an advisory body and the Colonial Office, who had the task of selecting the emigrants, welcomed the involvement of charitable organisations. The Colonial Office had no staff competent in the conduct of emigration and hence in practice this responsibility was devolved to charitable organisations, which sometimes paid part of the passage or the cost of the equipment for the emigrants in the early period of the scheme. The scheme was criticised in the colonies on the ground that it delivered poor quality immigrants, particularly female emigrants. It was claimed that a number of the emigrant ships were filled with paupers from workhouses. The colonial employers and officials complained that many of the early female arrivals were not qualified as servants or suitable as wives. Some critics also described some of the females as prostitutes. The Rev J D Lang, for example, asserted that the females assisted in the early 1830s rendered "the whole colony, and especially the town of Sydney, a sink of prostitution".[47]

The Commissioners for Emigration were dismissed in August 1832 and by 1833 had been replaced by the London Emigration Commission, which was formed from an emigration sub-committee of the Refuge for the Destitute. From 1833 to 1836 this was the official organisation through which emigrants were sent to the Australian colonies. The Colonial Office had effectively handed over the operation of the scheme to a charitable organisation. Thus from the beginning female emigration in particular was associated with workhouses and charitable institutions. The Commission had two roles: the selection of emigrants and arranging for their transport to the colonies. While the Commission took a personal role in vetting some of the applications in the London area it relied on its agents (largely ship owners) for selection, particularly in places other than London. The shipowners also provided the vessels. They were paid £16 for every person carried to the colonies and hence it was in their interest to send every vessel fully laden.

However, despite the criticisms levelled at these arrangements and the quality of the emigrants selected they did enable many females to

---

47. Madgwick, R. B. *Immigration into Eastern Australia, 1788-1851.* Sydney University Press, 1969. p. 105.

emigrate. For example, between 1832 and 1836 the 16 emigrant ships that had sailed delivered 2503 women, 475 men and 904 children (under 14 years) to New South Wales and about half these numbers – 1186 women, 286 men and 569 children, to Van Diemen's Land.[48]

Posters, like the one below, were used in 1834 to attract single women to the colonies.

Typical Poster Aimed at Attracting Female Emigrants
(By permission State Library of New South Wales)

---

48. Alford, K. Free Settlers Before 1851. In Jupp, James ed. The Australian People – An Encyclopedia of the Nation, It's People & Their Origins. Cambridge University Press, 2001, p.41.

With regard to the repayment of the passage cost by male emigrants it became increasingly clear that many had no intention of repaying the advance made to them. The colonial authorities found themselves unable to collect more than a very small proportion of the money due for the cost of the passage. This induced the home government in June 1835 to convert the loan into a free passage. Thus by 1835 assisted emigration became entirely free, with the whole cost being paid out of colonial funds.

The scheme to assist women emigrate to New South Wales was terminated in 1836. Even with significant numbers of females arriving through these early schemes there was still concern about the disproportionate ratio of men to women in New South Wales. In 1838, women were still outnumbered by men at a ratio of one to four. This increased to a ratio of one to twenty in rural areas.

Because of the continuing dissatisfaction with the conduct of the assisted passage scheme operated by the home government on behalf of the colonies, particularly of the poor quality of the emigrants selected (inappropriate skills, work ethic, morals, age, etc) a number of discussions took place about reforming the arrangements. While some changes in arrangements occurred there also emerged the desire for the colonies to control their own scheme. The colonies wished to have an arrangement over which the British Government exercised no control and where the colonies selected the emigrants through their agents and the emigrants were transported in ships engaged privately. Out of this discussion a new scheme of assisted emigration, to be known as the Bounty Scheme, emerged. The old assisted arrangements involving the British government would continue in parallel with the new Bounty Scheme and was referred to from that point as the Government Scheme (the funds for this scheme would continue to be provided by the colonies). By the end of 1836 the two schemes were operating side by side. It was decided that the governors of the colonies could apply one-third of the funds for emigration to the Bounty Scheme and the remaining two-thirds would be applied by the authorities in Great Britain to the Government Scheme. The London Emigration Commission was abolished and the position of Chief Agent for Emigration was created. Thomas Frederick Elliot was appointed to this position and took up his duties in April 1837 with the task of improving the administration of emigration arrangements and meeting the demands being made by the colonies.

It was thus on 20 October 1837 that a paper was issued by the Government Emigration Office, signed by T Frederick Elliot, Agent General for Emigration, setting out conditions under which the Crown would assist individuals to emigrate to New South Wales or Van Diemen's Land (although the document later added that "it is seldom that there will be an opportunity of sending a ship to Van Diemen's Land"). The paper indicated that the "practice of giving, or advancing on loan, sums of money in aid of private means of individuals desirous to emigrate has been discontinued". It further added, "the plan, which prevailed for some time, of sending out unmarried women separately, at the expense of the public, has also been discontinued". The arrangements outlined in the paper for assisting people to emigrate would involve the government 'occasionally' sending from different parts of the United Kingdom vessels that would provide free passage to persons falling into the following categories:

- They must belong to the class of Mechanics and Handicraftsmen or Farm servants;
- They must be married, and be accompanied to the colony by their wives;
- Neither the husband or the wife must be more than thirty-five years of age;
- They must be able to establish their character for industry, sobriety and good moral character.

The paper also indicated that the "number of ships dispatched in the course of a year cannot be very great" and that they "must be filled with persons who have an easy access to the Port whence they are to sail". Whenever a vessel became available it would be announced by "public advertisement". The paper also set out the following conditions and information:

- A surgeon would be appointed for each vessel;
- The surgeon would be responsible for investigating and selecting each emigrant by visiting the port of departure (his decision would be final);
- The surgeon's appointment would be announced and all applications to be made direct to him;
- The passage cost would be free but emigrants must meet any expenses involved prior to joining the vessel;

- Emigrants must bring "sufficient quantity" of clothes for the passage (the paper also provided a rather strange list of clothing considered 'indispensible' for the passage – suits, hats, flannel petticoats, multiple pairs of 'dark hose', neckerchiefs for men, 'dark gowns' for women);
- Emigrants will be provided with provisions, bedding and cooking utensils (a table was attached setting out the provisions to be provided each day of the week for female and male emigrants for biscuits, beef, pork, sugar, tea, flour, peas, oatmeal and vinegar);
- Emigrants on arriving would be free to work for whoever they choose and would not be 'bound to Government' or liable to repay the cost of the passage.

As a result of continuing criticisms by the colonies of the Government Scheme the position of Agent General for Emigration was abolished. In the period between appointment to the position and 1840 Elliot had worked hard to streamline and reform the organisation and to satisfy the needs of the colonies. The emigrants he sent were superior in economic and moral quality than previously (despite the considerable increase in numbers sent) and he tackled the problem of sickness and morality on emigrant ships with considerable success. He, however, failed to convince colonial authorities that he had not used colonial funds for the relief of funds in Britain. At the end of 1839 Elliot transferred a well-functioning emigration system to the new Colonial Land and Emigration Commission (CLEC). The establishment of the Commission was important in the further development of emigration from the British Isles to the Australian colonies. With the Commission came a more orderly system of emigration. This contrasted to the much larger but ill-organised migration to North America.

In addition to the continuing assisted passage arrangements under the Government Scheme there were periodically special short-term targeted programs of assistance. For example, one such arrangement was the Irish Orphan Scheme, which was aimed at girls and women aged between 14 and 18 from Irish workhouses. In 1848 and 1849 over 20 vessels carried 2000 to New South Wales, 1200 to Port Phillip (Victoria) and 600 to Adelaide (South Australia). This scheme of assisted passage, like many others, was short lived.[49] At the same time under similar arrangements a number of orphan girls were sent from English workhouses. The costs of these arrangements were borne in part by the parishes in which the orphans were selected and in part by the colonial government.

Under the British Poor Law Amendments Act of 1849 the Poor Law authority was permitted to assist not only the destitute but also poor people who wished to emigrate.[50] Similarly powers under the Irish Poor Law Extension Act allowed parishes in Ireland to provide assistance for the poor to emigrate. The parishes were required to contribute to the emigration costs. However, the colonial governments were increasingly taking a hard line on the type of person they would accept for assisted passage and were resisting pressure from British authorities to accept whoever was being put forward for emigration. Despite the criticisms by the colonies, between September 1849 and March 1852, 391 Irish were assisted to emigrate to the colonies by Irish parishes (mostly to New South Wales) and between January 1847 and December 1851, English parishes assisted the emigration of 3445 persons.[51]

Prior to 1850 it's clear that assisted passage arrangements operated by the British Government (sometimes with contributions by British philanthropists, parishes and charitable organisations) were often aimed at relieving poverty in Britain. Many of the women assisted were clearly poor because poverty was periodically a condition of eligibility.

After the 1850s there was a change in the types of people targeted for emigration under the arrangements operated by the British Government through the CLEC on behalf of the colonies. In the case of single female emigration, Janice Gothard believes that the chance to escape poverty was a key factor in influencing women to take advantage of the various programs

---

49. Hamilton, Paula. Tipperarifying the Moral Atmosphere, Irish Catholic Immigration and the State 1840-1860, in Sydney Labour History Group, What Rough Beast? The State and Social Order in Australian History. Sydney 1982, p.22.
50. British Parliamentary Papers, 1861, xxxiii, l, p.12.
51. Madgwick, R.B. Immigration into Eastern Australia 1788-1851. Sydney University Press, 1969, p.215.

of assistance to emigrate.⁵² Despite the criticism of the assisted passage arrangements in the first half of the century, 187,000 free settlers had emigrated to Australia by 1850; most had arrived under assisted passage arrangements.

Circulars continued to be issued periodically indicating that financial assistance with passage was available, the applying conditions and the target group(s). For example in March 1853 Colonization Circular No.13 was promulgated announcing that "funds have been provided to the British Emigration Commissioners, by colonial revenues, for assisted passage, by New South Wales, Victoria and South Australia" (the circular also noted that for the moment, funds were also available for Western Australia and Van Diemen's Land, but no funds were available for assisting persons wishing to emigrate to the North American Colonies). The rules for those wishing to apply for assistance from the available funds were as follows:

1. The emigrants must be of those callings, which from time to time are most in demand in the colony. They must be sober, industrious, of general good moral character, and have been in the habit of working for wages, and going out to do so in the colony, of all of which decisive certificates will be required. They must also be in good health, free from all bodily or mental defects, and the adults must in all respects be capable of labour and going out to work for wages, at the occupation specified on their Application Forms. The candidates who will receive a preference are respectable young women trained to domestic or farm service, and families in which there is a preponderance of females.
2. The separation of husbands and wives and of parents from children under 18 will in no case be allowed.
3. Single women under 18 cannot be taken without their parents, unless they go under the immediate care of some near relatives. Single women over 35 years of age are ineligible. Single women with illegitimate children can in no case be taken.
4. Single men cannot be taken unless they are sons in eligible families, containing at least a corresponding number of daughters.

---

52. Gothard, Janice. Pity the Poor Immigrant: Assisted Single Female Migration to Colonial Australia contained in Poor Australia Immigrants in the Nineteenth Century. Visible Immigrants: Two edited by Eric Richards. ANU, Canberra, 1991.

5. Families in which there are more than 2 children under 7, or 3 children under 10 years of age, or in which the sons outnumber the daughters, widowers, and widows with young children, persons who intend to resort to the goldfields, to buy land, or to invest capital in trade, or who are in the habitual receipt of parish relief, or who have not been vaccinated or not had the small-pox, cannot be accepted.

It's clear from these conditions that in 1853 the colonies were seeking healthy single females with particular qualifications and families with a 'preponderance' of females as their preferred immigrants. It's also clear that from this time the colonies progressively took greater control of the emigration process, largely by appointing agents to undertake selection and arrange transport. South Australia was the first colony to appoint its own Immigration Agent to London in 1858.

The various types of assistance offered by the colonies from the 1850s through the CLEC provided government assistance for either free or very cheap passage. Sometimes the assistance was limited to particular types of people. The rates of assistance often differed between the colonies and this frequently influenced the decision by the emigrant on the chosen destination. For example, in 1864 the New South Wales immigration agent reported that only by lowering the cost of the subsidised passage to that colony could it hope to encourage more single female immigrants. At that time Victoria, South Australia and Queensland were offering free passage to single women (although they were required to contribute 10 shillings towards the cost of bedding and ship kit).[53] It appears that some colonial authorities were sometimes slow to recognise that even a small difference in subsidy of only a pound or two made a substantial difference in attracting immigrants. However the agents they employed to make the selection were much more sensitive to the circumstances of the British working class.

For the Scots the nineteenth century was a period of enormous emigration and they played a disproportionate role in that mass migration movement. The population of Scotland late in the century was a little over 4 million and some 2 million emigrated by the end

---

53. New South Wales, Votes & Proceedings of the Legislative Assembly 1865-1866, vol. 2, p.218.

of that period.[54] In the case of assisted Scottish emigrants, many came from the highlands under special arrangements as a result of clearances and evictions. On a number of the highland estates emigration was used as an aggressive type of estate 'management'. The Dukes of Argyll and Sutherland and other large landowners financed emigration schemes. Offers of funding were linked to eviction, which left little choice to the crofter. However, the Emigration Advances Act of 1851 made emigration more widely available to poor people and the Highland and Islands Emigration Society was set up to oversee the resettlement process. Under the scheme a landlord could secure a passage to Australia for a nominee at a cost of £1. Between 1846 and 1857, approximately 16,500 people of the poorest types (mainly young men) were assisted to emigrate. The greatest loss occurred in the islands, particularly Skye, Mull, the Long Island and the mainland parishes of the Inner Sound. The British government was prepared to provide the funds for this scheme only because it felt that the emigration of large numbers was needed to overcome the highland problem and prevent famine in the future. It was against paying relief to the poor. The numbers choosing the Australian colonies as a destination were relatively small until around 1837, when a combination of factors led to an enormous increase in Scottish emigration to the colonies until around 1847. Many of those who emigrated were skilled workers (including many agricultural workers) and there were significant numbers of emigrants with capital (some came as unassisted passengers).

It's interesting to note that throughout the nineteenth century the Irish were one group that depended heavily on government assistance to be able to emigrate. Even after the gold discoveries, which changed the attractiveness of Australia as a destination, the Irish still largely depended on assisted passage. Where this was not available, or was insufficient, they sought other means of support such as an arrangement known as nominated chain migration. Under such arrangements friends or relatives who had preceded the emigrant paid part or the full cost of the passage and were reimbursed later from the earnings of the emigrant. This type of nomination scheme operated in Victoria from 1856 to 1861 and it

---

54. Baines, Dudley. European Emigration 1815-1930. Economic History Review, 47, 1994, pp.525-44.

allowed local Irish to deposit cash in relation to a specified migrant and the colonial government paid the remainder of the passage.

Clearly many of those who emigrated could not have done so without some type of financial assistance from government, or from philanthropic or private societies. Eric Richards concluded that the availability of government assistance led to the emigration to Australia of some of the poorest people in British society.[55] It's interesting to note that the British and colonial authorities responsible for administering these assistance programs saw the process as equivalent to acceptance of charity by the immigrant. This attitude seemed to prevail even though many of those who were assisted were targeted by the colonies to meet particular skill requirements (e.g. building, farming, domestic service). For single women the acceptance of this charity often implied that they would adopt the 'qualities' required of a servant (obedience, discipline, deference). On the other hand those who paid their own passage or made a substantial contribution were seen as having valued qualities such as independence, thrift and providence (these seemed to be particularly valued qualities in men). Another observation about assisted passage recipients is that it seems that for at least some of those who emigrated, particularly in the early years, there was probably no real choice.

Earlier in this chapter I talked about a push-pull effect at work in influencing the decision by those considering emigrating. However I believe that for some assisted passage emigrants there was a considerable push by government and charitable authorities in order to reduce or remove domestic problems (e.g. to reduce numbers on welfare, empty institutions, remove those considered troublesome). This was clearly more prevalent prior to the 1850s (at which time the colonies took more interest in selection) and was possibly more so for single women (e.g. from workhouses). There was probably more potential for this when the emphasis was on assisting paupers to emigrate and declined as the emphasis shifted to assisting those who were poor but probably semi-skilled or skilled.

---

55. Richards, Eric. Annals of the Australian Immigrant, in Richards, Eric, Reid, Richard, Fitzpatrick, David, Visible Immigrants: Neglected Sources for the History of Australian Immigration. Canberra 1989, p. 21.

Bounty Schemes

As stated above it was because of the considerable and ongoing criticism of the Government Scheme that the Bounty Scheme emerged. The colonies felt this arrangement would offer a greater certainty that the right type of immigrant would be brought to the colony and they felt that it would be a more effective and efficient use of colonial funds. It was asserted that the expense of maintaining the immigrant on arrival would be avoided because they would already be engaged to serve with the settler who imported them.

The principles underlying Bounty immigration were similar to those suggested by Edward Gibbon Wakefield in his persistent pressuring of the British Government about populating the colonies. He suggested that:

- The system of free land grants should cease and Colonial land should be sold.
- The revenue from these sales should be used to boost emigration from the United Kingdom.
- Certain conditions should apply to the type of emigrant accepted.

Wakefield and his followers were ongoing petitioners of the British Government about emigration, land use and assisted passage arrangements.

Under the Bounty System that was adopted the colonists would choose the emigrants in Britain and bring them to the colony. They would receive from the colonial government a bounty equal or nearly equal to the cost of the passage. On arrival in the colony the emigrant was required to appear before a Board appointed by the governor to examine the testimonials of character, which they were required to bring with them (signed by a responsible person). The Board was also interested to see proof of age, such as a certified copy from a baptism register. If the Board was satisfied with these documents and believed that the immigrant was in good health a certificate was issued entitling the settler to claim reimbursement for the funds advanced for the passage cost. The Board had the power to refuse bounties on immigrants they felt were unsuitable to the requirements of the colony.

The first set of Bounty regulations were contained in a Government Notice issued in Sydney by Governor Bourke in October 1835. The bounties being offered were:

- £30 for a married man and his wife (provided that neither was over 35 years of age);
- £5 for each of their children over 12 months old;
- £15 for every unmarried female between 15 and 30 years old (who must be under the protection of a married couple);
- £10 for an unmarried male 18 to 25 years of age (only permitted if the settler brings an equal number of females accompanying and attached to a family).

All the adult males must be either mechanics or farm servants.

In order to ensure that the scheme operated smoothly, and to keep a check on numbers, settlers were required to submit to the Colonial Secretary the names of people they wished to bring to the colony, together with a description of the health, character and trade or occupation of each person. They also had to provide a permit from the colony showing that the colony was prepared to pay the bounty.

The Bounty Scheme arrangements changed from time to time but always involved eligibility conditions, similar to those above promulgated in 1835, aimed at targeting the type of immigrants required in the colonies. For example, the conditions always involved age and skill requirements. Further to this, men generally had to be agricultural labourers, shepherds, carpenters, smiths, wheelwrights, bricklayers or masons and single women, domestic or agricultural servants. These regulations were devised to limit the number of non-productive immigrants, such as the elderly and children, and to establish a balance of the sexes. According to the colonies, the ideal immigrant was a young married couple with skills and no children.

However, the regulations were never effective in achieving exactly what the colonies required, despite the care taken by colonists in their drafting. The system gradually degenerated into commercial speculation controlled by British shipowners. While the conditions were set by the colonies, in practice, because of distance and isolation from England and the expense of maintaining an agent in England, the selection and recruiting was performed by English shipowners, hence the settler played a passive part. This meant that the system soon fell into the hands of shipowners and speculators. It wasn't long before the agents applied for and were granted permits in their own names and the shipowners transported any persons the agent's selected. The wishes of the settlers, in whose interests the Bounty Scheme had been established, were no longer considered.

The rates of the bounty that colonists could claim were changed a number of times. By 1840 the bounty levels were set at £38 for married couples, £19 for single adults and between £5 and £15 for children, depending on their age. As the bounties were gradually increased in value and the age limits extended, more shipowners found the returns attractive and entered the business competing with existing shipping firms. It seems that in these circumstances less care was taken of immigrants. With increased competition came instances of poor selection of vessels and of overloading with cargo. This led to criticism that the welfare of immigrants was being neglected. It also appears that the agents misrepresented the conditions in the colonies to prospective immigrants. Despite the problems and criticisms of the Scheme, between 1835 and 1841 about 40,000 bounty emigrants arrived in Australia.[56]

It was common for vessels to be commissioned to take bounty immigrants to the colonies and they sometimes departed from ports other than the usual ports in England used for embarkation for those emigrating to the colonies. An example of this is the embarkation at Tobermory, Scotland in 1837 of people chosen to immigrate to the colony of New South Wales. The vessel ***Brilliant*** had been engaged to take people from various parts of Scotland. This was reported as follows:

> *"A large body of emigrants sailed from Tobermory on the 27th September for New South Wales. The vessel was the 'Brilliant', and its size and splendid fittings were greatly admired.*

---

56. Bassett, J, Bomford, J, Abrahams, O. Voices from The Past. Australian History to Federation. Milton, Queensland 1994. p.65.

> *The people to be conveyed by this vessel are decidedly the most valuable that have ever left the shores of Great Britain; they are all of excellent moral character, and from their knowledge of agriculture, and the management of sheep and cattle, must prove a most valuable acquisition to a colony like New South Wales.*
>
> *The Rev. Mr MacPherson, of Tobermory, preached a farewell sermon before the party sailed. The total number of emigrants was 322, made up as follows: from Ardnamurchan and Strontian, 105; Coll and Tiree, 104; Mull and Iona, 56; Morven, 25; Dunoon, 28; teachers 2; surgeons 2. A visitor from New South Wales presented as many of the party as he met with letters of introduction, and expressed himself highly gratified with the prospect of having so valuable an addition to the colony. A government agent superintended the embarkation.*[57]

It's interesting to note that the sermon preached by the Reverend MacPherson was delivered in Gaelic. The letters of introduction given to the immigrants were to the colonists who would be employing them. It was reported that these letters were "joyfully received as passports to a secure and profitable employment".

From around 1837 entrepreneurs, merchants, shipping agents and landowners in Australia, acting in concert with Scottish merchants, shipowners and shipping agents began to take advantage of the bounty arrangements. It seems that they were able to work within the bounty conditions to deliver large numbers of skilled craftsmen, including agricultural labourers to the colonies (particularly to New South Wales and the Port Phillip District). Some of this activity occurred because Scottish commercial interests in Australia often had connections in Scotland.

The most common criticisms made of the Bounty Scheme were as follows:

- Settlers complained that not all migrants knew the trade they claimed;

---

57. *Inverness Courier Index*, 1837, p.212.

- Not many colonial settlers had the money to pay the Agents in the United Kingdom to act for them and the system soon fell into the hands of the ship owners or of speculators;
- There were not many checks to the system;
- The ship owners sometimes changed the arrangements;
- Discipline aboard ship was often neglected;
- The Agents in the United Kingdom created false impressions of life in New South Wales and Van Diemen's Land.

As a result of the criticisms the Scheme was reviewed several times and changes were made in an attempt to refine the processes and eliminate any abuses.

However, problems with the schemes persisted and in 1841 the Land Board in England was given power to be involved in an attempt to assist the colonies by detecting possible irregularities and attempts at fraud. From that time all persons desirous of claiming bounties on emigrants dispatched to either New South Wales or Van Diemen's Land were required to have a Land Board certificate for each person. The Land Board also exercised some control over publications produced by agents, the vessels to be used, the qualifications of the surgeons and matters related to the comfort and safety of passengers.

The Bounty Scheme never operated in Van Diemen's Land to the same extent as in New South Wales and in fact there was no assisted immigration in Van Diemen's Land between 1837 and 1840. This occurred largely because colonial revenues were not as buoyant as in New South Wales, combined with an inability to attract labourers and tradesmen due to the relatively low wages compared to the Port Phillip district and South Australia (the large number of convicts in Van Diemen's Land kept wages low in that colony). The Port Phillip District received some bounty immigrants from New South Wales. A public meeting in Hobart in April 1840 requested that the Scheme be resumed in Van Diemen's Land. The Governor agreed to the request and bounty rates and conditions similar to those in place in New South Wales were agreed. The Land Board was given the same powers and responsibilities that it exercised on behalf of New South Wales. Henceforth, except for minor differences in ages of immigrants and bounty rates, the two colonies were treated as one.

However, even with a greater role being played by the Land Board it seems that the regulations governing bounty emigration were never totally able to deliver the type of immigrant desired by the colonies despite a number of adjustments and increased care in their application. Madgwick contends that the "system gradually degenerated into a commercial speculation controlled by British shipowners."[58]

By 1841 it was clear that the Bounty Scheme no longer operated in the form of its original design. What had emerged was conflict in interests between the colonies, the shipowners and the British Government. The colonies were refusing to pay to the shipowners a bounty for some of the immigrants they delivered. In some instances this involved a substantial number of the immigrants. It became increasingly clear that the Colonial Office was not prepared to accept the opinion of the colony's Examining Board and Governor and was inclined to agree with the shipowner that they should receive bounties where they could demonstrate that every reasonable care had been taken. It seems that the experience with increased interference from England occurred in both New South Wales and Van Diemen's Land.

This increased interference by the Colonial Office and Land Board made the underlying principles for the operation of the Bounty Scheme unworkable. The final destruction of the original scheme took place in 1843 with the issue of a policy statement by the Land Board setting out principles on which disallowance of a bounty would be considered. The colonies would henceforth only have power to withhold bounties on people whose character was obviously unsatisfactory. They were to have no control over the machinery of emigration and were precluded from penalising shipowners they believed had infringed on the letter of bounty regulations. From that point onwards it would be sufficient for the shipowners to observe the 'spirit' of the regulations. The control of bounty arrangements was now firmly in the hands of the Land Board. The British Government (and the opinion of Wakefield and those who believed in systematic colonisation) saw the divided control of the original Bounty Scheme as inefficient and contrary to prevailing colonial policy.

---

58. Madgwick, R B. Immigration into Eastern Australia 1788-1851. Sydney University Press 1969, p.157.

By mid-1842 colonists were recommending that the Scheme be abandoned. There were also calls to radically overhaul the Scheme. However, in 1842 assisted immigration was suspended and not renewed until 1844 with at that time the Land Board exercising close control over arrangements. The Land Board issued new regulations and assumed the power to choose between the different shipping firms for the transport of immigrants. It made its selection on the basis of a tender process and selected three shipping firms. The Board released a list of rules applying to the shipping firms, which covered such matters as seaworthiness of vessels, dietary scale, medicines, berthing of emigrants, and duties of surgeons and officers.

During 1844 and early 1845 over 4000 immigrants arrived in the colonies under the new bounty arrangements and it seems that the colonies were largely pleased with these new arrivals.[59] However due to the state of colonial finances immigration was again suspended and not resumed until 1848. There were some colonists who were not happy about the suspension of immigration, as they still required labour (particularly in the farming sector). By 1847 there was an urgent call for renewal of immigration immediately as demand for labour was far in excess of supply. It was suggested that 5000 adults were required. This request was agreed to and would be financed by debentures issued in the colony. The immigrants would be divided equally between Sydney and Port Phillip District. Under these arrangements the British Government would select the immigrants and the shipowners would be left to find and fit out the vessels.

The regulations remained in force until 1852 with only minor alterations. In 1849, due to a substantial increase in the number of applicants, it was decided to seek some payment from the emigrants towards the cost of the passage. Charges were determined and were graduated according to the age and occupation of the applicant. For example, agricultural labourers, shepherds, herdsmen and female domestic and farm servants between the ages of 14 and 40 paid £2; between 40 and 50 years, £6; 50 and 60 years, £11, and over 60 years of age, £15. The suspension of immigration between 1844 and 1847 had significantly intensified the need for labour

---

59. Madgwick, R.B. Immigration into Eastern Australia 1788-1851. Sydney University Press, 1969, p.191.

in New South Wales (including the Port Phillip District) and hence the main objective of immigration from 1848 was the provision of labour for the primary industry sector.

For a short period after 1859, shipowners bore the costs of conveyance and were remunerated by the Immigration Board, and the small amount of government assistance that was provided for this scheme was allotted by legislative vote. In 1861 the scheme and the Immigration Board were abolished with the gold rush underway and large numbers emigrating at their own expense to New South Wales and Victoria.

Private Activities

As I indicated previously in the early years of the nineteenth century a major objective of the British government was to minimise expenditure on the colonies and consequently little was done to encourage emigration of workers to the Australian colonies. There was, however, during this period official encouragement for small capitalists to emigrate to the colonies. Between 1815 and 1830 the British Government gave land free to settlers. Only those that could afford the fare were able to take advantage of this offer. The small capitalists who came were a mixture of middle class people, a few professional people (such as lawyers), army officers retired on half pay, sons of landowners and tenant farmers from England and Scotland. Several hundred of these people emigrated to the Australian colonies each year. These people largely came because of the availability of grants of crown land. From 1818 these grants varied in size according to the amount of capital possessed by the recipient.

At the same time as these small capitalists were arriving to claim land there were also some large British investors, or groups of investors, who looked to obtain large grants of Australian land for development purposes. An example of this occurred in the Swan River area (Western Australia) where an English landowner, Thomas Peel, developed a plan based on settlers providing their own labour force. Generous land grants were offered proportionate to their capital, including an extra grant for each labourer brought to the colony at the settler's expense. A number of settlers followed Peel's example on a smaller scale.

They paid the cost of the passage from Britain for workers who were indentured to work for a specified employer in the colony. Because labour was scarce many employers preferred the indenture system as a means of retaining their labour force, at least for the period and the wages stated in the indenture. Breaches of indenture could be dealt with in court under the Masters and Servants Acts, which were biased against the workers. These schemes were at best only partly successful and were in fact something of a disaster in the Swan River area. It was clear that the large grants of land were of little use without the skilled labour to work them.

An attempt at large-scale immigration was undertaken in the 1820s by the Van Diemen's Land Company. Formed in 1825 by an Act of Parliament, the company's purpose was the raising of sheep for fine wool. The Company was granted 250,000 acres of land in the north-western part of the colony to encourage farming and immigration from England. Labourers were brought out at the Company's expense and indentured to the Company.

Sometimes wealthy settlers chartered vessels to bring out particular immigrants or family members. For example the first migrant ship to arrive in Van Diemen's Land on 20 September 1816, the **Adamant**, was chartered by settlers. It was followed by further chartered vessels the **Harriott** (1817), the **Caroline** (1820) and the **Skelton** in the same year.

There were a range of private schemes and ventures operating to assist the Irish to emigrate. They usually operated for a limited time and were often focussed on particular places. For example in the 1840s Lord Monteagle helped many of his Limerick tenants to emigrate to Australia. Significant sums of money were also raised by the Catholic Church in parts of Australia to bring Irish to the colonies. An example of this was the establishment of the Donegal Relief Fund, which used local funds to bring over 1000 emigrants to the colonies in 1859 and again in 1861.

Influence of Individuals and Groups

One of the most persuasive means of attracting emigrants to the colonies was by way of personal information and encouragement from relatives and friends who had emigrated. Although communications between the colonies and the British Isles were infrequent many settlers wrote home describing their experiences, and in some cases suggesting that others follow. An example of this is the following letter from Sydney in 1849 (note that the spelling corresponds closely with the spoken dialect in Buckinghamshire and that punctuation was inserted when the letter was first published):

> *"My Ever Dear frend*
>
> *I new write these few lines to let you know that we are safe Arived at sydney And A most beutful contery that ever was seen. my dear Isebela never stop in that Lousey cuntery and se yourself starv. com to sydney my Dear were we can save a litel money to keep us when we get in years with out being beolding to aney body and this is the place ware you could hurn more money then I could. A good cutter out in the Deres making can have aney money thay like to ask for in thear work. my Dear frend let me beg of you to com to sydney and let me purswade you all to com. I am satesfide that you will never Repent coming to sydney. give my best Respects to all inquring frends. I hope this will find you and my Dear litel lisey quite well as it leves me at present. new I must conclude with my kind love to you.*
>
> *I remain your Ever Dear frend and well wisher*
>
> *Charles Paine"*[60]

Various groups were also active in promoting emigration. Some resorted to the use of existing networks. For example, the following letter from the Bishops and Clergy of the Diocese of Adelaide to the Parochial Clergy of the Church of England in 1848:

---

60. Undated letter from Charles Paine in 1849. Reproduced in: Thomlinson, Gerry. Bring Plenty of Pickles. Buckinghamshire, England, 1986. pp. 16-17.

> "We the undersigned ... beg to assure you that abundant employment, good wages, plentiful and cheap subsistence, the means of grace in all the more settled districts, are to be found in this province and diocese, together with a tone of intellectual and moral sentiment superior in some respects to the average attainment of the industrial classes in England. We can safely advise you to direct those of your young people who desire to better their temporal condition, to emigrate to this colony...
>
> Adelaide, South Australia,
> October, 9, 1848."[61]

The press was also used extensively as a means of debating emigration issues and of providing information to prospective emigrants. An example of this was a letter published in the *London Times* on 1 November 1854, from one William Clements to his former Parish of St Martin-in-the-Field. The Parish Clerk to the Board, C R Griffiths, forwarded the letter to the *Times* explaining:

> "I am directed by the Board of guardians ... to forward you a copy of a letter ... by William Clements, of South Australia, one of the poor people who were assisted by the board to emigrate in 1852 from this Parish to Port Adelaide. The guardians think that the contents of the communication may be interesting to the readers of your paper....."

The paper then published the letter from William Clements:

> "Sir - I hope you will excuse the liberty I have taken in addressing this letter to you ....
>
> After leaving Plymouth, we had a pretty good voyage, with the exception of rough weather for a few days, were well treated on board, and arrived in good health and spirits. 26 of the number sent out by the board were engaged as shepherds and hutkeepers the first day after landing, and went away to Port Lincoln.

---

61. Hodgson, Arthur. Emigration to the Australian Settlements. London, Second Edition, 1849 (pages unnumbered).

> *I myself engaged on the same day with the gentleman I am now with as hutkeeper. I am about 300 miles north of Adelaide, and had to receive at the end of my first year 31L 4S, and have had a very good living indeed. i am still remaining in the same place; and it is impossible for me to express the feelings which at times occupy my mind, when I reflect on my past miserable life in London, earning only 2d. per day, and sometimes I might say not half fed and scarcely clothed, and my father also living at the union, whereas now I am not only well fed and clothed, but can save a nice sum of money every year that I should have looked upon in days gone by as a mass of wealth......*
>
> *I am, Sir, your most obedient servant, William Clements."*

This letter from William Clements is typical of many letters published in British newspapers. With time there were an increasing number of letters describing conditions in the colonies and providing an insight into a new life such as the following letter published on 27 March 1875 in the *Bury Free Press* under the heading of 'Letter from Queensland':

> *"My Dear Mother and Father, We have had a long voyage of 107 days before landing in Queensland, Harry, my husband was only 5 days before he got work, we live well and had a home till then, Harry get £1 a week, our food found of 12 lbs of beef a week, 3 lbs of sugar, ½ a lb of tea, 12 lbs of flour, a house to live in rent free, plenty of wood to burn, the master and mistress are like a father and mother to us. Dear Mother this is a fine place to live, my husband don't want to go to work without a good beef steak every day and one for supper every night, we long to get a letter from you to hear how you got on, make yourself happy dear mother for we are doing well and hope to do better, we will help you before long, your affectionate daughter Harriet and Harry Larter, Kelvin Grove, Post Office, Queensland, Australia".*

It was also common for papers to have 'correspondents' in the colonies who provided stories, about life in the colonies. They frequently provided a very optimistic outlook for the prospective emigrant. The following is an extract from a lengthy report by a *Times* correspondent which was published on Wednesday 16 June 1869:

"EMIGRATION TO AUSTRALIA
(From our own correspondent)
MELBOURNE, APRIL 24

By many good people in England, emigration is regarded as a 'leap in the dark'. They have frequently vague notions of our social status as of our geography.................. I propose to shortly sketch the position, and as nearly as I can, the prospects, of the immigrant immediately on his arrival on these shores.

In the first place he does not find himself on a desert strand, dependent on his own individual resources alone for food and shelter. We have in Melbourne an 'Emigrants' Home', a Government establishment in which new arrivals without means are provided for until they can obtain employment ... The home is situated at South Yarra, a healthy suburb of this city, and is daily resorted to by employers of labour, and no person, male or female, of any age to be useful, need be, or ever is, many days in 'the House' without being able to procure an engagement either in town or country. I have known several hundreds of newly-arrived immigrants engaged from this place in a few hours. When the new arrival puts forth from this temporary haven should his circumstances drive him to it at all, 'to take a look over the town', he is surprised that he has travelled so far to find so small a change from home. Streets, houses, shops, all seen to him to be English, and so they are, for the Englishmen carries his customs and fashions to every part of the world ...

Extensive tracts of country ... are rich and open forest land, as beautiful as an English park, and I have never ridden over them without a feeling of sadness coming over me at the thought of the many thousands of home toilers, without hope, who, if transported hither, could convert the now comparative solitude into a second county of Kent, but magnified indefinitely, and with a far more genial climate...."

The press article concluded with an account of the labour market, including a list of the wages that could be expected for various types of employment in the colonies.

I previously referred to the low education levels of agricultural labourers and how this initially led to confusion and misinformation about emigration and conditions in the colonies. As the century progressed, the growth of the railway network, the arrival of cheap newspapers and the general improvement in internal communications made country people more aware of the economic and social choices available beyond their own parish. An explosion of guides, pamphlets, tracts and newspaper articles about emigration accompanied these changes. It's clear that the wide circulation of advertisements for emigration suggests that officials and emigration agents expected a reasonably high level of literacy among prospective emigrants (particularly those who would be dependent on government or other assistance for the cost of their passage). While there is evidence to indicate that many agricultural labourers could not read or write there must have been reasonable numbers of rural people who were literate. Clearly there were significant numbers of assisted emigrants who were literate. For example during the period from the mid-1840s to the mid-1850s the proportion of assisted emigrants who could read and write was reasonably high.[62]

% of total emigrants	New South Wales 1848-60	Victoria 1848-56	South Australia 1854-60
Cannot read	19%	16%	21%
Read only	22%	20%	23%
Read and write	59%	64%	56%

There were a number of individuals who appeared to be on a mission to write and published a considerable amount of material encouraging people to emigrate and providing advice on how to go about it, what to bring, where to go, etc. One of those who wrote a large number of publications supporting the colonies was Samuel Sidney. In one of his publications in 1850 he included as an appendix a number of excerpts

---

62. Haines, R. Government Assisted Emigrants from the United Kingdom to Australia 1831-1860. Population Studies 48, 1994, p.234.

from letters from colonists indicating how well they had done since emigrating. They included:

> "PATRICK FLEMMING from Limerick - I arrived by the Comet in 1841, went into country service ... then went on a farm ... Have a set of ten bullocks and a good dray; fifty head of good cattle, and plenty of poultry and everything of that sort... I am very glad I came here - it's well I have done, thanks be to God...
> THOMAS BAKER from Sussex - I am from a place four miles from Rye-Uddimore ... I arrived in this country eight years ago; was four years in wages ...Having four children, found I would do much better on a farm. I began on the farm with nothing, as the saying is... I have fifteen head of cattle; four working bullocks; three pigs; ten ducks, plenty of fowls, at least ten laying hens, 100 chickens... use half pound of tea a week; six pounds of sugar; buy half a bullock at a time..."[63]

As I indicated previously it's clear that in some rural areas where access to written material was limited, particularly during the early part of the century or where many people were illiterate (such as among agricultural labourers), the most common way that information was passed around was by word of mouth. A rural newspaper reported in 1810 that "two thirds of the labouring people cannot read or write".[64] If this was typical of rural communities at this time then clearly the passing of information by word of mouth was important because it's evident that information about the colonies and emigration assistance was increasingly available

There were large areas of England, Scotland and Ireland where the collapse of the agricultural economy was not compensated for by the rise of industry. These areas were often in a state of recession for many years. It was from these areas that many people emigrated in a steady stream over a long period of time. As the nineteenth century went by, word came back from some who had emigrated and as the stories were passed around others were encouraged to emigrate. In 1874, at Wickham St Paul in rural East Anglia, when the school children sang *The Emigrant Ship* to

---

63. Sidney, Samuel. Female Emigration, As it is, as it may be. A letter to Right Hon. Sidney Herbert, MP. London, 1850. p. 41-42.
64. Bury & Norwich Post, 19 September 1810.

the school inspector[65] it was a poignant illustration of how engrained by then emigration had become a part of the culture of places with a rural population that the United Kingdom no longer wanted.

Agricultural Union Involvement

By the 1870s and the beginning of a new depression in agriculture the agricultural workers had increasingly become confident about possible options for the future and more ready to break with the land than their less educated parents had been. Many migrated to the towns but those who remained joined the burgeoning trade union movement largely because of their standard of living. These trade union movements became increasingly militant and were closely tied to the cause of emigration. The National Agricultural Labourers Union began to make emigration and migration central to its policies, exploiting the desire of young labourers to escape the farm.

It was hoped that this would lead to a long-term reduction in the labour supply and therefore put pressure on employers to settle individual wage disputes. The Union's policy of organised emigration had first been mooted at union meetings in early 1873. Rural union agitators such as Charles Jay took up the cause, visiting numerous villages in Essex to address farm workers on the advantages of joining the Union and promoting the possibilities of emigration. Jay had worked in North America where he had witnessed slavery before its abolition and had sympathised with the wrongs of the Indians. He had returned to Britain with a reforming mission and devoted his considerable energies to building the union in Essex. In his capacity as emigration agent of the Queensland Government he was to persuade many that, upon arriving in Australia, they would find higher wages and more pleasant living conditions. Jay toured central Essex, on one occasion speaking from the Shire Hall steps at Chelmsford. In keeping with the biblical rhetoric of many unionists of the time, he presented Australia as a 'promised land' of opportunity. In August Jay announced that *"on the 12th twenty five leave Essex for Queensland; on the 26th some more will go"* and claimed that *"I am now inundated with applications from Essex to emigrate"*. Such departures

---

65. The Foxearth & District Local History Society (www.foxearth.org.au).

aided the union's cause because they were presented as reluctant yet enforced renunciations of their homeland by labourers no longer able to tolerate poverty and subjugation.[66] The *Essex Standard* of 1872 noted:

> *"The Condition of the agricultural labourer is as bad as it can be. He toils like a slave, lives like a pig and too often dies like a dog, with no pleasure but an occasional debauch at the alehouse, no prospect but that of the Workhouse for an old age of rheumatism and misery."*

In what was seen as the crowning achievement of the National Agricultural Labourers Union, an entire ship, the ***St James,*** was chartered and filled with 300 people from Suffolk and Essex, sailing to New South Wales on 14 April 1874. Jay toured Essex branches offering free passages, free kit and grants of £1 per man, 10s. for a wife and 5s. for each child. Parties were formed in a number of Essex and Suffolk villages, supported by collections at religious services and socials. On a morning in April 1874 they converged on their nearest railway station to board the train for Tilbury, where the ***Saint James*** was waiting to bear them away. Jay described the scene at Witham:

> *"On the 14th inst. some of the finest peasantry of the Eastern Counties joined the Saint James for Queensland. It was a remarkable day in the Eastern Counties; every station from Woodbridge in Suffolk had passengers for Queensland. Kelvedon was rather a big gathering, but at Witham junction the largest party came together, some from Braintree, some from the Dengie Hundred and some from the neighbourhood around Witham ... It looked as if the Royal Family must be expected at Witham, every available space was filled by people come to see some 200 working folks leave the country. Cheer after cheer came from the onlookers and the starters; for miles from Witham every cottage seemed to expect the train to pass, for someone was prepared to wave a parting flag; hedgerows seemed to contain human beings for the purpose; ploughmen stood still and waved their hats, and at farm houses the servant appeared either at the door or window and excitedly waved her flag. At*

---

66. Brown, A. Meagre Harvest. The Essex Farm Worker's Struggle Against poverty, 1750-1914. Essex Record Office, 1990, pp.42-48.

the county town it will not be soon forgotten, and masters and parsons will be more persistent than ever in refusing to sign any emigration papers. Long streets in Chelmsford command a view of the rail; they were quite alive with women at the doors waving their parting flag."[67]

Individual Campaigners

There were also a number of other individuals who worked tirelessly to encourage people to emigrate from the British Isles and to support them in that process. Possibly the best known of this group was Caroline Chisholm.

Caroline Chisholm had first-hand experience of life in the colonies, having arrived with her husband and three sons in Sydney for a holiday in 1838 at the age of 30. She was quickly appalled by the conditions confronting many young women arriving in the colony, particularly the lack of support and the way they were left to fend for themselves. She witnessed young girls sleeping in the Domain at night and begging captains of ships to take them back to England. It was not long before she started organising support, accommodation and jobs for these new arrivals.

Mrs Chisholm returned to England in 1847 and continued her work in support of emigrants and emigration to the colonies. She was determined to spread the word about the benefits of emigrating to the colonies as widely as possible throughout the British Isles. This she did by a variety of means, including the publication of pamphlets and a book about life in the colonies. However, she understood that many of the working class were illiterate and that this would be a severe handicap to many potential emigrants in their ability to gain appropriate information about life in the colonies. As a result, she travelled extensively in England and Scotland and she visited Ireland preaching the benefits of emigration and the "moral improvement as God's cure for the poverty, drunkenness, prostitution and cruelty which muddied the reputation of mankind".[68]

---

67. Labourers' Union Chronicle 25 April 1874 quoted in Brown, A. Meagre harvest. Essex record Office, 1990, p.50.
68. Clark, C M H. A History of Australia. Part III, Melbourne, 1979. p. 241.

By the early part of the 1850s she was answering over 200 letters per day from people interested in emigrating.

A significant contribution to meeting the cost of emigration was achieved when she established the Family Colonisation Loan Society. Intending emigrants with families were encouraged to save two-thirds of the passage money and borrow the remaining third from the Society. She also worked to improve the conditions on board vessels for female emigrants. Her other achievements included pressuring the government to reunite convicts with their families. She had observed the plight of convicts on completion of sentence and their inability to raise the money to be able to bring their families to the colonies. She was also concerned about children who had been left behind when their parents emigrated. In 1846 she put forward a proposal for bounty assistance to enable children to be reunited with parents in the colonies. The proposal received support from the Secretary of State for the Colonies and was handed to the Land Board to implement. After investigation the Land Board recommended that the scheme be abandoned because of practical difficulties and concern about safety of the children. Mrs Chisholm protested and refused to believe that the scheme was impossible. The Colonial Office agreed to proceed. However, despite early interest in the scheme there were difficulties with children being reluctant to leave guardians or guardians refusing to allow the children to go. As a result only 76 children were ultimately assisted to re-join their parents.[69]

Mrs Chisholm also sought and won the support of other influential people in her work. For example, Charles Dickens was prepared to support her activities in his periodical: *Household Words*. However, as a Catholic she was criticised by some on the basis the she was attempting to Romanise the colonies.

Maria Rye, was another well-known and very active English social reformer who promoted emigration, especially of young women living in Liverpool workhouses. Rye began her emigration work by transporting adult middle-class women to Australia and New Zealand. She said that she acted on constant advice given to her to:

---

69. New South Wales, Government Gazette 1848 (http://trove.nla.govt.au/version/43775670).

> *"Teach your protégés to emigrate: send them where men want wives, the mothers want governesses, where the shopkeepers, the schools and the sick will thoroughly appreciate your exertions and heartily welcome your women."*[70]

In 1861 she set up the Female Middle Class Emigration Society (1861–1908), supported by many of the ladies of Langham Place. The society provided interest-free loans repayable over a period of two years and four months, to enable educated women to emigrate. It also established and maintained correspondents at most colonial ports to which female emigrants might travel. In 1862, Rye sailed to New Zealand with the first party sent out by the Society. Miss Rye went on to Australia and did not return to England until 1865. The society was most active between 1861 and 1867 when Rye was actively involved in its running. During this period she continued to organise vessels to transport young women to the colonies as shown in the following newspaper report:

> *"Miss Rye last week, from Liverpool, by the Government emigration ship Red Jacket, one hundred young women, the majority of whom are English, a considerable number Irish, and a few Scotch, to Melbourne. They are all girls qualified by physical health and moral character to take positions in domestic life as servants of various ranks when they reach the colonies."*[71]

In 1869 Maria Rye turned her attention to assisting young girls, usually aged between 5 and 12 years who were in the workhouses and managed to get funds through public appeal to take numbers of these girls to Canada. After a serious illness in 1895 Maria Rye retired, passing the management of the organisation onto the Church of England Waifs and Strays Society.

Another individual who worked to increase immigration into the colonies was the Presbyterian Minister, J Dunmore Lang. Lang was much more particular than Caroline Chisholm and Maria Rye in who he felt would be suitable immigrants for the colonies. He was concerned that the country would be flooded with the wrong type of person. His solution

---

70. *New Horizons.* Her Majesty's Stationary Office, London, p.1.
71. *Illustrated London News*, 8 September 1866, p.243.

was to devise a private scheme for mechanics of good moral character. Lang raised a loan, chartered ships and personally selected the migrants. In organising his scheme he travelled back to Britain six times and to America once. This would have involved an amazing amount of travel considering the time it took for each trip in those days.

In addition to the work of Maria Rye there were other individuals and organisations dedicated to the welfare and emigration of children. The Children's Friend Society was founded in London in 1830 (known then as the Society for the Suppression of Juvenile Vagrancy), with the objective of addressing juvenile vagrancy through the 'reformation and emigration of children'. The first group of children was sent to the Cape Colony in South Africa and the Swan River Colony in Western Australia in 1832, and in August 1833, 230 children were shipped to Toronto and New Brunswick, Canada. The main individuals who pioneered child migration in the nineteenth century were Scottish evangelical Christians, Annie MacPherson, her sister Louisa Birt, and as mentioned above Londoner, Maria Rye. Whilst working with poor children in London in the late 1860s MacPherson was appalled by the child slavery of the matchbox industry and resolved to devote her life to these children. In 1870 she bought a large workshop and turned it into the 'Home of Industry', where poor children could work and be fed and educated. She later became convinced that the real solution for these children lay in emigration to a country of opportunity and started an emigration fund. Home Children was a common term used to refer to the child migration scheme founded by Annie MacPherson in 1869, under which more than 100,000 children were sent to Australia, Canada, New Zealand and South Africa from the United Kingdom.

The Rush of the Fifties

While the range of factors described above were in various ways influential in the first half of the century there can be little doubt that the single most influential factor in the second half was the discovery of gold. Gold has throughout history had a magical like power to attract attention. Its ability to attract people was clearly evident in Australia in the 1850s. Nearly 700,000 people came to the colonies in the ten years after the discovery of gold – thus trebling the population. In this period Australia produced forty per cent of the world's gold.

Some three years after the discovery of gold in California, Edward Hargraves discovered gold near Bathurst, New South Wales, in February 1851. As soon as the discovery of gold near Bathurst reached Victoria a committee of wealthy citizens offered rewards for gold discoveries in Victoria. Early in August 1851 traces of gold were found in the Buninyong Ranges and these discoveries were soon followed by the discovery of richer deposits at nearby Ballarat. The gold rush in the colonies was underway.

The *Geelong Advertiser* reported on 6 October 1851:

> ### *The Gold Fever*
> *A medical friend informs us that the prevailing epidemic somewhat resembles ordinary fever at its commencement, as the pre symptoms are relentless anxiety, and disinclination to follow one's ordinary avocations. During the first stage of the attack, a sufferer may be known by an unshorn beard, a dirty face, and an embryo bandit appearance. As the disease advances, the patient sticks a short pipe in his mouth, and assumes a red shirt and pair of moleskin trousers. If the symptoms are unchecked by a rise in salary, all objects he views appear of a golden hue - excitement terminates in delirium - one morn we miss him from the 'customed spot' - and the answer to all the anxious inquiries of his friends, is that he was last seen on a loaded bullock dray, provided with straw mattress, a tin pannikin, a shovel and a cradle.*

While that piece in the *Advertiser* describes the state of mind of those inflicted by the gold 'fever' the following extract from an 8 October report in the *Advertiser* provides an insight into the mass movement to the diggings:

> "The cry is still they run 'off to the diggings'. Scarcely an hour of the day passes without five or six drays leaving town for the mines, and reports of those who have come in from the country all agree in declaring that the crowds of people passing along is astonishing; all attracted to the golden centre…"

People from everywhere left their jobs and rushed to the goldfields. Many city-based activities had difficulty in continuing operation. Significant numbers of the police force joined the rush and ships were deserted and left stranded in port because the crew had gone to find gold. It did not take long for the news to reach the British Isles. The result was an immediate rush of men to the Australian gold fields. By late 1852 some 15,000 were landing in Melbourne. Most of those arriving were young unmarried men from all classes of society. They had arrived to make their fortune having heard stories of large quantities of gold waiting to be mined.

> *"When first I left Old England's shore*
> *Such yarns as we were told*
> *As how folks in Australia*
> *Could pick up lumps of gold."*
>   *(Anon)*

Montage Showing Life on The Diggings Including the Welcome Nugget[72]
(State Library of Victoria)

---

72. Lithograph, which was published overseas including in Europe.

Emigration from the British Isles to Australia was generally only small compared to the number emigrating to America. However, in the 1850s and early 1860s British emigration to Australia reached almost half of the total that departed for America.[73] While the working-class emigrant, who had been arriving in significant numbers with assisted passage in the 1830s and 1840s continued to come in the 1850s, it is clear that the substantial numbers arriving after gold was discovered contained a new 'class' of emigrant:

> *"A new class of people, better educated and perhaps, more desperate, and needing only the powerful inducement that gold alone can supply, has for the first time found its native land too small and too poor to contain it. The middle stratum of society has been stirred."*[74]

One Hundred Years On

By 1888 Australia had undergone one hundred years of migration and settlement. According to the census of 1891, Australian-born sons and daughters of migrants made up the majority of the population and of those born outside Australia approximately half had been born in England.[75]

Throughout the nineteenth century the motives of those who chose to emigrate to Australia were complex. Despite the additional distance, difficulties and cost a significant number chose the Australian colonies in preference to emigration to North America.

In the first part of the century the prospect of jobs, higher wages and assisted passage must have been important factors in enticing many people from the working class to come to the Australian colonies. Clearly the discovery of gold produced a kind of madness that changed the mix of those coming to Australia. The continuing economic growth in the colonies in the four decades after 1850 ensured on-going growth in jobs. It was not until the onset of the depression of the 1890s that conditions changed markedly.

---

73. Sherington, Geoffrey. Australia's Immigrants. Allen & Unwin, 1990. p. 60.
74. Serle, G.R. The Golden Age. Melbourne University Press, Melbourne, 1963, p.47.
75. Sherington, Geoffrey. Australia's Immigrants. Allen & Unwin, 1990. pp. 84-85.

Governments stopped assisting immigrants and there was reluctance by prospective emigrants to pay for their passage when jobs were scarce. Thus the number emigrating from Britain fell dramatically in the last decade of the century. Australia became more inward looking during this period and a new sense of nationalism appeared to emerge. Australia for the Australians could be heard once again.

CHAPTER 4

Those Who Came

" 'Tis hard to part from those we've loved,
Whose friendships we have tried and proved;
To grasp the hand and say farewell-
Perhaps forever, -who can tell?"[76]

Three types of people settled in Australia in the nineteenth century – the convicts, the assisted emigrants and those who came at their own expense. The convicts and the assisted emigrants comprised the great bulk of the arrivals for the greater part of the period up to 1850. The convicts, of course, had no choice; but the emigrants we might suppose had a great deal of choice (with the possible exception of some of those people classed as paupers who in the early part of the century were very actively 'encouraged' to emigrate).

The early arrivals to the Australian colonies were, of course, largely convicts. As discussed earlier in this book the arrival of free settlers was at first slow and the numbers small. Two-thirds of the 160,000 convicts sent to Australia arrived in the three decades between 1820 and 1850. Not only did the total number of convicts rise during this period, but their percentage of the population in the colonies also rose. This percentage had declined from the 1790s but rose steadily in the 1820s.[77]

---

76. Higginbotham, George Brunswick, Assistant Surgeon, Marco Polo. Verse 1 of poem published in Marco Polo Chronicles, July/September 1854. Contained in Ship's Log. National Library of Australia Manuscript MS 6174.
77. Sherrington, Geoffrey. Australia's Immigrants. Sydney, 1990. p 23.

While the convicts came from all parts of the British Isles a significant number came from Ireland. In the 1820s and 1830s Irish convicts were arriving at an average of about 1000 per year. By the time transportation to the eastern colonies ended in 1853, just over 40,000 convicts had been sent direct from Ireland. Of those sent from England estimates suggest that about 8000 were Irish-born. In all, about one quarter of all convicts transported were Irish-born.[78]

Convict Population[79]
New South Wales

Year	Males	Females	Total	% of Population
1805	1,561	516	2,077	29.8
1819	8,920	1,056	9,986	38.3
1828	16,442	1,544	16,986	46.4
1836	25,254	2,577	27,831	36.1

Van Diemen's Land

1814	387	50	437	23.0
1819	1,928	262	2,190	47.1
1828	6,724	725	7,449	40.4
1835	14,914	2054	16,968	42.1

However, even though the number of those who arrived as convicts was substantial it was small compared to the scale of free emigration to the Australian colonies in the nineteenth century. The move to the Australian colonies was part of a mass migration from Europe, which was without precedent in human history. The majority of emigrants went to North America, particularly the United States of America. However, a significant group came to the Australian colonies. By the late 1830s the number coming as free emigrants had overtaken those arriving as convicts. It is possibly not too extravagant a claim to make that Australia was the scene for the first great attempt at assisted emigration. It is estimated that in the period 1831 to 1860 an average of 18,268 assisted

---
78. O'Farrell, Patrick. The Irish in Australia. NSW University Press, 1987, p.23.
79. Clarke, C M H. Select Documents in Australian History Vol 1 1788-1850. pp 406 & 408.

emigrants arrived each year and in the period 1861 to 1900 the average annual number was 10, 087 (these estimates give the total number of assisted emigrants in the period 1831 to 1900 at close to 1 million).[80]

There were not surprisingly a variety of views from within the colonies and the mother country to the type of person that would make the best settlers in these new colonies. Some of the early commentators contended that there should be a mix of those with capital and those able to supply the skills and labour needed to underpin the capital investment. This position appeared to generally prevail in the early years of the century, particularly with regard to encouraging those with capital to emigrate. Regarding the labour force there were again a variety of views, including a strong push initially to send to the colonies those who were a burden to the mother country (people on poor relief, those in work houses, the unemployed, those in poverty – the pauper class). However, as time passed there was a strong push to support only those people who could contribute to the development of the colonies; that is, those with the skills needed in the colonies. Others went further and advocated for a particular type of person with the right attitude and necessary drive. This latter position was put in 1848 by John Sidney, in his widely read publication: *Sidney's Australian Hand-Book*, as follows:

> *"...Action is the first great requisite of a colonist; to be able to do anything, to need the least possible assistance, to have a talent for making shift. With a young man the tone of his mind is more important than his previous pursuits. ....*
>
> *Dreamers of dreams, inventors of ingenious schemes, requiring for their success the labour and money of other people, had better stay at home.*
>
> *Without economy and sobriety a settler of small capital has not the most remote chance of success..."*[81]

---

80. Wray, Vamplew ed. Australians: Historical Statistics. Fairfax, Syme & Weldon Associates 1987 pp.2-22.
81. Sidney, John. Sidney's Australian Hand-Book. How to settle and succeed in Australia. Comprising every information for intending emigrants by a bushman. London, 1848. pp. 41-42.

Another writer of the same period by the same surname promulgated a similar message in his publications and writings:

> "...the emigrating classes will always consist chiefly of the most frugal and industrious of the working classes who desire to rise to a higher condition. All attempts to fill ships with the higher and middle classes have, after a brief period of enthusiasm, failed, because they are not the class who, in body, can succeed so well in a country where high wages are the cause of colonisation as the hard-handed; therefore any attempt to keep the working men down as hired servants will only end in keeping down the colony."[82]

While it's clear that there were a range of views about who should emigrate, and that some attempts were made through the various schemes to assist emigration to select particular types of people, it is also clear that many different types of individuals and families decided to make the long journey to the colonies as emigrants (some of course were given a push to assist in their decision-making process).

Of the 1.3 million people who made the passage to Australia from the United Kingdom before 1880, most came by sailing vessel (i.e. steam propelled vessels had little impact on the Australian run until late in the century). They were people from a broad cross-section of cultures. In addition to those coming from the United Kingdom, others arrived from a number of different countries, including China and Germany.

However, despite the arrival of people from several countries it is clear that the majority arriving in the nineteenth century came from the United Kingdom. Of those arriving in the colonies from the United Kingdom, which is my focus in this book, I have been curious to see if it might be possible to profile a typical nineteenth-century immigrant.

The largest group of those who emigrated to Australia were English born. This was evident from the 1891 Census, which found that approximately half of those born outside the Australian colonies had been

---

82. Sidney, Samuel. The Three Colonies of Australia; New South Wales, Victoria and South Australia. Their Pastures, Copper Mines and Gold Fields. London, 1852. p. ix.

born in England. However, the composition of the overseas-born varied somewhat in each of the colonies. This is illustrated in the table below.

Overseas Born in Australian Colonies, 1891[83]

Place of birth	NSW %	Vic. %	Qld. %	SA %	WA (1901) %	Tas. %
England	52.2	49.1	45.5	58.2	3.0	60.0
Scotland	13.0	15.7	13.5	11.0	11.3	13.5
Ireland	26.3	26.5	26.1	18.5	21.0	20.0
Wales	1.8	1.5	1.3	1.8	1.7	1.2
Germany	3.3	3.3	9.1	9.0	3.2	3.3
Scandinavia	1.6	1.5	3.1	1.2	3.1	1.2
Other European	1.8	2.4	1.4	1.3	5.7	0.8

While the English were clearly the largest group of emigrants, the Scots were nonetheless a significant group and the Irish, who made up a sizeable proportion of those transported, were also a very significant group of the emigrants coming to the Australian colonies.

For the Irish in the nineteenth century, emigration was an ever-present fact of Irish life, and, particularly with the onset of famine conditions, attitudes to emigration changed to a belief that anywhere would be better than Ireland. Hence the Irish emigrated in very substantial numbers. As one writer put it: "sad to leave, but glad to be gone".[84] When Mary Robinson became President of Ireland in 1990, one of her first, and most symbolic, actions was to light a lamp in the kitchen window of her official residence to acknowledge the many millions of Irish people overseas. Until then, Irish emigration had been one of the great unspoken topics of political life, while simultaneously being one of the great themes of Irish drama, fiction and poetry. It seems that the majority of those who emigrated in the first part of the nineteenth century went to

---

83. Lyng, James. Racial Composition of the Australian Population, in Sherrington, Geoffrey. Australia's Immigrants. Sydney, 1990. p. 85.
84. O'Farrell, Patrick. The Irish in Australia. New South Wales University Press, 1987, p.57.

North America. It has been said that America absorbed many who were traumatised by the famine conditions prevailing in Ireland. These people were largely poorly educated and unskilled.

The situation with regard to most of the Irish who came to the Australian colonies appears to be different. The small numbers who came in the 1830s and 1840s were mainly poor and destitute semi-skilled farm workers largely from Cork, Clare, Limerick and Tipperary. There seems to be evidence that the emancipated Irish convicts were reasonably successful in business developing modest entrepreneurial skills and that those who emigrated to the colonies in the period from the 1850s to 1880s (when the majority of the Irish came) were a different 'type' of person to those earlier emigrants who had fled the famine conditions. O'Farrell believes that there is evidence that the Irish coming after about 1850 were "in search of gold, land, fortune and adventure: they were a much more accomplished, venturesome and happy lot than those the Famine had dumped on America".[85] It seems that the Irish emigrants were fairly well dispersed in the cities, towns and rural areas of the colonies. The tie of family rather than individualism was the mark of nineteenth-century Irish emigration. This was possibly a reflection of the continuing rural nature of Irish society. After the discovery of gold there were considerable numbers of emigrants willing to pay their passage to the colonies. However, for the majority of Irish emigrants assisted passage was important throughout the century.

The Scots were different to the Irish as they were relatively sparse among the convicts, but came later as assisted and unassisted emigrants. In the early years they were attracted to Van Diemen's Land, but in later years they were attracted to districts with prospects for pastoralism, including the Western Districts and Gippsland in Victoria and the Darling Downs in Queensland. Those who came in relatively small numbers in the 1820s and first part of the1830s often came as paying passengers and frequently brought significant capital with them. It's clear that in the 1840s and 1850s there was an unambiguous element of coercion applied to the highland crofters to emigrate both by the government and the landowners. The majority of those who emigrated from the highlands

---

85. ibid. p. 63.

in this early part of the century went to America or Canada. However New South Wales appointed Dr Boyter as Colonial Emigration Agent in 1836. Prior to this London had appointed two government emigration agents, partly in response to criticisms that the Scots were not being provided with the opportunity to emigrate to the colonies. These two agents were based at the ports where emigration vessels were most likely to depart (Greenock and Leith). The three agents began to work together to promote emigration and to explain the government assistance that was available. Boyter travelled extensively explaining the assisted passage and the virtues of New South Wales and the Port Phillip District. The work of these agents clearly had an impact because 1837 saw a dramatic increase in emigration to Australia and this trend continued through the peak years of 1838 to 1841. The following report in the *Inverness Courier* of 30 May 1838 is an indication in the growing interest in emigrating to the colonies:

> *"After some months of expectation and anxiety, Dr. Boyter, the Government emigration agent for Australia, arrived at Fort William... The news of his arrival, like the fiery cross of old, soon spread through every glen of the district, and at an early hour on Monday, thousands of enterprising Gaels might be seen ranked around Caledonian Hotel, anxious to quit the land of their forefathers and to go and possess the unbounded pastures of Australia.......While we regret that so many active men should feel it necessary to leave their own country, the Highlands will be considerably relieved of its over-plus population."*

The sudden growth in Scottish emigration to the colonies in 1837 possibly occurred because there was an alignment in Scotland of, on the one hand, improved information and facilities for selection with a changing attitude to emigration and, on the other hand, a growing weariness (particularly amongst destitute highlanders) with conditions in Scotland. It was also in that year that the Colonial Office decided to extend bounty emigration to agricultural labourers and married couples. These changes fitted well with the desire to emigrate from the highlands and from some lowland areas where little interest had previously been shown in emigration to the colonies.

With further highland clearances and famine conditions later in the century it seems that the geographic focus for emigration shifted further to Australia and New Zealand. The Scots emigrating to Australia tended to be generally better educated than other emigrants. This is possibly because many had trade qualifications and were skilled labourers. There clearly were large numbers of artisans and shepherds among the Scottish emigrants. It seems that the agricultural labourers from Scotland were highly regarded and sought after in the colonies. In fact many of the agricultural workers were employed in the colonies as overseers because of their experience and skill level. Another characteristic about Scottish emigrants, particularly those from the highlands, is that ties with kinsfolk and friends were very strong. This caused some problems for colonial authorities. However a compromise was reached and those family members not eligible for bounty assistance were permitted to emigrate through a payment to cover costs. An example of family ties can be seen from the passenger list of the vessel, **British King**, which sailed from Tobermory in October 1838 with 332 passengers, including 146 with the surname Macdonald. As the nineteenth century drew on the Scots became fairly well-distributed throughout the colonies, but remained significantly higher in number in Victoria.

Some groups of emigrants tended to congregate in particular geographic areas. An example of this is the Cornish, who clustered around mining communities. The Cornish had a long history of emigration, often taking their advanced mining methods and machinery to many parts of the globe (in each decade from 1861 to 1901 around twenty per cent of the Cornish male population migrated abroad – three times the average from England and Wales).

It is clear from the above table that the proportion of those who emigrated to the Australian colonies from Europe was small. However, it is interesting to note that significant numbers of Germans were attracted to South Australia and Queensland. Nevertheless, while there were these cultural differences between the colonies the ethnic differences were subtle.

Another group who were very evident at various times during the nineteenth century were the Chinese. They were present in the first half of the century in small numbers, but began to arrive in considerable numbers from 1848. Some were brought to the colonies as indentured labourers (often referred to as coolies) up until the end of 1851. After the discovery of gold shiploads of Chinese arrived in New South Wales and Victoria. By 1859 the Chinese made up almost twenty per cent of the male Victorian population and by 1861 they were about 3.3 per cent of the total population of the Australian colonies.[86] The large numbers of Chinese on the goldfields prompted cultural and economic insecurity and unrest amongst the other miners. They were accused of affronting civilised behaviour because of the clothes they wore and of threatening the economic livelihood of other gold diggers. There were anti-Chinese riots on the Victorian and New South Wales gold fields. As a result of the riots, the governments of Victoria and New South Wales tried to control the number of Chinese immigrants by imposing poll taxes and residence fees on the Chinese. Many of those who emigrated during the gold rush years eventually returned home. By 1881 the Chinese made up only 1.7 per cent of the total Australian population.[87] Those who stayed moved to country towns and into large groupings in Melbourne and Sydney (the basis of the Chinatowns in those cities), where they became merchants and shopkeepers and a number were cabinetmakers.

Indians were also brought as cheap indentured labour for a few years from 1848. The practice of importing Chinese and Indian coolies then declined. However, the powerful pastoralists (squatters) wanted to have a continuing source of cheap labour and as the number of convicts available declined, with the last ship load arriving in New South Wales in November 1840 and there being a growing number of people calling for the complete cessation of transportation, some squatters resumed coolie importation during the gold rushes. They were also calling for assisted British immigrants to be indentured. There was an outcry from opposing groups. Some saw the possible emergence of a plantation style economy. While there was some opposition on moral grounds there was an emerging fear that an unskilled and uneducated labour force could become a separate lower class. According to Irving, the opposing forces comprising radicals and capitalists expressed a common view that "the independence of all workers would be jeopardised, class distinction

---

86. Searle, G. R. The Golden Age. Melbourne, 1963, p. 320 in Sherington, Geoffrey. Australia's Immigrants. Sydney, 1990. p. 66.
87. ibid. p.332.

would be widened and political rights restricted".[88] The gold rushes had a major impact on reinforcing these views. In the ten years after 1851 the population of Australia almost trebled to 1.2 million. Following the initial dislocation, which the gold rushes produced, they brought an increase in capital and supply of labour. The emigrants who came as a result of the gold rushes rapidly produced a workforce with a high level of literacy and skills and a new market. Apart from the feelings about the Chinese there was little interest on the gold fields of a person's origin or past position. A kind of social democracy emerged. As time passed gold mining reinforced this with a blending of capital, skills and labour. This led one commentator to say:

> *"Gold is the mainspring of commerce; commerce the forerunner of civilization; and civilization is the handmaiden of Christianity.'* [89]

The importation of labour occurred again from the 1870s when squatters and sugar plantation owners brought Pacific Islanders to north Queensland. For the following three decades the numbers of Pacific Islanders in north Queensland fluctuated, and by 1901 there were 9324 in Queensland.[90] Most were later deported under legislation passed by the new Commonwealth parliament.

Some writers contend that ethnic and cultural differences among the nineteenth-century emigrants were related to regional differences present in Britain. In other words there were differences between the Irish (who resented being classified as British), the Welsh, the Scots and the English. However, a counter view contended that Australia in the nineteenth century did not reflect the regional differences in Britain and was a more homogeneous society. It was said that emigrants to the colonies in the nineteenth century remarked on the sense of cultural familiarity that they found. Rickard describes this as "a kind of British amalgam which did not exist in Britain

---

88. Irving, T.H. 1850-1870. In A New History of Australia ed. Frank Crowley. William Heinemann, 1974, p.137.
89. *Sydney Morning Herald*, 14 February 1853.
90. Corris, Peter. White Australia in Action: The Repatriation of Pacific Islanders from Queensland. Historical Studies, Volume 15, No.58, 1974, p.238.

itself".[91] He went on to remark that the diverse group that made up nineteenth-century Australia shared a common sense of autonomy over their lives.

Clearly government policies and attitudes had an impact on the type of people that emigrated to the colonies. For example, there was a clear change in emphasis during the 1820s with the arrival of Sir Thomas Brisbane as Governor of New South Wales. Both Brisbane and the British Government were interested in encouraging, not the unemployed working classes of the British Isles, but capitalists who could support themselves and employ convicts. The arrivals during this period therefore contained a growing proportion of military and naval officers and well-to-do middle class merchants and farmers. The call for mechanics and small shopkeepers became correspondingly smaller. Nearly all the regulations established during the 1820s reinforced this shift in policy by discriminating against the poorer emigrants. Madgwick contends that government policy during the period from 1815 to 1825 appeared to go a step further by aiming to turn New South Wales into a nineteenth-century equivalent of a plantation colony. Thus, under such an arrangement, convicts would provide the labour force as they had done before in America, and their employers would comprise a few large property owners (pastoralists or squatters).[92]

The policy during this period appeared to be largely driven by suspicion of small landholders as they had proven a liability to the British Government in the past. It is clear that this policy was also strongly motivated by a key element of overall government policy, which was focussed on economy and certainly not systematic colonisation. Many of those who came during this period brought varying amounts of capital and possibly helped to form the basis for a prosperous free population. It is reasonably clear that those who came during this period were determined to improve their status by hard work in the colony. As time passed government policy on emigration was modified and schemes of assisted passage introduced. These changes had the effect of shifting the balance back in favour

---
91. Rickard, John. Australia A Cultural History. Harlow, England, 1988. p.39.
92. Madgwick, R.B. Immigration into Eastern Australia 1788-1851. Sydney, 1969. p.50.

of the working-class emigrant. At first this was mainly a change in composition rather than magnitude but numbers of working-class emigrants increased as time went on, particularly as assisted passage arrangements took effect.

From the arrival of the first ships in 1788 the number of males arriving was significantly higher than female arrivals. This imbalance started with the convicts and continued with the arrival of the early immigrants to the colonies. A number of attempts were made to address the colonial imbalance between males and females. For example, the Emigration Committee in 1834 made special efforts to attract female emigrants to the colonies, including assessing the suitability of applicants to emigrate. In a report to the Parliament dated 30 December 1834 the Emigration Committee commented:

> *"In the execution of the delicate and onerous duties which devolve upon them, the emigration committee have been fully alive to their highly important ... and ... serious responsibility resting on them. They have strongly felt that as respects the colonists, among whom the grievous disparity between sexes, and the state of morals obviously arising from such a state of society, render the occasion of females of virtuous and industrious habits in the highest degree essential, they owed the utmost care and caution in sanctioning and aiding the transit of such females only as were likely to become really useful ... they have anxiously endeavoured to guard against the admission of improper subjects, by previous personal inquiry in all cases within a reasonable distance, and in the case of persons living remote from London, they have uniformly required the certificate of a resident minister ..."*[93]

The report also contained tables of numbers of females assisted to emigrate through the efforts of the Emigration Committee. The details are as follows:

---

93. Papers presented to and printed by order of the House of Commons, on 27 March, 1835. Emigration to the Australian Colonies. Report by the Emigration Committee to the Colonial Secretary of State, 30 December, 1834.

Passengers	Ship: *Strathfieldsaye* 476 tons - for VDL 1 May	Ship: ***David Scott*** 778 tons - for Sydney 10 July	Ship: ***Sarah*** 488 tons - for VDL 16 October
Females on whose behalf a bounty was allocated towards their passage	256	247	115
Females married or above the age of 30 (paying own passage)	14	26	21
Female children	18	32	21
Male children	18	35	18
Married men with families	3	16	21
Total passengers	309	356	196

The early attempts to address the gender imbalance in the colonies by recruiting women to emigrate and then arranging special vessels for their transport were sometimes criticised for sending unsuitable women of poor character. It's clear that for the colonists the ideal female immigrant was single, between the ages of 18 and 30, trained in domestic service, preferably with a knowledge of farm life, of good health, strong and, above all, of good moral character. As time passed the selection process was improved and the selection requirements were changed to focus attention on recruiting women of 'good character'.

The following extract from a London newspaper is typical of the advertisements used in the 1830s:

> "*The COMMITTEE for promoting the EMIGRATION OF SINGLE WOMEN to Australia, under whose management the Ships Bussorah Merchant and Layton were last year despatched with Female Emigrants, acting under the sanctions of His Majesty's Secretary of State for the Colonies, hereby give Notice, that a fine Ship of about 500 tons burden, carrying an*

experienced surgeon, and a respectable person as superintendent to secure the comfort and protection of the Emigrants during the voyage, will sail from GRAVESEND, on Thursday, 1st of May next (beyond which day she will on no account be detained) direct for HOBART TOWN, VAN DIEMEN'S LAND. Single Women and Widows of good character, from 15 to 30 years of age, desirous of bettering their condition by emigrating to that healthy and highly prosperous Colony, where the number of females compared with the entire population is greatly deficient, and where consequently from the great demand for servants, and other female employments, the wages are comparatively high, may obtain a passage on payment of Five Pounds only.

Those unable to raise that sum here will be allowed to give notes of hand payable in the Colony within a reasonable time after their arrival, when they have acquired the means to do so...

The Females who proceed by this conveyance will be taken care of on their first landing at Hobart Town; they will find there a list of the various situations to be obtained, and of the wages offered, and will be perfectly free to make their own selection...

....It will be necessary for the application to be accompanied by a certificate of character from the Resident Minister of the parish, or some other respectable person to whom the applicant may be known..."[94]

These special government-financed recruiting measures to attract females ceased in 1836, but other schemes were in operation and individuals like Caroline Chisholm worked to support emigration of females to the colonies. Despite these various efforts to increase the number of female emigrants coming to the colonies the balance of male to female emigrants, according to official figures for the period 1843 to 1872, was ten males to every eight females.[95]

---

94. Villiers, Alan. Vanished Fleets, Sea Stories from Old Van Diemen's Land. Cambridge, 1974. p. 293.
95. Hassam, Andrew. Sailing to Australia. Manchester, 1994. p. 15.

Hassam, in his analysis of the shipboard diaries of nineteenth-century British emigrants, makes some interesting observations about the literacy levels and the occupational backgrounds of emigrants. Although it seems that some nine out of ten emigrants travelled steerage passage and that most of the steerage passengers would have been working-class people, it cannot be concluded that the majority of these would be illiterate. It seems that the figures for literacy among assisted passengers of the 1850s show a surprisingly high proportion who were literate: eighty-one per cent of the Scots, seventy-two per cent of the English and Welsh and forty-nine percent of the Irish could both read and write.[96] However, it does appear that for many of those classified as literate they would have only had basic competency or proficiency. Hassam comments further that the more able in these areas, that is, those more likely to be fully literate, were the skilled workers, such as blacksmiths, carpenters, boot makers, who had undergone an apprenticeship. These types of skilled workingmen comprised about nineteen per cent of adult males entering Australia in the period 1854 to 1876. This compared to agricultural labourers, twenty-six per cent; general labourers, thirty-seven per cent; and middle class occupations, thirteen per cent.[97]

Some idea of the skill level of the emigrants who arrived in the second half of the century can be gained by looking at occupation. It seems that while there was a significant number of unskilled labourers in the 1850s and 1870s that number increased significantly in the 1860s. This is evident from the following table.

UK Emigration to Australia – Occupation per 10,000 Adult Males[98]

	1854-60	1861-70	1871-76
Commerce, finance, insurance & professional	964	1,489	1,568
Skilled trade	2,346	1,253	2,036
Transport	65	43	82
Agricultural	2,856	1,713	3,224
Other labourers	3,367	5,173	2,427
Others	402	329	663

---

96. ibid. p.12.
97. ibid. p.13.
98. Carrier, N.H. & Jeffrey, J.R. External Migration: A Study of the Available Statistics. HMSO London, 1953, p.386.

History records that there was some criticism by settlers of the quality of those who followed as emigrants, particularly in the early years of the century. The settlers had demanded of the United Kingdom strong, active and resourceful agricultural labourers and shepherds. It seems that very often they received instead men and women who had been very demoralised by long periods of unemployment or by the operations of the Poor Law; or whose occupations did not fit them for the work that colonists expected them to undertake. Complaints by the colonists were loud and persistent. It is most likely that the disappointment of the colonists led them to exaggerate the defects of the immigrants. There was also suspicion in the colonies of the Colonial Office, which led to a suspicion of those people selected or recommended by that organisation. It is also very possible that there would have been a natural prejudice of settled inhabitants against newcomers. It seems that the New South Wales Legislative Council and the colonial press were unduly influenced by the large landholders and condemned any immigrants that they spoke against. One writer of the time suggested that squatters considered the perfect immigrant to be "an able-bodied single man from an agricultural county – humble, ignorant and strong"[99]. Against this test mechanics, artisans and professional men would have been undesirable immigrants. We know that about half of the emigrants from the United Kingdom in the nineteenth century were assisted and that this proportion varied from colony to colony. In two of the popular destinations, New South Wales and South Australia, the vast majority of emigrants were assisted. Victoria on the other hand attracted the highest proportion of unassisted emigrants.

Despite the criticisms (largely coming from New South Wales), these early emigrants held on in the face of hardship and uncertainty. They laid the foundations of a society, which by the time the gold rush began in the 1850s, was able to absorb the newcomers that poured in to dig for gold. The rich lodes in Victoria attracted most of the new arrivals. In the years from 1852 to 1860, 290,000 people moved from Britain and Ireland to Victoria, which was equal to over half of the total British emigration to Australia and New Zealand in those years.[100] Although assisted passage arrangements continued during this period most of the emigrants paid their own passage in the 1850s. While manual labourers were amongst

---

99. Sidney,, Samuel. The Three Colonies of Australia. London, 1852, p.128.
100. Searle, G. R. The Golden Age. Melbourne University Press, 1963, p.44.

those arriving the backgrounds and occupations of the 1850s emigrants were much more diverse. These new arrivals were more self-reliant, reformist, often looking for a place free from political prosecution and economic insecurity. Charles Dickens describes the crowds who gathered at the offices of shipping merchants as follows:

> *"Legions of bankers' clerks, merchants' lads, embargo secretaries, and incipient cashiers; all going with the rush, and all possessing but faith and confused ideas of where they are going or what they are going to do; beg the hard-hearted shipbrokers to grant them the favour of a berth in their last-advertised, teak-built, poop-decked, copper-bottomed, double-fastened, fast-sailing, surgeon-carrying emigrant ship."* [101]

It's clear that of those emigrants arriving during the 1850s many came not to dig for gold but to seek their fortune by providing goods and services required for an expanding country. These included professional people, including lawyers and skilled tradesmen, such as stonemason. It's also interesting to note that considerable numbers of women arrived during this period, including numbers of unmarried middle-class women. What is clear is that the gold rush generation were far more diverse in skills, education, occupation and background.

Throughout the century many families emigrated to the colonies. These families often included a number of children. Because of the high mortality rate among children during the early years of emigration the British authorities attempted to limit the size of families and to prevent pregnant women from emigrating. However, large families and pregnant women continued to emigrate throughout the century. On some vessels the number of children exceeded the number of adult passengers. Hence it should be remembered that large numbers of children arrived as emigrants during the nineteenth century. Up to 1839 it has been estimated that about thirty per cent of passengers on Bounty Scheme vessels, and a little over forty per cent on Government Scheme vessels, were children[102].

---

101. ibid. p.44.
102. Madgwick, R.B. Immigration into Eastern Australia 1788-1851. Sydney University Press, 1969, p.139.

While an examination of the types of emigrants reveals that there were common themes and threads and several broad groupings there was nevertheless considerable diversity amongst nineteenth-century emigrants. Thus it would seem reasonable to conclude that there was no such thing as a typical British emigrant. Clearly the emphasis on type of emigrant coming, being sought by the colonies or being encouraged to emigrate by the home government, changed periodically during the course of the nineteenth century. It also seems that, despite government policies, programs or preferences that some people just decided to come anyway. The broad groupings of those arriving from the start of the century can be summarised as follows:

- In the first few years of the century the early governors sought to encourage people from farming and agricultural backgrounds that might be able to establish and maintain crops that could feed the growing colonies of New South Wales and Van Diemen's Land. These attempts were successful in attracting small numbers of emigrants but largely attracted people from an urban background who were not equipped to farm.
- The emphasis then changed as the colonial government and the home government decided that people with capital and expertise would better serve the colonies. They were encouraged to come by offers of land. In the three decades from about 1815 significant numbers from the more 'respectable' parts of British society came to the colonies. Some Scots with capital also arrive in this period. The expansion of rural New South Wales into the western districts after the crossing of the Blue Mountains in 1813 and the expansion of the profitable wool industry provided promising new fields of investment. Southern English agriculture was undergoing a period of depression and re-adjustment at this time and opportunities in Australia were attractive to these farmers.
- The establishment of schemes of assisted emigration during the 1830s and 1840s made it possible for poor or labouring class people to emigrate either by having their passage subsidised or paid in full. Some philanthropic schemes also emerged at this time. The requirements of the colonies during this period were for skilled labour and single women. There was clearly success in attracting significant numbers of women (some were poor, including a component from the workhouses,

some came as part of family groups and a number were unmarried middle class women). The schemes of assistance were only partly successful in attracting skilled male workers. Many men came during this period but they were often unskilled or semi-skilled labourers, often from a rural background, escaping limited opportunity at home and taking a risk that life in the colonies would be better.

- The discovery of gold dramatically changed both the numbers emigrating and the mix of people arriving during the 1850s. While assisted emigration continued during this decade some eighty per cent of arrivals paid their passage. The assisted emigrants were much the same as the previous period; families and individuals from the working class. However, the other emigrants were a very broad cross section of British society including those with skills and trade qualifications, professional people, some with capital, shopkeepers, merchants and of course miners and labourers. Some were seeking to escape the cultural, political and religious constraints of British society. Regardless of how successful the gold rush generation were in becoming rich it's interesting that few of the British-born returned home.
- From the 1860s to the end of the century emigration continued with the colonial governments taking firm control of the various assisted passage schemes. This ensured a steady stream of emigrants departing for the colonies during this period, including some who came unassisted. Many of the emigrants came from areas that already had links with the colonies, particularly from the southern counties of Britain. London, Middlesex and Kent were very prominent as sources of immigrants for the colonies. During much of this time the colonies sought to attract skilled labour and agricultural workers. However, at least until the 1870s the majority had little or no skills and no capital. The twenty-year depression in British agriculture and industry from the 1870s encouraged increasing numbers of skilled workers to emigrate.

It's clear that those who came as emigrants during the nineteenth century were far from an homogenous group of people. They comprised a wide variety of people whose backgrounds, problems, hopes and aspirations were far from uniform. However it does seem that they were optimistic or at least hopeful that Australia would offer a better life. Many came from depressed areas of the United Kingdom and they bore the scars of battling unemployment or underemployment, poverty, mistreatment, rejection and coping with the Poor Law stigma including trying to keep a family together and stay out of the poorhouses. For some of the emigrants the Australian colonies may have been a place of last resort. They arrived in colonies where development and economic conditions were sometimes primitive and frontier like (compared to England which was highly industrialised by 1830) and job requirements were often alien but most were able to rise above these difficulties and make a new life in their new home. These people were the true pioneers.

CHAPTER 5

The Emigration Vessels and their Crews

*"And now and then of the dwindling number
Of proud square-riggers there, slim and tall,
The wonder of her spars above them all."* [103]

Clearly those who came to Australia from Britain in the nineteenth century had but one mode of transport, which required a long journey by sea. For a significant part of the century this involved for most emigrants a voyage in a square rigged sailing ship. Bowen[104] described the period between 1780 and 1870 as the golden age of sail, because it marked the beginning of a period of 'scientific shipbuilding over the old rule of thumb', trade was increasing rapidly forcing ship construction to keep pace with it and the risk of war served to increase speed and strength. He also commented that 'the history of sailing ships and sailing ship design is fascinatingly interesting and every voyage was a romance'. However, for the majority of those who emigrated to Australia by sailing ship in the nineteenth century the voyage in the emigrant ships was far from a 'romance'. Life on board for passengers and crew was cramped, uncomfortable, at times damp, and frequently poorly ventilated, smelly, unhealthy and, of course, often dangerous.

The vessels that undertook the voyage from the British Isles to the colonies and return were a critical link for the people of the colonies with the old world. They were a vital part of nineteenth-century Australian history, or as Martin expressed it:

---
103. Smith, Cicely Fox. Sea Songs and Ballads.
104. Bowen, Frank. The Golden Age of Sail. London, 1925. p. 1.

> "Maritime history is very much nineteenth-century Australian history." [105]

The early emigrant ships were blunt nose box-like vessels. They were built with a flat bottom because of the lack of docking facilities and the need to be able to rest easily on the mud in a tidal river or harbour. They had a relatively blunt bow (front), sailed badly and as a consequence moved slowly through the sea pushing a great bow wave in front, but were relatively safe.

Falconer commenting on these vessels said:

> "most immediately is their boxy shape, flat bottom and great depth in relation to length." [106]

Despite developments in ship design and construction during the century these wooden sailing ships continued as regular passenger carriers until the 1860s and beyond. The nature and standard of service that the majority of these vessels offered at the end of this period was much the same as at its beginning.

These wooden vessels tended to "ride like a cork on the great rollers of the Southern Ocean on their way from Cape Town to Australia......They shipped little water and in very bad weather they could drift more or less bows on to the wind for days on end in relative safety."[107]

The words 'ship' and 'vessel' are often used interchangeably. This is in keeping with the current practice of describing any vessel as a ship. However, in the nineteenth century the term ship was only applied to a sailing vessel, which was square rigged on all masts (i.e. all the masts on the vessel carried yards (spars or cross pieces) with square sails. The ship had three or more masts – the fore, the main and the mizzen – all rigged

---

105. Martin, Terry. Maritime Paintings of Early Australia 1788-1900. Melbourne University press, 1998, p.105.
106. Falconer, John. Sail and Steam, A Century of Maritime Enterprise 1840-1935. Boston, 1993. p. 11.
107. Greenhill, Basil and Giffard, Ann. Travelling by Sea in the Nineteenth Century. London, 1972. p. 11.

with square sails. The rigging on a full-rigged ship can be seen from the sail plan of the *Lady Ebrington* (launched on 3 June 1852 and fitted as an emigrant ship to Australia).

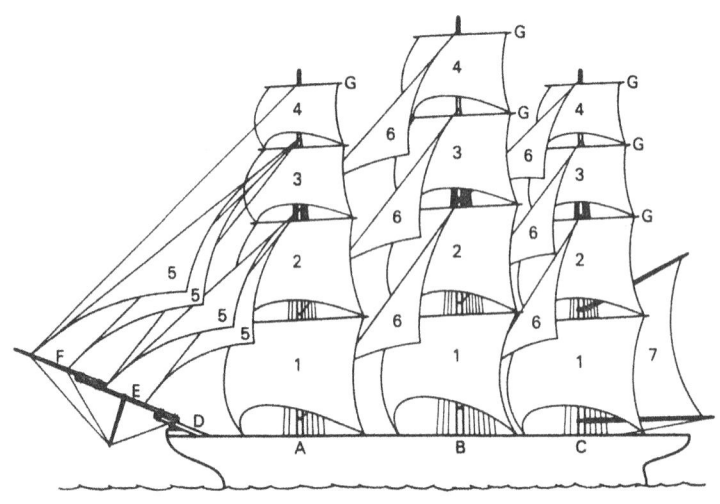

Sails

1. Courses
2. Topsails
3. Topgallants
4. Royals
5. Headsails
6. Staysails
7. Spanker

Spars

A. Foremast
B. Mainmast
C. Mizzen Mast
D. Bowsprit
E. Jib – Boom
F. Flying Jib – Boom
G. Yards

Sail Plan - Lady Ebrington[108]

Some shipowners preferred vessels rigged as barques, which had the square sails on the mizzenmast (back) replaced with sails carried fore and aft (i.e. along the same plane as the vessels fore and aft line – the line of the keel). These fore and aft rigged vessels were generally more manoeuvrable and efficient when working in changing wind conditions close to the coast. However, long ocean voyages required a large sail area to take advantage of the prevailing wind and current patterns of the globe. This was for many years the domain of the square-rigged vessel. On a square-rigged mast the sails had names,

---

108. Grant, Alison. Sailing Ships and Emigrants in Victorian Times. London, 1872. p. 29.

which indicated their position on the mast. The lowest square sail was the course, the next sail up was called the topsail and the next the topgallant sail. Some large ships had a fourth sail above the other three called the royal. The diagram below shows the difference in rigging between a ship and a barque.

Diagram Comparing the Rigging on a Ship & a Barque

During the course of the nineteenth century many vessels that started life as a ship ended life as a barque. There were some who thought that barques sailed better than ships, but given that many ships were still being constructed well into the second part of the century it is doubtful that this was the reason. It may have had more to do with economics. Up to about the mid-1850s, in addition to the fully rigged ships and barques there were also a variety of other smaller vessels carrying passengers to Australian ports. These smaller vessels were usually rigged as brigs, schooners or snows. They were frequently privately owned, sometimes the owner being a wealthy emigrant, who possibly obtained financial assistance to transport emigrants to the colonies. These ventures were not subject to the same strict control as official emigrant ships. Many of these vessels were sold at the end of the passage and a number remained in Australian waters working in the coastal trade.

Masts were constructed of pine, and were crossed by the yards, which were usually made from fir and designed to support and spread the sails. Since a single tree was insufficient height for the masts of very large vessels, such masts were composed of three sections: lower, top and topgallant mast. Most designs underwent few changes other than the continual endeavour to strengthen the joints between the mast sections and thus reinforce them against the ravages of weather.

The masts and yards were supported by an elaborate maze of rigging to accommodate the ever-growing profusion of sails. The rigging required constant highly skilled attention to keep it in working order. The bowsprit, projecting forward from the stern of the ship, gradually became longer to accommodate staysails, spritsails and jibs – all designed to maximise wind power. The sails took quite a beating and were frequently damaged, necessitating prompt repair. The sail maker was thus an important part of the crew of every large vessel.

In bad weather the crew sent the upper sections of the mast (each section is called a 'mast' in its own right) down to the deck, thus reducing the resistance of the rigging.

The sailors had to be able to respond swiftly to the captain's orders and this necessitated a complete understanding of the vessel. The on-board directions referred to the various parts of the vessel. The bow or fore, being the front of the boat and the back being the aft or stern. The right side became known as the starboard because the steering board was held on the right side of the vessel. The left side is the port. The weather side is the side from which the wind blows and the sheltered side is referred to as leeward.

Many British harbours at this time possessed only rudimentary docking facilities, so ships had to be able to rest on the ground in ports that dried at low tide and hence the flat bottom was a necessity. A second major consideration was the 1773 tonnage rules under which ships were built. These rules provided a formula for calculating the tonnage of a ship based on her length and breadth but they did not take account of her depth except as a nominal value. As port dues, pilot charges and other fees were based on tonnage, it made commercial sense to build vessels to the greatest possible depth, thus increasing cargo capacity while registering the lowest possible tonnage.

Although old tonnage laws were changed in 1836 and again in 1854, many ship builders continued to construct vessels to the old patterns for years afterwards. These changes to the way that vessel tonnage was calculated resulted in more than one tonnage figure being provided for many vessels of that period. Regardless of the measurement used it is clear that many of these early emigrant vessels were small. According to Parsons[109] the average measurement of vessels carrying migrants from Great Britain and Europe to South Australia in the first twenty-four years of colonisation (i.e. from 1836) was about 450 tons, although some exceeded 1200 tons and some were as small as 100 tons or less. An 1843 emigrant commented:

> *"The vessel in which we have now finally set out on a voyage of 16,000 miles is not large, being only 188 tons. She is however a good sailer and a light craft and has earmarked herself a good name by two very quick passages, made in succession. The Captain of the* **Mona** *is William Milligan, a Scotsman by birth...."*[110]

There was little difference between the early naval ships and the emigrant ships. Many ships were used interchangeably as naval ships, convict ships and emigrant ships, with only some changes to the ships' fittings.

Over time, hull design witnessed several important changes, and by the beginning of the nineteenth century the steep sides had flattened out until they appeared almost vertical. The design of vessels in the early part of the century was influenced by the East Indiamen (considered to be the aristocrats of the sea in the late eighteenth century). The East Indiamen were all built to much the same plan, heavy frigate-like ships, with no pretentions to speed. Their hulls were of stout construction and some finished their lives as convict ships. In the middle of the century, the development of the large merchant sailing ships was considerably influenced by external economic and political events. In 1831 the East India Company lost its exclusive right to trade with India. This marked the end of the long line of East Indiamen built by private owners, to a highly standardised design and leased to the Company. Existing vessels were redeployed to other use as private ships. To remain competitive there was a move to increase the speed of vessels. During this period of change

---

109. Parsons, Ronald. Migrant Ships for South Australia 1836-1860. Gumeracha, South Australia, 1983, p.16.
110. Wood. Journal of Voyage from London to Launceston in 1843 (20 June). National Library of Australia, Manuscript MS 9113.

in design some of the best and fastest ships were the Blackwall frigates, descendants of the old East Indiamen. These Blackwall frigates, originally built at Blackwall on the Thames, were the British version of the American tea clipper. They were rounded and full in the bow above the waterline, but sharp and wedge-like below the waterline. They were generally square rigged on three masts with a single deck. They were later employed on the Britain to Australia passenger and cargo run and recorded some fast passages. These vessels were much loved by the shipbuilders and sailors and often had songs and poems composed about them.

> "At the Blackwall Docks we bid adieu
> To lovely Kate and pretty Sue,
> Our anchor's weigh'd and our sails unfurl'd
> And we're bound to plough the wat'ry world,
> Sing hay, we're outward bound
> Hurrah, we're outward bound."[111]

The growth of shipping tonnage slowed considerably in the first half of the nineteenth century. The second half of the century saw a considerable growth in demand and also technology, which developed the merchant sailing ship to its highest form. The construction of sailing ships particularly prospered between 1850 and 1870. Although the most famous British ships came from the great yards of Scotland and North England, there was such demand that almost every small shipyard in every small seaport was kept busy. At this time there were few who believed that the beautiful wooden sailing ships would be driven from the oceans by the iron steamers. The number and size of ships launched during this period increased even from the small shipyards. However, while this was happening there also occurred parallel development of the steamship. During this period the sailing ship also sought out and found specialised routes and cargos where it could operate in viable competition with the steamship.

Possibly because Britain had borne the burden of the Napoleonic Wars, she lagged behind America in the design of swift sailing ships. America also had a ready supply of softwood. American shipbuilders started

---

111. Lubbock, Basil. The Blackwall Frigates. Glasgow, 1922. p. 24.

developing the new breed of sleeker and faster ships in the 1840s. Competition from steam on the Atlantic run spurred designers of sailing ships to their greatest efforts and this eventually improved ships used in the Australian trade. These new style ships, unlike the older box-like design, were much longer in relation to the beam. They were often referred to as 'clippers', a fairly vague term without any specific origin other than some commentators saying that they seem to clip along.

The mid part of the century saw a number of improvements, both legislative and technical, which set the scene for the transformation of merchant shipping. In 1850 an Act was passed by the British Parliament for improving the conditions of Masters, Mates and Seamen and the maintenance of discipline in the merchant service. The Steam Navigation Act of the following year made further provision for the safety of sea travel. In 1854 the Merchant Shipping Act provided 548 clauses relating to the merchant service. In the following decade there were further improvements in training, signalling, navigation and general safety. These changes reflected the increasing volume of trade and passenger traffic, with colonial expansion, the discovery of gold in Australia and America and the creation of new markets. The conflicts in Europe and America, with the Crimean War and the American Civil War, also contributing to the shipping boom in the 1850s and 1860s.

The developments in the second part of the century also saw a gradual move from wooden to iron ships. There were problems with the wooden ships as they became waterlogged and were subject to rot as they aged. They were also subject to attack by a shipworm (*toredo navalis*), which could bore large holes and cause ships to founder. It can grow up to 60 cm in length and 1-2 cm in diameter, and has a small shell that acts like a drill bit boring circular burrows into wood. The great shipworm causes extensive and costly damage to unprotected and untreated timber structures. Wood that is attacked is damaged beyond repair by the many burrows bored into it. In order to overcome these problems wooden ships were at first treated with tar and then later sheathed at first in lead and zinc and then copper. From around 1846 a mixture of copper and zinc was used – referred to as 'yellow metal'.

The use of iron also offered possibilities of greater internal space because its strength meant that the structural members used in construction could be much smaller than the alternative wooden members. Iron ships were of two types: those built entirely of iron and those built with an iron frame planked on the outside with teak. The latter type were referred to as 'composite' ships. For many years the two types were developed and existed side by side. The extra room available in these iron ships made them ideal for carrying large quantities of bulky cargo. There was, of course, some reluctance by a conservative ship building industry to move to iron construction; after all, wood had been used for shipbuilding since time immemorial. The composite method offered a compromise for many as it allowed the use of an iron skeleton for strength to carry the tall masts and an immense spread of canvas, but also allowed a fine timber finish of the hulls and decks to be achieved. Between 1863 and 1879 most of the ships built were of composite construction.

Thermopylae duelling with the *Cutty Sark*
(Brodie Collection, La Trobe Picture Collection, State Library of Victoria)

Possibly the best known of the composite ships was the clipper, **Thermopylae**, which completed the journey to Melbourne in 60 days in 1868, the year of her construction. She was 991 tons registered,

210 feet long, 36 feet beam and 21 feet deep. Another famous composite clipper used on the Australian run was the ***Cutty Sark***, built specifically to challenge the ***Thermopylae***. The ***Cutty Sark*** was almost the same size and had her maiden voyage in 1870. From the early 1880s both vessels were engaged in the wool trade for a number of years. Towards the end of the nineteenth century the hulls of all large ships were wholly of iron or steel construction, with steel also used for the masts, yards and rigging.

Cutty Sark **(watercolour by F Brown)**
(State Library of Victoria)

A detailed description of a composite ship, the **Schomberg**, built for the Australia run, was contained in the *Argus* on Saturday 6 October 1855 (the day she departed for Melbourne). The *Argus* referred to her as "this magnificent addition to the Australian fleet of clipper ships" and then proceeded to provide the following details:

> "The Schomberg registers 2600 tons, builder's measure. She is 288 feet of length between perpendiculars on deck, 45 feet extreme breadth of beam, and 29 feet depth of hold. As mentioned at the time of the launch, the vessel is built on the diagonal principle, which is calculated to secure the greatest strength. Her thickness consists of four courses of Scotch larch, each 2 ½ inches thick, and between each is a layer of hair felt, the outside or skin being pitch pine 5 inches thick - the whole combined by means of screw trenails. The beams of her two upper decks are of malleable iron, the lowest being pine pitch, and the whole supported by three courses of malleable iron stanchions. She is of the regular Aberdeen clipper build. She has three decks. On the first or main deck there is a full topgallant-forecastle, a round-house, forming a passenger saloon, poop, etc. Part of the forecastle is fitted for the accommodation of the crew, and in the vicinity is large space for working the chains of the vessel. The deck-house extends to the main hatchway, and contains staterooms, storerooms, etc. also protecting two staircases which lead to the deck below. A moveable house covers the main hatchway at sea. Before the poop is a house which extends nearly to the mainmast, and along its sides, and indeed generally on the deck, there is ample room secured for the working of the vessel. The lower cabin contains sixty large staterooms, finished with white and gold, and furnished with every convenience. The ladies cabin or drawing room is inlaid with rosewood, set off with Grecian arched panels, and ornamented with pilasters, papier machee cornices, gilding, and flower work, the windows filled with transparencies, and altogether the furnishings are in the best style, and include a handsome piano. The dining saloon is about 30 feet long, and symmetrical breadth; it has many windows, admitting a flood of light, and is also splendidly furnished. The top of the poop affords space for a promenade. Descending

by double staircases to the second or middle deck - the height between decks being 7 1/2 feet - we come to have some idea of the immense size of the vessel viewed internally. A large part of the deck is for second-class passengers, at the aft end being the first-class passenger's sleeping berths. Along the sides are square portholes, with plate-glass windows in them, which can be opened; and above, through the topgallant-forecastle, the house amidships, etc., there are ample ventilators, which render this deck light and airy. This arrangement has also been made, and with excellent effect, in the case of the third deck, for third-class passengers - a compartment usually hitherto in almost all passenger ships almost intolerable, from deficient ventilation and other causes. It may here be stated that the greatest possible attention has been given to secure ventilation as perfectly as possible, and with complete success. Altogether, for extent of accommodation, as well as for the utmost provision being made for the comfort of the passengers - we might say the gratification of their tastes - it would be difficult to conceive it possible what more could have been done in the case of a ship. For instance, to descend to a particular or two, there are baths, a library, a smoking-room on the poop; a cow is to be kept on board to afford fresh milk; indeed, it would be difficult to say what is not to be had, in its best condition, either for health or sickness; whilst there are eight boats on board, besides two fire-engines, and other means of protection and precaution. She will carry 1000 passengers with ease and comfort.

Below the third deck is the hold for goods, the bottom of which may be said to form a fourth deck, being laid with immense iron water-tanks, capable of containing 350 tons of water, for the use of the passengers and crew.

Her lower masts and bowsplit are of pitch pine, and hooped with iron, and her topmasts, jibboom, and lower yards also of pitch pine. She is a full-rigged ship, and when her dimensions are taken into account some idea may be formed of what a spectacle she will present, with all her sails set, holding on her noble course. Indeed, the masts and yards are extremely symmetrical and beautiful, and to give an idea of *their proportions, we may mention that from the step to the maintop the length is about 210 feet. The mainmast is taut; the bowsprit is proportionately short; and there are no less than 16,000 yards of canvas in her sails.*

.........It is right to mention that this really magnificent vessel - the largest of her class (ie apart from steamers or ships of war) ever built in Great Britain, or with one exception in the world - is with all her equipments, rigging, chains, ropes, etc., in short from the keel to the main truck, the work of Messrs Hall. How much credit she does them requires no laudation here - the vessel herself furnishes their best eulogium, and for the rest, deeds not words, may be left to speak.

The Schomberg will proceed direct to Liverpool, from which she will sail on 5th September for Australia."[112]

Ship *Schomberg*
(Phillip Doak Collection, State Library of Victoria)

---

112. *The Argus*. (Melbourne). Saturday. October 6, 1855, p.4 (with details of the vessel taken from the Aberdeen Journal by the Argus).

While this account of the ***Schomberg*** is rather lengthy and reads somewhat like an advertisement on behalf of the shipping line, I nonetheless felt it worthy of repeating most of the article, as it gives a good account of the latest shipping technology and an insight into conditions on board a large emigrant ship. At that time she was the biggest wooden ship ever built in a British yard and was dubbed the 'monster emigrant clipper'. Built at a cost of £43,103, she was well-equipped and set new standards in size and comfort. In this respect she was very atypical of the standard of accommodation that confronted most emigrants travelling to Australia at this time on board the square-riggers.

As a postscript to the ***Schomberg*** story, which started with such fanfare, there is an unhappy ending. On her maiden voyage to Australia, 81 days out, on 26 December 1855, she ran aground at Peterborough, 35 miles west of Cape Otway in Western Victoria. While the vessel was a total loss the steamer, *Queen*, bound for Portland, saved all on board next morning. Thus 'this magnificent addition to the Australian fleet of clipper ships' had a very short career and the 'monster emigrant clipper' was no more.

Another steel vessel that is worthy of special mention is the ***S S Great Britain***. She rates special mention because of her advanced design and because she carried more passengers to Australia than any other nineteenth-century emigrant ship. The ***Great Britain*** was designed by Isambard Kingdom Brunel for the Great Western Steamship Company in 1838 for the transatlantic service between Bristol and New York. After a number of construction delays she was launched in 1843, weighing 3500 tons and measuring 320 feet long (more than 100 foot longer and 1000 tons larger than any vessel previously built). The iron keel plates were an inch thick and the hull seams were lapped and double riveted in many places. She was rigged like a clipper, but had auxiliary steam power. Following the launching there were further delays in fitting the vessel out and on 26 July 1845 she finally embarked on her maiden voyage from Liverpool to New York with forty-five passengers. The final cost of construction was £117,000 (£47,000 more than the original estimate). The maiden passage was made in 14 days and 21 hours, which was slower than the prevailing record. The propeller proved unsatisfactory and so was replaced. On her next crossing to New York with 104 passengers the vessel ran into heavy weather and lost three propeller blades and a mast. After repairs in New York she set out for Liverpool and lost four propeller blades during the crossing. By this time another design flaw became evident. The vessel rolled heavily, especially in calm weather without the steadying influence of sail, causing great discomfort to passengers. To remedy these problems the six-bladed propeller was replaced with a four-bladed cast iron model, the third mast was removed and the iron rigging replaced with conventional rigging and a major alteration saw the addition of two bilge keels to each side to lessen the tendency to roll.

In her second season of service the **Great Britain** successfully completed two round trips to New York but was then laid up for further repairs. Embarking on her third passage of the season to New York a number of navigational errors resulted in her being run aground in Dundrum Bay on the north coast of Ireland. She remained aground for almost a year. In August 1847 she was floated free at a cost of £34,000 and taken back to Liverpool. After some time she was sold to Gibbs, Bright and Co. for a mere £25,000. The new owners decided to give the vessel a total refit. This included replacing the keel, strengthening the bow and stern, replacing the engines with more efficient and lighter engines and replacing the three large boilers with six smaller ones. The refit took two years. Following the refit she was again put on the Atlantic route. After only one further trip she was again sold. The buyer this time was Anthony Gibbs & Sons who planned to place her into the England-Australia service.

The new owners may have intended to employ the **Great Britain** to exploit a temporary demand for passenger service to the Australian goldfields following the discovery of gold in Victoria in 1851 but she found long-term employment on this route. For her new role she underwent a further refit. Her passenger accommodation was increased from 360 to 730 and her sail plan altered to a traditional three-masted square-rigged pattern. She was also fitted with a removable propeller, which could be hauled up on deck by chains in order to reduce drag when under sail power alone. She made her first of thirty-four passages to Australia in 1852, carrying 630 emigrants. She created great interest by the people of Melbourne, with 4,000 people paying a shilling to inspect her. Although fitted with a steam engine, the days of the true long voyage steamship being sometime away, she operated much like a steel clipper, generally using steam power only at the beginning and end of a voyage and, of course, in the doldrums in tropical waters. Her passage times were remarkably good with an average time in the mid-sixties and her best time of just under 56 days. She carried an estimated 20,000 people on the Australia run before being withdrawn from service in 1877.

Great Britain - **Among the Icebergs**[113]
(National Library of Australia)

It's interesting to note that on her 1861 passage to Melbourne she had a crew of 143 and 544 passengers plus a cow, 36 sheep, 140 pigs, 96 goats, 1114 chickens, ducks, geese and turkeys. She also transported on that passage the first English cricket team to visit Australia. That passage to Melbourne (her ninth) took 64 days.

---

113. *Illustrated Sydney News*. 21 January, 1971. p. 125.

In 1882 the *Great Britain* was converted to a vessel for transporting coal but after a fire on board in 1886 she was found on arrival in Port Stanley in the Falkland Islands to be damaged beyond repair. She was sold to a company in the Falklands Islands for use as a coal storage hulk. In 1937 she was towed away from Port Stanley, scuttled and abandoned. In 1970 a decision was taken to salvage her and return her to Bristol for restoration. On 5 July she was towed up the River Avon to Bristol. Following the long process of restoration she was ready to receive visitors in July 2005. As part of the restoration and dry docking, at the Great Western Dockyard a glass plate was installed across the dry dock at the water level incorporating dehumidifiers to ensure that the hull does not corrode further.

Great Britain **on Display, Bristol**
(Photographs taken by author 2009)

Although steamships had been in existence from the latter part of the eighteenth century they had little impact on the Australia passenger trade until almost a hundred years later in the latter part of the nineteenth century. Steamships (of a kind) had been in existence since 1788 and had been proven to be potential seagoing vessels from around 1810. The first British steam navigation company was formed in the 1820s, and the development in 1836 of the screw (to replace the paddle wheel), the use of iron and later steel in ship construction enabled the development of the steamship to move ahead.

Even with these developments the use of the steamship was limited because of practical difficulties. For example, with the development of the screw as a means of propulsion this only partially solved the problem of finding a better method of propulsion than the paddle. The screw introduced a further difficulty because the vibrations and the torque of the shaft imposed stresses on the wooden hull. By the 1850s several shipping yards were building ships in both iron and wood, and by 1880 in Britain only smaller sailing ships (i.e. under 500 tons) were still built of wood.

The early steam engines were very inefficient and the quantity of coal needed to fire the boilers left insufficient space for cargo. These new vessels belching smoke and steam were also regarded with some suspicion as the work of the devil. The early steamships that attempted the long Australian run often-encountered difficulties. This is illustrated in the following extract of the account of the return voyage from Melbourne of the **Croesus**, which took some three and a half months:

> "SOUTHHAMPTON, Dec 14.
>
> *The General Screw Steamship Company's steamship Croesus, Captain J.V. Hall, arrived here this afternoon.... The steamer brings about 30 passengers, and on freight 3,805 ounces of gold from Sydney, 42,406 ounces from Port Phillip, 41,350 sovereigns from Sydney...*
>
> *Like the outward passage of this noble steamship, the homeward one had been marked by mishap, and attended with delay. On 12th of September, at 8 pm, only two days after leaving Melbourne, one of the fans of the propeller broke off; and on 3rd of October the remaining one gave way. The remains of the screw were then hoisted up and unshipped. The weather was extremely unfavourable, with baffling easterly winds, between New Zealand and 126 long. In lat. 55, long. 105 ice was fallen in with, and continued for several days. Cape Horn was rounded on 19th of October under sail only, as the new propeller could not be got into place, owing to the heavy weather and the rolling of the ship, till the 29th October..."*[114]

---

114. *London Times*. December 15, 1854.

The Steamer *Croesus* on her Voyage to Sydney, 1854
(Rex Nan Kivell Collection NK2106/74, National Library of Australia)

The development that finally saw the emergence of the steamship as the dominant form of sea transport was the introduction of Siemens steel, which made it possible after about 1878 to construct boilers that could operate at high pressures and thus achieve greater efficiency and lower fuel consumption. One of the first vessels built as a result of these developments for the Australian emigration trade was the ***Aberdeen.*** On her maiden voyage in 1882 she went from Plymouth to Melbourne in 42 days with one coaling stop.

However, countries had for years sent ships around the world under sail and unlike the steamship, propulsion occurred by wind, which was generally available and was free. Development of the sailing ship had occurred very slowly over as long period of time. Travel by ship was a slow affair, voyages were leisurely and they stayed that way for centuries. It was not until the latter half of the nineteenth century that a quest for speed (largely for economic reasons) led to the development of fast sailing ships.

These faster sailing ships were capable of carrying large amounts of cargo and could 'clip' along at a considerable speed. After gold was discovered in Australia there was an immediate demand by thousands in Britain to get quickly to the gold fields. Ships, such as the *Marco Polo,* set new records on the Australia run. The *Marco Polo*, a large ship (1625 tons), was built in New Brunswick, Canada, and purchased by the Black Ball Line for the Australia run. She first sailed to Melbourne in 1850 carrying 950 passengers and 30 crew, arriving in 68 days. However, of the passengers 327 were children, 52 of whom died of measles during the passage.

Ship *Marco Polo* (painting by Thomas Robertson)
(State Library of Victoria)

The *Marco Polo* made many trips carrying emigrants to the colonies and returning with cargo and at times passengers. The first page of the colonial papers carried shipping news and advertisements relating to vessels returning to the British Isles. The following advertisement relating to the return passage of the *Marco Polo* in 1856 is a typical example of what appeared daily as part of the shipping news:

> **BLACK BALL LINE OF BRITISH AND AUSTRALIAN ROYAL MAIL PACKETS FOR LIVERPOOL** – The celebrated royal mail clipper ship **MARCO POLO** 1625 tons register, James Clarke, commander, having arrived with the English mail of 7 December, will be despatched with the return mail to England on 25 March.
>
> This famous clipper has superior accommodation for salon, second cabin and intermediate passengers, and her commander Capt. Clarke, is well known for his urbanity and kind attention to passengers.
>
> Gold, wool, and general cargo taken at current rates.
>
> For plans of cabins and other information apply to MACKAY, RAINES and Co, Hall of Commerce, Collins Street West.

On her first passage to the colonies in 1850 *Marco Polo* was the largest vessel at that time to have carried passengers to Australia. The round trip to the colonies and back to Britain was completed in 5 months and 21 days. Her captain for the 1850 voyage was James 'Bully' Forbes, who developed something of a reputation for hard sailing. He later captained another Black Ball Line clipper, the *Lightning*, also noted for her fast voyages to Australia, and was captain of the *Schomberg* on her fateful voyage to Australia in 1855.

These new, sleek, fast vessels were impressive and captured the attention and imagination of those interested in shipping and maritime life. Some of this feeling of design and speed is captured in the following verse:

> *"A ship there was, and she went to sea*
> *(Away O, my Clyde-built clipper);*
> *In eighteen hundred and seventy-three,*

Fine in the lines and keen in the bow,
The way they've forgotten to build 'em now,
Lofty-masted and heavily sparred,
With stunsail booms to every yard,
And flying kites both high and low
To catch the winds when they did blow
(And away O, my Clyde-built clipper!)[115]

The **Lightning** was rival to the White Star Line clipper, **Red Jacket**. The **Red Jacket** (named after an American Indian), built in 1853, was 2560 registered tons, 260 feet long and had a beam of 44 feet. This compared to the **Lightning's** slightly smaller measurements of 2096 tons registered, 245 feet long and a 44-foot beam. These two vessels departed on the same day (14 May 1854) for Australia; both determined to be the first to arrive. The **Red Jacket**, under the captaincy of Samuel Reed, arrived in Melbourne in 69 days compared to the 77 days that the **Lightning** took. The rivalry between the two vessels, including this trip to Melbourne, was reported to readers of the *London Times*:

> "**THE CLIPPER RED JACKET** - *Much interest and curiosity were manifested last May, it will be remembered, as to the relative sailing merits of the clipper ships Red Jacket and Lightning, and numerous wagers were made by the friends of the respective "crack" ships, that they would go out in less than 70 days. The Red Jacket has performed her task admirably, having arrived at her anchorage at Melbourne in 69 days 11 hours and 15 minutes, of which she was under sail only 67 days 13 hours, and we feel assured that the homeward passage would have been made in the same, or even less time, had she not unfortunately fell in with large masses of ice off Cape Horn, which materially interfered with her progress. The qualities of the Lightning have yet to be ascertained, her run out not offering a fair comparison, and we feel confident that she will recover her prestige for speed on the trip home........*"[116]

---

115. Smith, C Fox. Rhymes of the Red Ensign. London 1919. The Clyde-Built Clipper, verse 1. p. 15.
116. The Clipper Ship Red Jacket. London Times. October 17, 1854.

American Clipper *Red Jacket*, 1853 (watercolour by D M Little)
(State Library of Victoria)

On a later voyage to Australia the **Lightning** 'recovered her *prestige* for speed' and also made the trip in 69 days. This was to be her best passage to Australia. In 1856, under the captaincy of Anthony Enright, she carried 47 saloon, 53 second cabin, 20 intermediate and 253 steerage passengers to Australia; returning with 104,000 ounces of gold (said to be the biggest shipment ever dispatched). These early clipper ships, unlike the later composites, were entirely of wooden construction and were built in North America.

There was considerable competition between the various shipping lines and the competition extended to committing those praises to verse. For example:

> *When I was a lad and went to sea*
> *In Seventy-seven or six maybe,*
> *There was ten tall ships on Merseyside*
> *Did sail or berth with every tide;*
> *There was "Hills" and "Halls" and "Dales and "Bens",*
> *'Counties' and 'Cities' and 'Lochs' and 'Glens';*
> *But none there was so fast and fine*
> *As them that sailed in the Blue Star Line.*

They had tough skippers as hard as nails
To crack 'em along in Cape Horne gales,
And hard-case shellbacks thirty-two
They used to be in a Blue Star crew,
To man the capstan, and raise the shout
at tacks and sheets when she went about,
And brassbound reefers eight or nine
In them tall ships of the Blue Star Line.[117]

Ship *Lightning* (watercolour by D M Little)
(State Library of Victoria)

The management of a clipper was demanding as every change of wind meant a change of sail, in order to maintain speed and avoid problems or even disaster. For emigrants sailing under such conditions for days and weeks at a time it must have appeared that the captain was frequently taking intolerable risks. Despite the development of these fast sailing ships most passengers coming to Australia arrived in slower, square-rigged sailing vessels. The Flagstaff Observatory in Melbourne recorded 300 passages between Europe and Melbourne in the period 1858 to 1863. Only one of the 300 bettered 70 days; seven completed the voyage

---

117. Fox Smith, C. Rhymes of the Red Ensign. London, 1919. p.55.

in 70 days; fifty in 71 to 80 days; eighty in 81 to 90 days; sixty-eight in 91 to 100 days and ninety-four exceeded 100 days.[118]

The gold rush not only brought an enormous number of people to the colonies seeking their fortunes but it put considerable pressure on shipping available to bring assisted passengers to the colonies. With large numbers of people deserting farm and other work to go to the goldfields there was an urgent demand for replacement workers and pressure was exerted on the Colonial Office to relax its regulations relating to suitable vessels to transport assisted working class people to the colonies. Employers in Adelaide, Melbourne and Sydney were desperate to obtain replacement labourers as quickly as possible. These circumstances resulted in poor decisions in the early 1850s by the British authorities regarding the engagement of vessels to transport large numbers of assisted emigrants, which had fatal consequences.

The decision involved chartering four large American-built vessels, which could accommodate steerage passengers on two lower decks. This meant that these vessels could carry twice as many emigrants below the decks. The Commissioners also relaxed the rules relating to the number of young children under the age of ten that could be transported. One of the four double-decked vessels the **Bourneuf**, a ship of 1495 tons, sailed from Liverpool on May 26 arriving at Geelong some three months later on 3 September 1852. The passage had been a horrific experience for the passengers with 88 dying of measles, diarrhoea, scarletina (better known now as scarlet fever a bacterial infection) and marasmus (a severe form of malnutrition). Most of the deaths were amongst the Scottish children under seven years old.

The deaths were the subject of an investigation by the Victorian Health Officer. The following extract from a report gives a clear indication of the nature of the passage:

> *"Five women had died of consumption, puerperal fever, or been lost overboard. Of the 180 children under seven years of age who embarked, nearly half died of diarrhoea, measles, and other complaints...*

---

118. Charlwood, Don. The Long Farewell. Ringwood, Victoria, 1981, p.37.

Arrangements for hygiene were primitive or non existent. The main deck leaked, so that the two migrant decks were usually damp. The water-closets were 'of inferior construction and leaky'…

The upper immigrant deck had a 'disagreeable smell' while the lower deck was dark and 'difficult to ventilate'. There was insufficient hospital accommodation or spare bedding, so that infected mattresses had to be used again. The matron was almost useless 'owing to physical want of activity or energy', while Surgeon McKevit was accused by the passengers of being 'so grossly intoxicated that he could not attend to his duty'…."[119]

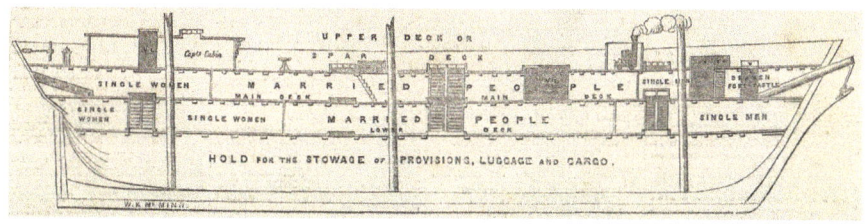

Below Decks Sketch of Ship *Bourneuf*
(Rex Nan Kivell Collection, NK4182/89, National Library of Australia)

The story of the passage of another of the double-decked vessels, ***Ticonderoga*** is even more horrific. On 4 August 1852 in Birkenhead, 795 migrants, predominantly Highland Scots, boarded the ***Ticonderoga*** a four-masted ship of 1089 tons. The vessel was captained by Thomas H Boyle and carried 48 crew, which included Dr J C Sanger as the surgeon superintendent and Dr James William Henry Veitch as his assistant. Provisions included over 36000 lbs of flour, 12000 lbs of split peas, 93 cwt of sugar, over 6000 lbs of raisins, barrels of Navy bread, preserved beef and pork, canned soup, over 400 gallons of pickles and 7000 lbs of treacle not to mention the 25000 lbs of oatmeal and 3 chests of tea left over from the previous voyage of the ship.

Dr Sanger reported that disease had been noticed about two weeks after the ship's departure: red rashes, strong delirium bordering on insanity and the ever-present diarrhoea and dysentery. On 5 November 1852, 90 days after their departure, the ***Ticonderoga*** crawled into Port Phillip Bay flying the yellow flag and carrying the stench of death. The *Argus*,

---
119. Cannon, M. Who's Master Who's Man? Australia in the Victorian Age. 1971, pp. 159-60.

Melbourne, reported on Tuesday 9 November 1852 that the Port and Harbour Master at Williamstown, Captain Charles Ferguson, stated that:

> *"100 deaths and nineteen births had occurred on the passage, seven of the former since the ship anchored at the Heads. There are at present 300 cases of sickness amongst them, principally scarletina".*

There were in fact, 311 cases of "fever" (typhus), 127 cases of diarrhoea and 16 cases of dysentery on the ship's arrival. At that time it was not known that lice spread typhus, which most of the deaths were later attributed to. The report given by the Immigration Board in Melbourne to the Emigration Commissioners in London on the condition of the **Ticonderoga** on its arrival, stated that:

> *"The ship, especially the lower part was in a most filthy state, and did not appear to have been cleaned for weeks, the stench was overpowering, the lockers so thoughtlessly provided for the Immigrants use were full of dirt, mouldy bread, and suet full of maggots, beneath the bottom boards of nearly every berth upon the lower deck were discovered soup and bouille cans and other receptacles full of putrid ordure, and porter bottles etc, filled with stale urine, while maggots were seen crawling underneath the berths, and this state of things must have been prevalent for a long time as the 2nd Mate describes the ship to have been in the same state when he supervised the cleaning of her by the Captain's order five weeks previously".* [120]

Captain Boyle landed the **Ticonderoga** at Portsea at Point Nepean, so chosen because of its isolated but accessible position and good anchorage. A quarantine ground was marked out with yellow flags and white paint on the trees, and tents were erected using the sails and spars from the ship. The government purchased two houses that had been occupied by lime-burners and converted them into hospitals. The **Lysander** sailed over from South Australia, and was outfitted as a hospital for the worst cases. The surviving passengers arrived in Melbourne on 22 December 1852, most without one or more of their family members. In memory of the enormous number who lost their lives (100 passengers -17 adult males, 29 adult

---

120. Welch, J H. Hell to Health - The History of Quarantine at Port Phillip, Victoria: The Nepean Historical Society 1969 p28.

females, 39 children between 1 and 14 years of age and 15 infants under the age of 1 yr) the bay between Observatory Point and Police Point on the Nepean Peninsula was named 'Ticonderoga' and a memorial to those who lost their lives on this ill-fated vessel, lies in the Point Nepean Cemetery.

Another of the double-decked vessels engaged during this brief period was the ***Beejapore,*** which arrived in Port Jackson on 6 January 1853 after a relatively quick passage of 86 days. On arrival she was immediately placed in quarantine due to an outbreak of measles and other illnesses on board. The vessel had carried on that passage to Sydney 967 emigrants, including 342 children. During the passage 56 emigrants were buried at sea 55 of them children or infants and a further 52 children and ten adults died during the quarantine period. The vessel made another passage in 1857 to Sydney (the only double decked vessel to sail into Port Jackson in the 1850s) and a further trip to the colonies in 1863 to Keppel Bay, Queensland and then she disappeared on the return to her homeport.

There were clearly unforeseen problems associated with the double-decker aspect of these ships. Poor ventilation and lighting were the major two. As a result, washing the decks wasn't commonly practiced as the water would leak from deck to deck and it was almost impossible to dry out the 'damp'. As the passage progressed the atmosphere between decks grew more and more polluted. The risk of disease was also heightened by a lack of space for exercise on the upper deck (due to overcrowding) along with poor personal hygiene, an aversion to medical treatment and ignorance about the incubation of disease. There is no doubt that any infection or "fever" would thrive amongst such shocking sanitary conditions.

After the relatively short experience with double-decked vessels bringing emigrants to the colonies the Commissioners took a decision not to charter these large vessels in the future and also reversed its decision about allowing such large numbers of children to travel on assisted emigrant vessels (i.e. no family would be accepted for emigration in which there were more than two children under seven years, or three children under ten years).

While there was an increase in the use of steamships towards the end of the century there was never the less continuing development of the sailing ship into the early part of the twentieth century. Possibly the ultimate development in sailing ships was the ***Preussen,*** built in 1902. She was a five-masted fully-rigged steel ship, 433 feet long and some 54 feet at the beam. The ***Preussen*** was propelled entirely by her 60,000 square feet of canvas, providing a best speed of about 17 knots. She was, of course, something of an anomaly in the twentieth century as the age of sail for transport had largely passed. However, in the first decade or so of the twentieth century many believed that there was still work for well-designed square-rigged ships, particularly as the steamers had a usual speed of around 8 knots, with an average of about 6 knots on a long voyage. These fast sailing ships lasted longer on the long-haul runs, like Australia and New Zealand because of their speed, economy and because of an absence of coaling stations for steamships.

Ship *Preussen* (watercolour by C Dickson Gregory)
(State Library of Victoria)

However the demise of the sailing vessel was assured by the end of the nineteenth century despite several comebacks. In the mid-1880s, for example, the introduction of cheap high-quality steel led to the building of hundreds of big four-masted barques, which were able to compete profitably with steamships until well into the 1890s. Many were over 300 feet long and could carry over 5000 tons of cargo. These sailing vessels built after the end of the clipper era embodied some of the finer points of clipper design.

Most of the paying passengers travelling on the long haul to Australia in the second half of the century found that the cheapest passage was obtained in the older style square-rigged ship. These vessels were generally referred to as 'packet' line ships. Shipowners wanting to attract passengers to a mediocre vessel were likely to advertise her as a clipper. Thus, as time went on the term 'clipper' became widely applied to signify that the vessel had desirable qualities. The advertisements in the shipping columns of the newspapers described passenger vessels in very attractive terms. The following advertisement from the *Melbourne Argus* of 6 October 1855 is a good example:

> "*BLACK BALL LINE OF BRITISH AND AUSTRALIAN ROYAL MAIL PACKETS* - *For Liverpool, forwarding passengers, gold, and cargo to London, the magnificent new clipper ship CHAMPION OF THE SEAS, 2447 tons register, J. McKirdy, commander, will be despatched with the return English mail on Thursday 25th October.*
>
> *This ship is now on her second voyage, and in point of speed, comfort, and accommodations as a passenger conveyance, stands second to no vessel afloat. Her magnificent saloons are fitted up in a style of luxurious elegance, the state rooms are spacious, lighted by side ports, and are furnished requisite, including bedding.*
>
> *Second Cabin passengers are provided a good table and steward attendance. Intermediate passengers receive a liberal supply of the best provisions.*
>
> *The ship is fitted with iron tanks to carry an ample supply of water. She also carries a milch cow for the use of the cabin passengers.*
>
> *Captain McKirdy is well known in the trade, and has uniformly won the respect and esteem of his passengers by his kindness and attention, as well as by his ability as a commander.*
>
> *A qualified Surgeon accompanies the ship...*"

While there was a tendency to exaggerate when describing vessels in the second half of the century there is little doubt that vessels constructed in this period benefited from developments in shipping technology. The early developments led to lighter sails and rigging. Then came the use of steel for masts. Some of the changes also reflected the need for economy and hence for a smaller crew.

Prior to the development of the faster style vessel the square-rigged wooden ship operated as an integrated enterprise with the crew being capable of undertaking a range of tasks, requiring of the crew many skills. The seaman's life throughout the nineteenth century was hard, dangerous and insecure. For example, between 1872 and 1884 an average of 3000 seamen a year lost their lives through drowning and accidents, and in 1865 alone, 2259 seamen also died from diseases, such as cholera and dysentery.[121] The loss of crew overboard can be readily seen from an examination of ships' logs. In the log of the **Comus**, a 376 ton vessel which had departed for Sydney on 20 April 1865, Captain Thomas Black records the drowning of an apprentice as follows:

"8.30 am 56 15 South 70 14 West
October 18 Wednesday

> *At the above hour heard the cry of a man overboard (the ship hove to under close reefed main topsail) ran to the life buoys and pitched it close to the man as he came towards the quarter of the ship, the crew had been endeavouring to get ropes to him... The chief jumped the quarter with a rope in his hand... as he was being hauled up he slipped the rope, went down and was seen no more. We had great difficulty getting the mate up afterwards."*[122]

It appears that a boy, Thomas Ambrose, was shifting the Main Royal Halyards to windward at night, slipped and fell overboard. The second mate, Malcolm Malcomson, jumped over the side holding a rope to rescue the boy. There was a high sea and it was raining lightly. Neither was seen again. The log records on 18 June 1868 all items of clothes and personal effects of the two lost crew and on the 27 June at 4 pm

---

121. Falconer, John. Sail and Steam. A Century of Maritime Enterprise 1840-1935. Boston, 1993, p.13.
122. National Library of Australia. Manuscript MS. 2569.

that all items were auctioned. This was the practice and the proceeds of the auction were passed on to the next of kin when the ship returned to homeport.

The log of the **Albert William**, a 505 tons vessel, returning to England after a passage from Liverpool to Adelaide in 1867, records on 18 June 1868 that two crew were lost overboard:

> *"Heavy gale the day before we hove the ship round under small sail and steering as near as possible the opposite course to where we lost the men to try if we could hear or see anything of them but could see nothing but the life buoy which was hove over the side..."*[123]

The *South Australian Register* reported on 7 January 1850 the arrival of the **Coromandel** with news of a similar tragedy:

> *"The Coromandel for this port and Port Phillip anchored in the Bay on Friday evening...*
>
> *There were four births and one death on board. Off the Cape a sea apprentice was lost whilst furling the jib in a heavy gale. The poor lad, who was one of the smartest on board, slipped from the boom, and all efforts to save him were unavailing..."*

The fast sailing ships were only part of a steady stream of sailing ships, which connected Australia and New Zealand to the rest of the world between 1870 and 1900. During this period many of the slower sturdy ships belonging to well-known shipping lines, such as Loch and Holme (the names of the ships always included these words), ran with considerable regularity to Australia. There were also the older plodders, which continued to make their annual round trip from Europe to Australia and return. During this period it was common practice to cut back fully-rigged ships to barques by removing the square sails from the mizzenmast, thereby reducing sail handling by about one-third. Most big sailing vessels from 1880 onwards were three or four masted barques.

---

123. ibid.

The Suez Canal was opened in 1869 and this provided a further opportunity for steam to emerge as a serious contender for the carriage of passengers on the Australia route. One of the steam ships to take advantage of the shorter route was the **S S Lusitania** a relatively large vessel of 3877 gross tons, with one funnel and three masts (rigged for sail). She was of iron construction, had a clipper stem, single screw, a maximum speed of 12 knots and made several trips on the London – Australia service. In 1885 Australian painter Tom Roberts travelled on the **Lusitania** back to Melbourne after four years in Europe. During the passage Roberts made a number of sketches and used these to paint *Coming South* in 1886 (see book cover). On that passage the vessel carried a number of "salon" class passengers but the majority were travelling steerage class beneath the decks. It has been suggested that in the painting Roberts attempted to show a mingling of different ethnicities and classes. For example in the background women in elegant dress mingle with men without jackets and there are some men in outfits that suggest a rural or country background. National differences appear as well: there is a man wearing a tam o' shanter (traditional Scottish bonnet worn by men) and there is a women doing needlework and wearing a red shawl and black hat which was typical Welsh dress at that time.

While steam powered vessels like the **Lusitania** were beginning to take advantage of the shorter passage afforded by the opening of the Suez Canal wind remained the major source of power for most emigrant vessels for the remainder of the century.

The large square-rigged ships used for so much of the emigrant trade in the nineteenth century were complicated things to operate. While it is true that there were many components that required attention by the crew, in order for the vessel to sail effectively and efficiently, these workings were well understood by the seamen of the day, many of whom had lived aboard such ships since they were children. The ships were always with them and they knew them intimately. The crew of these ships had to be able to find every piece of rigging in the blackest of nights in a gigantic sea with gale force wind blowing. The seamen had to face extreme conditions of hardship in handling the sails in heavy weather. For example, in the southern latitudes winds of sixty miles per hour were common and the sails were often frozen stiff. There was also the presence of ice in the water. A letter to the *London Times* of 21 March 1850 published on 28 March from 'A Sailor For A Quarter of A Century' lists some of these difficulties in his effort to caution against great circle sailing for emigrant ships:

> *"Sir - Having seen a paragraph in your valuable journal relative to the great circle sailing, I beg to offer a few remarks should you deem them worth of insertion. Having navigated the India and China seas, and those seas applicable to the circular sailing, I consider it my duty to caution those who might be led to pursue the same course as mentioned in your paper in making the passage to Australia in high south latitude, knowing it is fraught with much danger.*
>
> *In December 1841, I sailed from England to New Zealand, and made the land in less than 100 days. I adopted the plan of sailing on a small circle, varying in latitude from 46 to 48 S. On the 10th of March, in latitude 45 30 S., and on the meridian of Cape Leewin, we fell in with immense blocks of ice, approaching to the size of small islands, and measuring from angles taken with a quadrant upwards of 200 feet above the level of the sea; we were amongst these for seven days. We also passed several pieces level with the water's edge, the wind during the time being generally from the north with hazy weather, which precluded distant view on the horizon, and rendered the passage extremely dangerous. I think that commanders of emigrant ships should consider, and not risk the lives of so many persons for the sake of a quicker passage..."*

Great skill was required in determining the amount of sail to carry in heavy weather conditions. Without sail a ship could not be steered and would be at the mercy of the sea, but too much sail could have perilous results with the ship being 'driven under', dismasted or capsized. When rigged for rough weather the vessel was said to be running under storm canvas. Often the conditions were extreme and crew had to react instinctively as evident in the return trip to England on the **Dover Castle** in 1867 as reported in the vessels newspaper:

"On Wednesday (1 May) night the first appearance of rough weather caused a reduction of canvas, and two men were placed at the wheel, owing to the heavy running. Thursday commenced with a perfect gale, and our ship was pitching and heaving very heavily in a furious sea. At 11 am we were flying before the gale under double reefed mizen topsail, lower fore and main topsail, reefed upper, foresail and jib. Very few passengers appeared on deck, and those who did found great difficulty in keeping a footing - sea sickness again prevailed, and what with confusion, pitching about, and constant soakings, everything was chilly and miserable as possible...

Of a sudden a heavy sea struck on the starboard quarter sweeping with great force over our labouring ship, and causing everyone to hold fast to prevent being swept overboard. The vessel trembled violently after the blow - a second of quietness followed - and down came tons of water on our decks, rushing with frightful force down the main hatchway and flooding the cabins on the 'tween decks to a depth of about three feet; here were assembled upwards of a hundred passengers, amongst whom the consternation was indescribable - yelling and shouting from the men - screaming, praying and cries for salvation from the women - crying from the children - the surging waters rushing to and fro with the motion of the ship.

...A quarter of an hour elapsed and confidence was again restored, when of a sudden the vessel heeled over to port, and coming up again, was struck by another sea of still greater and more frightful force than the first... the trembling vessel hove down again on her beam ends, and deluge of water fell upon her decks, flooding again the salon, second berths, deck and intermediate cabins.... Fortunately no lives were lost..."[124]

(The author of the above article from the Dover Castle News, the ship's paper, finished the account of the storm with the words: "nearly all passengers had retired before nine o'clock to their wet bunks.")

---

124. Horsey, John G. A Voyage from Australia to England. An Account of the Voyage of the Dover Castle, 18 April to 30 July 1867. London, 1867, pp.5-6.

Dover Castle - **1003 tons, built Sunderland 1858**
(Brodie Collection, La Trobe Picture Collection, State Library of Victoria)

Working under such conditions also required that sailors be able to comprehend immediately orders that related to any of the many functions that had to be carried out, to not only propel the vessel, but to also ensure that it came to no harm. There were sets of orders for most of the manoeuvres that were carried out on these ships. The merchant ships were operated without an excess of crew. It was therefore important for each crewmember to understand his role. The sailors of merchant vessels were not drilled; they had simply absorbed through a life at sea all that was needed of them to do the job effectively. Most took pride in being competent at their job. Of course, for a complex sailing vessel to operate efficiently and safely, there had to be order - everything well organised and in its place. This was the pattern to be followed by competent captains responsible for the many and varied sailing vessels plying the emigration trade to Australia in the nineteenth century.

In 1890 David Syme & Co. published in Melbourne the following wood engraving montage of vessels "old and new" involved in "bringing mail" to the colonies. Those included represented the range of vessels that served the colonies during the nineteenth century.

Montage of Vessels - Great Britain, Marco Polo, Ellora, Red Jacket, Ormuz & Britannia " Past & Present" Involved in the Colonial Run
(State Library of Victoria)

CHAPTER 6

Preparation and Embarkation

"There is scarcely any human act so important in its consequence as that of exchanging one country for another."[125]

Leaving one's country as an emigrant destined for another land is a very difficult and traumatic experience for most people who venture to take that step. No matter how difficult home circumstances might be, and how attractive the new destination, it is nonetheless an uprooting experience leaving a birthplace, familiar territory, family and friends.

In the nineteenth century the decision to emigrate was not simply about a long voyage, but would have involved an awesome uprooting experience. The communication difficulties of the nineteenth century, and the cost and difficulties associated with a return passage, would have added to the impact of this uprooting experience for the nineteenth-century emigrant. Hence for most of the emigrants it meant dislocation and separation from family and country forever.

Change is an underlying theme of emigration and change causes most people to become anxious. As embarkation time drew near and preparations were made for the voyage this anxiety would have been heightened. Each step in the process of preparing to leave would have acted as a reminder of the enormity of the decision, and for some this would have heightened the anxiety and no doubt raised (or re-raised) doubts about the wisdom of the decision to emigrate.

---

125. Howitt, Richard. Impressions of Australia Felix, 1845.

The decision to emigrate would have precipitated for some emigrants actions and decisions that had, in the past, been considered relatively unimportant and hence were often deferred or neglected. For example, some couples who had been living together suddenly decided to marry. For other families, unbaptised children and adults were quickly baptised. Others who had not had any strong connection with a church sought some assurance and a blessing from a clergyman.

The process of preparing to leave tended to increase in complexity as the income and wealth of the emigrant increased. In the case of people of substance there would have been the matter of liquidating any unwanted land, property, equipment, furniture or stock. Arrangements also had to be made to ship items that the emigrants wished to take with them. Wealthy emigrants would usually employ an agent to arrange freight space and to assemble any equipment and luggage at the place of embarkation. There was also the difficulty of safely transferring any surplus funds to the port of destination.

However, most of the emigrants to Australia during this period were people of little or no means and hence this component of the emigration process was relatively simple. While disposal of possessions for these people may have been much less complicated there would nonetheless have been possible trauma because of sentimental attachment and because these few possessions may have represented the only material possessions accumulated over a lengthy period of time and with some difficulty. There would also have been a feeling of uncertainty about the ability to acquire replacement possessions in the new country.

It was possible that the middle class family with a number of possessions faced the greatest difficulty, in liquidating unwanted possessions and then moving the remainder to port to await embarkation. Breaking up a household was difficult yet it had to be done.

Emigrants were generally advised to take with them only necessities. This advice was offered on the basis that furniture and other large items could prove to be an encumbrance, freight costs were high, and in any case all such items were readily available in Australia. This advice was often accompanied with a reminder that work was readily available in the colonies and wages were higher than in Britain. For those with any funds the advice was to take only a little in cash and the remainder as bank drafts.

On the matter of what to take, emigrants were given a range of, sometimes conflicting, advice. This advice was often proffered by people who had never been to the colonies and had little knowledge or factual information on what conditions were really like. Frequently intending emigrants were advised to take a good supply of clothing, china and cutlery, brushes and combs. Some advised that a gun and pocketknife was also advisable.

Poor advice often led to unwise decisions about what to take. For example, many took unsuitable clothing, which in some cases did not even survive the storage conditions in the hold during the long passage to Australia. Most passengers were only able to take with them a small handbag or portmanteau as hand luggage containing articles needed during the passage. The remainder of their possessions were stored below, in areas that were often subject to dampness. These conditions were often the cause of the deterioration of the contents of luggage stored in this way. Luggage stored in these areas of a vessel were not easily accessible to passengers, although on most Australian passages passengers would have been provided access to this luggage on at least one occasion. This baggage was always stored in the lower hold and that meant the area was dark and would require a lantern for light. Due to the haphazard method of stowing this cargo it was often impossible to locate some items without emptying the hold of all cargo. The captain would only permit baggage to be taken from the hold on a calm day and would usually allocate a couple of the crew to assist. However, with three hundred or more passengers on board most emigrant vessels this meant that it would be extremely unlikely that all passengers would get access to their luggage on the one day. There were many reasons for suspending this arrangement and thus a common complaint of passengers on long passages was that the luggage hold was not opened for the entire time. Such limited access to stored luggage meant that passengers had to carefully select what they would take with them as hand luggage. This was a difficult assignment for most emigrants, given the duration of the passage and the fact that most of them had no experience of any kind of travel, let alone a long sea trip of the kind they would face in sailing to Australia.

Advice was also given to emigrants about the best way to carry personal effects so as to best ensure their preservation and to fit the storage requirements on board ship. It was recommended that passengers use a strong chest that could withstand a rough passage similar to the type used by seamen. This type of chest would be about five cubic feet in capacity. Ideal dimensions for a chest of this size were felt to be around 2 foot 6 inches by 1 foot 6 inches. The chest should ideally have a handle at each end so that two people could carry it.

There were, of course, restrictions on what could be carried by each passenger and the allowance size varied depending on the class of passage. The following is an example of typical passenger luggage allowances:

- 1st Class Passengers   40 cubic feet;
- 2nd Class Passengers   30 cubic feet;
- 3rd Class Passengers   20 cubic feet.

The 20 cubic feet allowance for the third or steerage class passengers was equivalent to approximately two large trunks (which were not to exceed 10 cubic feet each). Passengers were charged for excess baggage at a rate of about 1/- per cubic foot. On steamers the allowance was frequently less than for sailing vessels.

In addition to their personal effects, all but first class passengers were generally required to bring on board certain items that would be needed for the passage. In some instances these items were provided by the shipping agent as part of the fare arrangements or at a fixed charge. Hence the first class passengers would have everything supplied while the second-class passengers may have been required to provide their own bedding, linen and soap, but glassware and crockery might be provided. In third class the passengers were expected to provide most items, including bedding, linen, soap, eating utensils, drinking vessel, teacup and water container. However, in the case of assisted steerage passengers these items were provided by the Commissioners and the emigrants were permitted to retain them on disembarkation. Those emigrants required to bring bedding had to secure it in a canvas bag.

Intending emigrants were advised to travel with a companion or other people of 'good reputation and character' with whom 'mutual confidence exists'. This was particularly the case in steerage where little privacy existed and where support and assistance may be required on such a long passage. For example, in the case of sickness assistance may be required in the preparation of food, tending to needs and generally safeguarding property.

There were many who were prepared to offer the emigrant advice despite the fact that much of this advice was based on little practical experience. Some resorted to writing and selling pamphlets on emigration designed to advise the prospective emigrants. One such paper concluded with the following 'Hints for Emigrants'[126]

> *"A few drops of chloridine in water will often stop the violence for sea sickness.*
>
> *TENTS - Emigrants, especially those likely to take up land, will save much expense by providing themselves with tents, as by this precaution they save rent til they can erect a homestead. The simplest and least expensive tents are made thus: Raise .... a framework of saplings to the size required, strain and nail over these a covering of unbleached calico; then erect upon a second ridge pole supported by two forks, and rising about seven feet from the ground and four inches higher than the inner tent, an outer covering of the same material; this will secure the inmates from wet and render the habitation cool and comfortable......*
>
> *MOSQUITO CURTAINS - These will be found especially in hot climates and in the country, almost indispensable to comfort, and emigrants will do well to provide themselves with materials to make them, fine muslin or tarlatan is best............*
>
> *COOLING DRINK - As an emigrant's success depends much on his abstinence from whisky and strong drink, the following recipe for lemonade may be useful. One pound of brown sugar to five pints of*

---

126. Barlee, Ellen ed. Emigration Papers for the Working Classes. Kensington, 18??.

boiling water, and one ounce of tartaric acid, add when cold sixpennyworth of essence of lemon. A wineglassful of this mixture in a tumbler of water will be found the right proportion.

SUN BONNETS - Female emigrants are advised to provide themselves with these articles, which are simply made in the form of a large cap with a full boarder and a long curtain falling behind. A yard of print makes one.

CURE OF BITES OF INSECTS - Tincture of arnica diluted in twelve times its own quantity of water.

FOR DESTROYING FLIES - Infusion of quassia one pint, brown sugar four ounces, pepper two ounces, mix together and place in a shallow dish."

Advice also came in the form of letters from the colonies that sometimes found their way into print in the newspapers. The following advice from a colonist, which was put together with other letters and published as a pamphlet is an example:

"As there is much unoccupied time on ship-board, women should take with them some linen to make up or materials for knitting, and a few books, if they possess any; by no means forgetting the book of books, the Bible. Not only on the passage will it be found a valuable acquisition; but under the various trying circumstances and situations of after-life, it will be found a comfort...

The spirit taken out should only be used medicinally; every labouring man must learn to do without liquor. The time of passage will prove to him the possibility of so doing; and where indulgence in them has commenced, it may happily prove the means of breaking so pernicious a habit..."[127]

It was widely known that many of the emigrants would suffer from seasickness during the long passage to Australia. Hence there was much

---

127. Barlee, Ellen ed. Emigration Papers for the Working Classes. Kensington, c 18??

written about the effects of seasickness, warning people what to expect, how to avoid it and how to remedy it. The advice included:

- living in moderation a few days before embarkation (especially abstain from celebrating or over indulging);
- remain on deck as much as possible during the passage;
- when below decks remain whenever possible in a recumbent position;
- never rise without at first eating something (a dry biscuit is ideal);
- never allow the stomach to become empty;
- as a precaution tie a handkerchief or towel tightly round the body over the stomach and take some effervescing drink; and
- in the case of onset of sea sickness the following mixture was recommended:

Hydrocyanic Acid	12 drops
Acetate of Morphine	1 grain
Carbonate of Soda	1 drachm
Water	16 ounces

There were also manufactured products being offered to help the sea traveller overcome seasickness. One such product was a potion called the Sir James Murray Fluid Magnesia, the qualities of which were said to have been testified by people of repute. Another device recommended to ladies and gentlemen was Joseph Browne's Patent Anti-Sea-Sickness Sofa Bed. This ensured that the person lying upon it remained perpendicular even in the roughest of seas. For infants there was a swinging cot.

There were those in business who sought to take advantage of the commercial opportunities that emigrants offered by providing a range of special equipment and 'essentials' that the emigrant might require in the new country. Implement makers advised that emigrants could select from their warehouses a vast array of agricultural, trade and domestic appliances, tools and equipment, which could be shipped immediately. Some suppliers specialised in tents. The shopkeepers were busily offering at ports of embarkation a range of wares to make the journey more comfortable and to equip the traveller. Clark tells of the offer by Samuel Brothers of London who "respectfully begged to inform the public in August 1848 that they had added an important feature to their extensive and well-known establishment in Ludgate Hill, namely 'AN OUTFITTING DEPARTMENT FOR EMIGRANTS'"[128]. The emigrant was frequently reminded that products of the best materials and workmanship could be purchased at much lower prices than in the colonies.

Many passengers had to travel some distance to get to the port of embarkation. This meant leaving home several days before the vessel sailed and for some the journey to the port would be made with very heavy heart having departed the home town and left family and friends behind. The goodbyes were usually traumatic as illustrated in the following diary excerpt of an emigrant who was farewelled in Scotland before travelling to St Katherine's Dock, London:

> *"It was on the afternoon of Friday, the 2nd June 1843 that my sister Ann and myself left our beloved home. The bitterness of our parting I shall never forget. All were in tears. My cousins, my brothers and sisters, and my parents, were over come; and as we said adieu to those whom we left behind, how each wrung the others hand, and sobbed with bursting sorrow. But all was little comfort with the pain of parting with our dear mother. I cannot describe it but the remembrance of it will never fade. My heart bleeds yet, and must long bleed when I think of it, may the Heavenly Comforter cheer her heart, and the hearts of all whom we are united by love."*[129]

Passengers were usually required by shipping companies to be at the port of embarkation the day before sailing. This was necessary to enable final arrangements to be made and in some cases to collect the balance of the passage fare. Although sailing dates were advertised in advance vessels frequently departed later than the advertised date. This could mean that some passengers would be required to spend several

---

128. Clark, C M H. A History of Australia Part III. Melbourne, Victoria 1979, p.231.
129. Wood. Journal of Voyage from London to Launceston in 1843 on the **Mona**. National Library of Australia, Manuscript MS 9113.

nights and days at the port of departure. Some also chose to come to the port of embarkation as soon as all preparation arrangements had been made.

The early arrival of passengers or the prolonged delay of departure provided opportunities for enterprising people to separate the emigrant from any spare funds. Many of the emigrants were unaccustomed to city or port life and were left to their own devices while awaiting departure. The 'harpies', as these people were known, devised a variety of schemes to separate awaiting passengers from their money. These confidence people often included those connected with lodging-houses, who sought to exploit the need for accommodation and at the same time separate the emigrants from the precious savings in their possession. Others posed as the local emigration agent in order to trick the emigrants. Brokers often charged exorbitant prices for lodgings.

As a result of these practices there was growing concern in ports of embarkation about the welfare of emigrants while waiting to sail. Meetings were held by concerned citizens in some ports to devise ways of protecting emigrants. The following report of a meeting in Liverpool is typical of the type of concern being expressed for the welfare of emigrants:

> "*PROTECTION OF EMIGRANTS - LIVERPOOL, Monday.*
> -*A large and influential meeting of clergymen, merchants, and others was held at the Clarendon rooms today, to take into consideration a proposition for providing an emigrants' home in Liverpool. The Venerable Archdeacon Brooks occupied the chair, and several addresses were delivered showing the necessity for the establishment of such an institution as the one proposed. Lieutenant Hodder, the Government emigration agent, stated that when the Irish emigrants landed at the Clarence-dock, of this port, they were beset by a body of men banded together, who were known as the "forty thieves", the most unscrupulous set of scoundrels that could possibly be conceived. These men acted as porters, and handed the poor emigrants over to "land sharks", who obtained a percentage from the passenger-brokers for each customer they obtained. The lodging-house keepers and provision-dealers also gave*

a further commission to these unprincipled agents; and the emigrants were plundered on all sides to the greatest extent. He characterised the emigration system as one vast combination of fraud, with the most extensive ramifications. .... The Rev. H. McNiele moved a resolution to the following effect: - "That this meeting, feeling the great influence that emigration has on this country, as well as on the colonies, deem it of the utmost importance that measures, should be taken for the protection of the emigrants, and for the improvement of their temporal and moral conditions, especially in this great port of Liverpool." This motion was unanimously agreed to, and a committee was appointed to devise a plan, it being the general opinion that one large building should be fitted up for the emigrants, and that such an institution would not only be self supporting when once established, but would afford the emigrants greater comforts and much greater advantages, at much smaller cost, than those they at present derive from the doubtful sources which are open to them."[130]

The practices commented on in this newspaper account were particularly prevalent in the first half of the century. In order to provide protection for the emigrant the Colonial Land and Emigration Commissioners drafted rules and regulations to shield the awaiting passengers from exploitation. Progressively every embarkation port to Australia had a depot capable of housing four or five hundred people, in which the emigrants were comfortably lodged free of charge until their vessel sailed. This protected them from the confidence men. A doctor and clergymen visited them to watch over their health and spiritual well being.

Emigrants were often accompanied to the port of embarkation by friends or relatives. On some occasions they were farewelled by relatives and neighbours in their hometown or village. The Irish often held wakes as a symbol of the permanency of the departure. The clergy would often bless them and remind them that given the perils of such a passage, they should be prepared to meet their Maker.

---

130. Protection of Emigrants. *London Times*, May 7, 1850.

Irish Emigrants Leaving Home - The Priest's Blessing[131]
(National Library of Australia, BibID: 1574658)

Although accommodation and support for the emigrants gradually improved as a result of new regulations and provision of depots for housing those awaiting embarkation, there were nonetheless a variety of people in port cities who spent much time devising new ways of relieving emigrants from their money. Some of these unscrupulous people worked as agents for shipping companies engaged in the emigration trade. They devised ways of encouraging prospective emigrants to use the vessels of a particular shipping line. For this they received a commission. The following extract from an 1850 account illustrates these practices:

> *"MAN-CATCHING IN LIVERPOOL - A few months ago some of the more respectable firms connected with the emigrant trade of this port resolved to dispense with the services of the passenger agents, who had been previously in receipt of commission from their offices for the passengers whom they secured. These passenger agents have obtained*

---

131. *Illustrated London News*, 1851.

a rather disreputable notoriety, and are, now popularly known by the designation of "man-catchers", and so glaringly dishonest were their practices, and so unequivocal was the condemnation pronounced against the system by Government and local authorities, that the more respectable shippers at this port at the period referred to met and resolved not to employ "man-catchers" for the future. Whether the agreement entered into was ever strictly observed we know not, but up to a very recent date it was not openly broken through. Now, however, the mask is thrown away, and the system of "man-catching", with all its attendant evils, flourishes in all its "rank luxuriance"; emigrants are fleeced in every possible shape, and after the most approved fashion, and those who fleece them receive a bonus when they have "plucked the pigeons" to hand them over to the emigration-offices..."[132]

While these practices were prevalent in most ports some of the more reputable shipping lines attempted to improve conditions for the emigrants and to provide some protection and comfort while they awaited embarkation. Shipping advertisements often referred to assistance at the point of embarkation and some of the material contained in pamphlets about emigration made reference to the assistance provided by shipping lines. The following extract from a pamphlet providing hints to emigrants illustrates the type of information provided:

"...in order to render every arrangement as perfect as possible for securing the health, comfort and well being of the emigrants proceeding by regular line of the Australian Packet Ships despatched by Mr. Marshall, extensive and conveniently situated premises in Plymouth have been taken and fitted up by him, where all bounty passengers proceeding to Australia by his ships will be lodged and boarded free of any charges whatever, while waiting at that Port for the arrival of his ships from London. A man and his wife of ascertained respectability of character,

---

132. Man-Catching in Liverpool. *London Times*, Saturday May 11, 1850 (reprinted from the Liverpool Times).

fulfilling the duties of master and matron, reside on the premises as well as respectable assistants, and the arrangements with tradespeople fully secure the regular supply to the establishment of the best provisions...."[133]

Francis Taylor, who emigrated steerage class as an assisted emigrant on the vessel ***Stag*** to Adelaide in 1850, reported in his diary his arrival and accommodation at one of the special depots for emigrants awaiting embarkation:

"Friday 19th hired a cab to convey myself and boxes to Deptford, seven miles distance, paid four shillings, much the best plan, no shifting from one conveyance to another but taken direct to depot, arriving there at 12 o'clock. The depot much like a workhouse and the manager, Mr Cooper, not very agreeable in his manner, but Mr Banks, assistance manager, quite the reverse and generally beloved. Provisions are here supplied to the emigrants by the Commissioners, they are of excellent quality and sufficient quantity. No emigrant after arriving at the depot is allowed to leave without special permission of governor, Mr Cooper.

6 o'clock nearly all arrived here that are going out, on board the Stag. We are summoned to prepare for our meals by the ringing of a bell, we are now going to tea. 9 o'clock just going to bed never slept with so many in the same room in my life. "[134]

Liverpool played an important role as the port of departure for millions of people seeking new lives in North America, Australia and New Zealand. In the nineteenth century thousands of emigrants from the British Isles and mainland Europe left from Liverpool. The establishment of regular sailing packet lines from 1818, and the huge demand for North American timber and cotton as raw materials for

---

133. JBW. Emigration: Its Necessity and Advantages. 2nd Edition. London, 1841, p.23.
134. Taylor, Francis diary transcribed in Limbrick, Doug: The Stag Diary Passage to Colonial Adelaide 1850. Xlibris Corporation, 2012, p.48.

Preparation and Embarkation

Government Emmigrant Depot Birkenhead 1852
(Rex Nan Kivell Collection NK4182/89, National Library of Australia)

British industry, led to well-established transatlantic links and emigrants, along with British manufactured products, provided a useful return cargo for the shipping lines. It has been estimated that between 1830 and 1930 over nine million emigrants sailed from Liverpool bound for America, Canada and Australia.[135] By 1851 Liverpool had become the leading emigration port in Europe. Large numbers of emigrants departed from Liverpool to join the gold rush in Australia, but this traffic, together with emigrants to New Zealand, which began to grow in the 1860s, was shared with other British ports including Southampton, London and Plymouth.

A number of emigrants were assisted to emigrate by societies established to promote emigration. These societies often provided clothing and other items required for the passage. There were general emigration societies and there were those that directed their assistance to the emigration of

---

135. British Maritime Archives & Library. Information Sheet 64. Liverpool and Emigration in the 19th and 20th Centuries, p.1.

women or children. By the late 1880s there were a considerable number of such societies as the following list for 1886 shows:

General Emigration

The British and Colonial Emigration Society, London.
The Central Emigration Society, London.
The Christian Home for Emigrants London.
The Church Emigration Society, London.
The Clerkenwell and Central London Emigration Society.
The Colonial Emigration Society.
The East End Emigration Fund.
The East London Family Emigration Fund.
Miss J. E. Groom's Emigration Fund.
The Jewish Board of Guardians.
The Jews Emigration Society.
The Kensington Emigration Aid Society.
The London Colonisation Aid Society.
The London Samaritan Society.
The National Association for the Promotion of State-directed Emigration and Colonisation.
The St Andrew's Waterside Church Mission.
The St Katherine's Mission Emigration Fund.
The Self-Help Emigration Club.
The Brighton Emigration Society.
The Bristol Emigration Society.
The Crystal Palace Self-Help Emigration Society.
The Young Men's Emigration Advice Society, Manchester.
Oldbury and Langley Self-Help Emigration Club.
The Somerset and Bristol Colonial Emigration Association.
The Wimbledon Emigration Society.
The Winchester Emigration Loan Society.
The Scottish Emigrants' Aid Association.

Emigration of Women

The British Ladies' Female Emigrant Society.
Female Middle-Class Emigration Society.

The Girls' Friendly Society.
The United Englishwomen's Emigration Society.
The Aberdeen Ladies Union.

Emigration of Children

Dr Barnardo's Homes.
The Boys' Home, Southwark Street, London.
The Boys' Home, Regent's Park Road, London.
The Children's Home.
The Church of England Central Society for Providing Homes for Waifs and Strays, London.
The National Refuges for Homeless and Destitute Children.
Miss Rye's Home for Destitute Girls.
St George and Bloomsbury Refuge.
The St Vincent Home for Boys, London.
The Children's Emigration Homes, Birmingham.
The Canadian Home for Girls, Bristol.
The Catholic Children's Protection Society, Liverpool.
The Manchester and Salford Boys' and Girls' Refuges, and Children's Aid Society.
The Redhill Farm School.
The Orphan Homes of Scotland, and Destitute Children's Emigration Homes.[136]

It was not uncommon for such societies to offer advice to the intending emigrant to assist with preparation and members of such societies often attended the final preparation, embarkation and departure. The following article from the *London Times* of 1836, while lengthy, provides considerable insight into this practice:

"EMIGRATION TO VAN DIEMAN'S LAND
Yesterday morning Mr Foster, the chairman of the committee for promoting emigration to the Australian colonies, accompanied by Mr Parker, Mr Sterry and several other members of the committee, attended St Katherine's

---
136. Carrothers, W A. Emigration from the British Isles. London, 1929, pp.319-320.

dock to superintend the embarkation of the male and female emigrants who have volunteered to go out by the William Metcalfe to Van Diemen's Land. The greater part of the baggage of the parties was sent on Monday last by a steamer down to Gravesend, where the William Metcalfe was then moored, and yesterday the emigrants mustered at St Katherine's dock in order to be conveyed from thence to the same vessel. At 9 o'clock the Albion steamer, which was engaged for the occasion, having taken them on board, started from the wharf and proceeded down the river to Gravesend, where they arrived at 12 o'clock. The embarkation of the passengers on board the William Metcalf immediately took place under the inspection of Mr Marshall, the emigration agent, and a small body of the metropolitan police. As each emigrant stepped on board, he or she received a ticket fixing the birth (sic) which they were to occupy during the voyage, and to that birth (sic) they immediately proceeded, with such of their baggage as they had with them for immediate use. The scene was full of bustle, and to judge from the outward demeanour of the majority of the parties, was not much disturbed by those feelings of sorrow which one would have anticipated as natural on the part of a number of individuals about to quit the land of their father for ever. Shortly after 2 o'clock most of the females were assembled in the central part of the ship, which is assigned as the place of their berths, and though there was some confusion among them, owing to a waste of knowledge of the precise localities which they were to occupy, there was an evident desire to rectify it as soon as possible, and to avail themselves of such comforts as were provided for them. The female emigrants and the young children accompanying them, amount to upwards of 150, and in the space allotted to them there are births (sic) for 20 more than that number. The height between decks is something more than 8 feet; there are two ranges of births (sic), one above the other, in this space, to which ventilation is offered not only by the ordinary number of portholes, but also by a double hatchway, one at each end of the apartment, if we may use the expression respecting that portion of the vessel which is barred off from the rest for the exclusive use benefit of the women and children. The male emigrants amount to 53 or 54 and in the space allotted to them is room for four births (sic) more than that number. The vessel is painted white between decks and this gives it a very light and cheerful appearance. As far as we could judge, from the hasty inspection which we gave it, the beds and bedding provided for the parties by the Emigration Committee are such as not to be liable to any just objections. As to the provisioning of the ship, with which fault has been found by some of the passengers by former vessels, we can say nothing of our own knowledge: but we were of course informed that care had been taken by the committee to prevent any just complaint on that score. We have again to repeat that the emigrants appeared in better spirits than we could have anticipated - not more than two of them were in tears, whilst the majority were cutting jokes upon the novelty of their situation, and were evidently indulging in flattering hopes as to the future, which we sincerely hope may not be disappointed. The committee we were told, consider this as the most respectable party of emigrants which they have not yet sent out. The majority of them are married; and to secure the women from the attention of the sailors, the husbands have agreed to keep watch and ward in turns during the night over the hatches leading to their wives' cabins.* They are mostly English, and of the agricultural class. There are 23 Scotch emigrants among them, but not half that number of Irish. The reason why the emigrants from Ireland in this vessel are so few is, that the Emigration Committee have chartered another vessel for the Irish, and have sent, or are about to sending it, to Cork for their reception. A few minutes before 3 o'clock notice was given to all strangers to leave the vessel, as the anchor was weighed; and at the moment a Scotch woman, apparently nearer 40 than 30 years of age, declared that it would break her heart to leave the country, and insisted on having her boxes taken out of the hold and put into a boat alongside the ship, for go with the William Metcalfe she would not. She was immediately told that if such was her determination she should have every facility given her to carry *it into execution, and on her repeating that it was, her trunks were handed over the ship's side, and she followed them. From a conversation which we subsequently had with her, it appears that she had come from Aberdeen in the Minarch steamer, and had suffered so much from sea sickness on that voyage, that she dared not encounter the inconvenience of another. The poor creature said that she had not a farthing of money in her possession, that she had no acquaintance in London, and that she knew not how she should ever return to Scotland. These facts were afterwards communicated to a member of the committee, and he we were told, directed one of its agents to take care that for the present the women was provided for.*

As soon as the surprise occasioned by this incident had subsided, the passengers were mustered on the poop of the vessel. The Emigration Committee wished them a happy voyage, and recommended them to the care of the captain and his subordinate officers. Shortly afterwards they left the vessel, the Albion steamer immediately took her in tow, and at 3 o'clock the William Metcalfe, with its crew of exiles was proceeding down the river to its place of destination.

* Surely if the 150 women are tolerably decent persons, they can protect themselves against a score of sailors, unless the committee have selected a crew ten times as desperate as Don Juan."[137]

One of the final matters confronting the emigrant prior to sailing was a medical inspection. In some cases the inspection occurred prior to embarkation at the government depot while in some cases it took place on board ship. In the case of the ship-board inspection passengers were mustered to a particular part of the ship and passed in a single file before the medical officer. The purpose of the inspection was to determine fitness to make the passage. In most cases the application for assisted passage would have required the applicant to obtain from a doctor (sometimes the Poor Law doctor attached to the parish) a certificate of health. However the vessel's surgeon was required to complete a further examination prior to departure.

---

137. Emigration to Van Diemen's Land. *London Times*, 7 October 1836.

Many of the immigrants sought by the colonies, agricultural workers rural tradesmen, shepherds, husbandmen, dairymaids, were often the lowest paid occupations in the home country and hence they were amongst the poorest and possibly under-nourished people in Britain. For example, the Irish and Highland Scots had been subject to deprivation and famine for many years and their fitness and health was possibly marginal. It seems from surgeons' reports that many of the emigrants were weakly and lacked vigour. While it would be difficult to deny passage to a person on the verge of commencing the journey it was never the less the responsibility of the surgeon to ensure that no person made the passage who had symptoms of an infectious disease. Again from the surgeons' reports it seems that numbers of people were rejected at the point of embarkation.

The assisted emigrants to the Australian colonies usually departed from Plymouth, Southampton, London and sometimes Liverpool. Thus at the time of embarkation the emigrants often found that for the first time they were in a large town where their immune systems would have possibly been tested. The children from remote areas would have been exposed to infectious diseases that were endemic in these port towns, such as measles, whooping cough and scarlet fever. It's therefore not surprising that some people arrived at the port of embarkation in a relatively healthy state but boarded carrying an infectious disease that would not appear until the passage was underway.

The surgeon was also required to vaccinate emigrants against smallpox where they could not provide proof of previous vaccination, or where they could not show smallpox marks from a previous attack (this requirement proved very successful in preventing smallpox outbreaks on emigrant vessels). The clothing of the emigrants was also inspected (usually in the company of the agent of the Emigration Commission). Each person was expected to provide clothing and personal items as set out in the regulations. Poor emigrants could apply to a range of charitable or philanthropic organisations, or their parish or Poor Law Union, for assistance to obtain these compulsory items. Poor parents travelling with children would have required a considerable amount of charitable aid to be able to meet the clothing and other requirements for children.

At the important ports there was always considerable activity with vessels coming and going, people embarking and cargo being loaded and unloaded. Shipping movements were reported in the local newspapers, including details of those that had sailed and those preparing to sail. The following notice of 1854 is typical of those appearing in the newspapers of the day:

The Embarkation, Waterloo Docks, Liverpool[138]
(State Library of Victoria)

"EMIGRATION - PLYMOUTH, Oct. 29 - The following ships, under charter to Her Majesty's Colonial Land and Emigration Commissioners, have been despatched from Plymouth during the week, after embarking their full complement of emigrants from the Government depot: - The Samuel Boddington, 669 tons, Captain Mowatt, with 259 souls, equal to 220 statute adults, for Sydney; the Oithona*, 857 tons, Captain Taylor, with 334 souls, equal to 287 statute adults; the Shand, of 836 tons, Captain Christie, with 332 souls, equal to 278 statute adults, for Portland Bay, Victoria; besides which the Fortitude, 800 tons, Captain Harrison,

---

138. *Illustrated London News*, 6 July 1850, p.17.

Preparation and Embarkation

for Adelaide and Hobart Town, has embarked a considerable number of passengers paying their own passage for Adelaide, and a large number of persons proceeding on the bounty billet system for Hobart Town, and has been ready for sea for some days, but detained owing to the captain's indisposition. She will probably sail this day. The following ships, also chartered by the Emigration Commissioners, are appointed to embark the whole of their emigrants at this port during November - viz, the Amazon, for Melbourne; the Marchioness of Sailsbury, for Geelong; the Lord Hungerford, for Sydney; and the Nile and Rodney, for Adelaide. There are also the first-class passenger ships Abdalla, for Sydney, and the George Marshall, for Melbourne, to embark their passengers here. The Shand sailed hence on Friday morning. The Telegraph, which embarked her emigrants at Southampton on Wednesday, put in here on Friday evening, from stress of weather. All these ships are consigned to the agency of Mr. Wilcocks, the agent for the Emigration Commissioners, through whose exertions a considerable number of emigrants have been selected. The Josephine Willis, Captain Cooney, for New Zealand, has also taken her departure hence during the past week"[139]

[*The **Oithona** has particular interest to the author as she carried paternal great-great-grandparents, Richard and Ellen Limbrick and five of their children, including great-grandfather, George, to Australia on this passage of 1854].

Passengers were usually taken on board by means of a short trip in another vessel. Steamers were sometimes used to ferry passengers to their ship. The responsibility for getting luggage to the ship lay with the passengers, who sometimes enlisted relatives and friends to assist in this process. Despite the picture that is conveyed in the above *London Times* article of order and organisation during the embarkation, this appeared to be an exception, particularly for the steerage passengers. For the first class and cabin passengers there was some order about the embarkation process, as cabins were allocated and varying levels of assistance given to

---

139. EMIGRATION -Plymouth, Oct. 29. London Times, Monday 30 October, 1854.

Emigrants Embarking[140]
(State Library of Victoria)

aid the settling-in process. The orderly nature of the final arrangements for cabin passengers can be seen from the journal of William Johnstone, about the journey by himself and his wife to Van Diemen's Land in 1842:

> "We left Gower Street on Monday morning 1 November 1841. I proceeded by the 11 o'clock Steamer to Gravesend - circumstances detained the **Arab** there during the week, which time we spent very happily in lodgings in St George's Terrace, in the society of those kind relatives who had accompanied us from London. "All that's bright must fade however" and accordingly at about 10 o'clock on Saturday night we were once more compelled to take a sad adieu from our friends, and escorted by I.I.M.J. Hills and Gets and G Biewe entered a small boat at Gravesend Pier, which quickly put us on board the **Arab** (350 tons), Captain Westmorland, bound for Launceston, Van Diemen's Land. Our feelings at this moment, may, as the newspaper would say, be more easily imagined than described. We were leaving our home, country, and all the beloved companions of our youth to seek our fortune in a strange and distant land ... After arranging our cabin, the rest of the

---

140. Australasian Sketcher. 18 December, 1880. p. 336.

party left us to the sad reflection of 'Our friends are gone'. We employed ourselves for some time in pursuing the scraps inscribed on the walls of our cabin, and soon afterwards turned in..."[141]

A further example is contained in a letter by Rachel Henning in 1854:

"My dearest Etta

I begin to write to you as we hope to reach St Vincent's on Sunday or Monday and shall be able to send home letters from there.

Amy, Tregenna and I watched you from the deck of the steamer on that raining morning till we were so far from the shore that we could not see you any longer, and then returned to cover of the cabin where you left us, and whence we did not move again till we arrived alongside the **Calcutta.**

We three betook ourselves to the saloon, where we sat and talked about you on your way homeward, and got rid of the time as well as we could till we were called for dinner.

Amy and I had been looking about and speculating upon the passengers, and had pitched upon a pretty looking girl of about eighteen, dressed in mourning, as the only one we should like for a cabin companion, and when we went down to look at our berths after dinner, there she was. She is very pleasant and good-tempered, and I think, a lady, so we are very well off in that respect. She is going to Melbourne with her uncle and brother...

... We found our berths more comfortable than we expected. Miss Maunder has the one under the porthole, and Amy the upper one on the opposite side, and I have the lower. We put away all our things after dinner and found plenty of room for them. The

---

141. Cited in Greenhill, Basil and Giffard, Ann. Women Under Sail. Newton Abbott, Great Britain, 1970. p. 78.

two boxes which Mr Arnold conveyed on board were safe in the empty berth.....".[42]

Emigration Ship *St Vincent* Being Towed Out[143]
(Rex Nan Kivell Collection NK4182, National Library of Australia)

The story of embarkation for those travelling steerage, which was the majority of those who emigrated by sailing vessel (as cabin passengers rarely exceeded ten per cent of total passengers on any vessel) bore little resemblance to the orderly process described previously in the quotations from the diary and letter. Steerage passengers suffered from a major disadvantage: lack of space. The process followed for allocation of sleeping space was also generally on a first come first served basis. Unlike the smaller spaces afforded by cabins allocated to the first and cabin class passengers the steerage class passengers were housed in large open areas located between the decks.

---

142. ibid. p. 78.
143. *Illustrated London News.* 13 April 1844. p. 229.

The best accommodation on board the nineteenth-century sailing vessels was located under the raised poop deck in the stern of the vessel. The most sought after rooms were those at the very stern of the vessel, because of the stern windows. These rooms were also often the largest rooms on the ship and were naturally reserved for use by first class passengers. The other first class cabins adjacent to these rooms were smaller, being about six feet by six or seven feet in size. The captain and the surgeon usually had their cabins in this area. These cabins would generally either lead to or open off a salon area, which was frequently lavishly decorated and was used for meals and recreation by the cabin passengers. The poop deck immediately above this area was available for the exclusive or almost exclusive use of the first class passengers. In some vessels other paying passengers had use of the poop during specified times. The poop deck looked down on the main deck, some eight feet below, where all other passengers sought space for their exercise and recreation. In some vessels the first-class cabins were located below a quarter deck, also located at the stern of the vessel but, only projecting a foot or two above the main deck to provide more cabin head room than was available below the main deck. On these vessels the quarterdeck would be reserved for certain classes of passenger.

Vessels offering second-class accommodation would generally provide this at the same level on the vessel as the first-class cabins but located on the main deck. Thus these cabins were constructed on the main deck and were sometimes referred to as 'house on deck' accommodation. These rooms comprised small shared cabins, opening onto a small dining 'salon' area. On some ships the term 'salon' was applied to this class of accommodation.

A clear distinction was generally maintained between the various classes of passenger during the passage, particularly between the first-class passengers and the others on board. This distinction sometimes caused ill feeling among passengers during the long passage. It is interesting to note that this distinction extended to the paying passengers not considering themselves to be emigrants. In their eyes an emigrant was someone who was financially assisted to make the voyage. The 'emigrants' were also viewed as people lacking any refinement and frequently thought to be vulgar and dirty.

The class distinction, the feeling of superiority and the difference in service is illustrated in the following comments made during a passage to Port Phillip on the **Kent** in 1852:

> *"The intermediates pass back and forth, with their tins of food while we are at meals, also they claim the right to walk on the Poop deck....They all seem to rely on me and I flatter myself that I have really been able to help matters......the immense advantages we enjoy on the Poop deck are the cool breeze and the prospect but both are denied to the intermediates, they see us [in the cuddy] eating all sorts of good things, and drinking our wine .... or water made pleasant with limejuice and they envy us ..... numbers of them come up on the Poop, and the Captain has to order them down or soon the whole body of them would be there, and we should have paid our extra fees for nothing."*[144]

The **Kent**, a White Horse Line frigate-built East Indiaman of 1200 tons, carried only 17 cabin or first-class passengers and 252 'intermediates' on that passage to Australia.

Immediately beneath the first and other cabin passengers could be found the mass of the ships passengers those travelling third or steerage class. This area was between the decks of the vessel and was referred to as 'tween decks and accommodated other facilities, including the ship's hospital. These early sailing ships were not designed to carry the large number of passengers that were carried by emigrant ships. The accommodation of such large numbers required of most vessels a special fit-out of the lower decks. This fit-out was usually undertaken in accordance with the requirements of British legislation (i.e. the prevailing Passenger Act). However, the design and requirements were largely based on experience in transporting large numbers of convicts on similar types of vessels. In some instances more emigrants than convicts were carried on vessels formerly used to transport convicts. For example, the **Lady**

---

144. Extract from diary of William Howitt during a journey on the *Kent* in 1852. Quoted in Walker, Mary Howitt. Come Wind, Come Weather. A Biography of Alfred Howitt. Netley, South Australia 1971. p.28.

McNaghten had carried 300 convicts, but carried 405 emigrants. This occurred largely because, in the early part of the process, emigration agents were paid according to the number of people and hence they were eager to cram as many as possible into the emigrant vessels.

Once all passengers were on board it was the duty of the surgeon superintendent to ensure that all passengers were aware of the rules relating to shipboard life. For the steerage passengers this would often involve a briefing on the deck. In the case of some Highland Scots and Irish, who only spoke Gaelic or Irish, an interpreter was required (occasionally this was a Gaelic speaking clergyman). It was important before the passage started for all emigrants to understand the housekeeping and other routines of the vessel. It's interesting to note that some emigrants were unfamiliar with plates, knives, forks and spoons and the workings of a water closet. Attempts were usually made to explain the uses of these things and to impress upon the emigrants the need to maintain personal hygiene and cleanliness of their bunks and space. Surgeons were also expected to advise passengers of their rights. A copy of a document setting out the requirements (behaviour, cleanliness, meal and bed times, and prohibitions) and the daily meal allowances was usually posted on the steerage deck. On arrival the emigrants were given the opportunity to complain about the surgeon, crew, diet and treatment and it seems that many chose to do so.

In the early days of emigration to Australia a few of the old East Indiamen were employed, such as the **Prince of Wales** (built 1842 by Green's of Blackwall). These ships had a reputation as high quality vessels (even if slow), longer and deeper than most other vessels at that time. British shipbuilders developed a type of vessel modelled on the Indiamen, sometimes referred to as the Blackwall Frigates that were similar in size and finish. Most other vessels were fitted in much more spartan style and this was particularly evident below decks where the steerage passengers were accommodated. The *South Australian Register* on 18 October 1866 described the **Prince of Wales** when she arrived as follows:

"The Commissioners were determined to secure a spacious ship when the Prince was chartered, for being one of the old East Indiamen, she has aspar-deck, main-deck, and tween-deck, each of which was devoted to passengers."

Ship *Prince of Wales*
(Brodie Collection, La Trobe Picture Collection, State Library of Victoria)

Lubbock commented on the different standard in accommodation on these vessels:

"For first class passengers the splendid Blackwall frigates of Green, Money Wigram and Duncan Dunbar, and the beautiful little clippers of the Aberdeen White Star Line, provided excellent accommodation and a comfortable and safe, if not a particularly fast passage. But the ordinary steerage passenger had to content himself as a rule with a ship that was little better than a hermetically sealed box; one as deep as it was long, with clumsy square bows and stern, with ill-cut ill-set sails - its standing rigging of hemp a mass of long splices; and

> *with a promenade deck no longer than the traditional two steps and overboard.*"[145]

The steerage accommodation comprised simply constructed berths, of plain timber. They included four posts, fixed top and bottom to prevent movement and held two wooden platforms. These platforms were like open topped shallow boxes. Each berth was about eighteen inches wide usually grouped together in eights (four up and four down). Thus, there were two bunks of four berths on top and two below. This meant that within each space of six-foot square eight people could be accommodated. In the married quarters adults would occupy the two top bunks with two children below each couple. Couples without children would have children from another family below. The bunks usually had a dividing board between them for 'privacy', which in early ships was less than a foot high. The height of this board was later required to be at least twenty-three inches. Some vessels included curtains at the ends and sides of bunks, but they were often unsuitable because of the ventilation and lighting problems below decks. The bottom bunks had a small space of about six inches below them for luggage. The bunks were constructed row upon row with a long trestle table along the central area. These sleeping areas were separated into three sections using timber partitioning: a large area for married couples (and any children) and two smaller areas for single women and single men. Head room varied but was usually between six and seven feet, but was reduced in some parts of the vessel because of the presence of heavy beams that projected a foot or more down from the ceiling. On some much larger vessels there was a further deck below this area for yet more steerage passengers. The accommodation arrangements were similar in the steerage areas from deck to deck.

It's clear that many of the vessels that were used on the Australia run were used flexibly to carry passengers and cargo and to also at times carry convicts. The internal fit out below decks would have been capable of being quickly transformed at the start of a passage to meet the needs of that part of the voyage. The rudimentary fit-out to accommodate emigrants below decks was thus easily removed to make room for bulky

---
145. Lubbock, Basil. The Colonial Clippers. Glasgow, 1924. p. 3.

cargo. The timber would have readily been sold in the colonies. In reality the steerage passengers were placed in the cargo hold. The 1850 passage of the *Stag* to Adelaide is a good example of this flexibility, where some 300 emigrants and crew were carried on the passage out and copper and lead became the cargo for the return passage. The illustration below shows the usage of space below decks when the vessel is set up to carry passengers and their baggage.

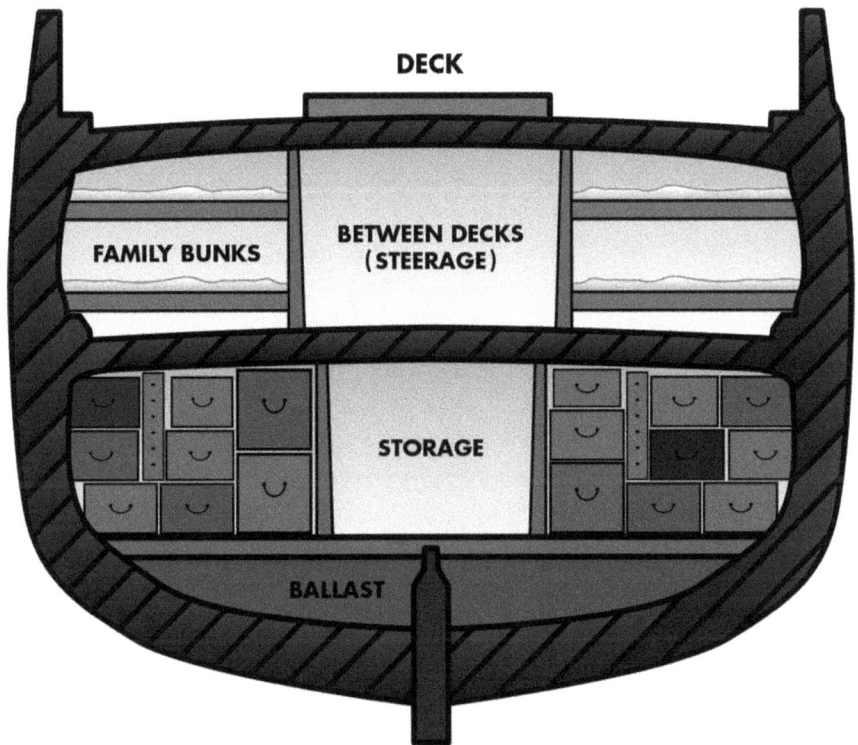

Cross Section of Square Rigged Vessel
(By Permission of Jeremy Limbrick)

Arrangements on board for steerage passengers is described by a writer in the *London Times* in 1850:

> "*EMIGRATION - At the present time there are no less than 14 vessels in the London and St Katherine's Docks bound for Australia, New Zealand and Port Natal, for the most part with passengers. The gross tonnage of these 14 vessels is 9,183, and they are all advertised*

to sail in the present or next month. It is calculated that they will take away from this country no fewer than 1,200 emigrants to the distant colonies mentioned. A few words on which these vessels are fitted up for the accommodation of passengers may not be uninteresting at the present time. Of course, it is not necessary to mention the cabin passengers, as their comforts are attended by a regular steward; steerage or intermediate passengers, as they are called, depend to a great extent on their own exertions for comforts of cleanliness, ventilation and consequent health. The between decks of the ship is used for their berths. All ships which carry passengers have two decks, or if not a temporary deck is made by laying planks along the beams. The height of the between decks varies from 6 to 7 feet, according to the size or build of the vessel. It extends the whole inside breadth of the ship, and the berths are fitted along the sides. Each berth contains from two to six beds, one placed above another, that is two people sleeping lengthways with the ship, and one, two or four across, according to the capacity of the cabin. Along the length of the ship a table is placed about two feet and a half broad, and securely fastened to the deck in case of heavy weather. Along the sides of passenger ships there are spaces cut at about every seven feet, and fitted with strong glass panes, which can be pushed outwards for the purpose of ventilation. These panes of glass are about six inches in diameter, and the berths are frequently so fitted that one pane serves as a light for two cabins. Of course these small windows are chiefly used in heavy rains, when it is impossible to open the hatches. Once fairly at sea intermediate passengers are divided into gangs of eight or twelve and over each gang a passenger is placed whose office it is to enforce order and superintend, generally, in the way of seeing that the proper amount of provisions is weighed out to his gang, and of course to look to the quality of the food. It will be easily understood that the captain of a ship of 800 tons, even with two officers under him, has enough to do in looking after the proper navigation of his vessel to have much time to bestow upon passengers. It is the duty of every one, therefore, to look to himself for those little comforts which all more or less require. A passenger on board an emigrant ship should make up his mind to rough it in the best way he can, to be sparing at meals, so that his allotment of provisions may not be expired before the day expires. But, above all, it is necessary to husband water with the *greatest care. A few hours of hunger can easily be endured, but under warm tropical sun thirst is intolerable. Passengers should always remember that there are no more men on board a ship than are absolutely necessary for her navigation. They must, therefore, bestill themselves in the way of cleaning their berths, or their own health, and that of every one on board is endangered. The scale of dietary is always advertised with the vessel, and it is, therefore unnecessary here to mention it. Only let every passenger to look to the scale and remember that at sea he can eat about half more than on land. Competition has so lowered the price of a passage to Australia, that there is a difference of 25 per cent on the charges of different brokers. Of course there must be some cause for the difference in price, which every passenger should ascertain for himself. The voyage to Australia takes from four to five months, according to the sailing qualities of the ship or the prevalence of favourable or unfavourable winds."*[146]

Emigrant Ship Between Decks

From the "Illustrated London News", 17 August 1850

Emigrant Ship, Between Decks
(Rex Nan Kivell Collection NK4182/70, National library of Australia)

---

146. *London Times*. 19 January 1850.

Adequate ventilation and light were significant problems for passengers below decks. They were never satisfactorily resolved until the advent of electrically-driven fans and electric lights. Hatches were opened in good weather but it was not possible to drive fresh air from this source into the hold. Ships utilised wind sails to capture and circulate air below decks. These sails were suspended from the rigging in order to direct a breeze into a canvas tube or funnel. It was also not possible to use this apparatus in bad weather because of the risk of directing water below decks. Primitive pumping arrangements had difficulty in handling small amounts of water from other sources and hence every effort was made not to increase the volume of water below decks. Even with hatches open and wind sails in operation, ventilation was not adequate. This was very apparent in the humid and hot conditions in tropical waters. It was common practice for male passengers to sleep on the open deck when weather permitted.

These British emigrants were of course not accustomed to the excessive heat and humidity of the tropics and consequently many were distressed and became ill. The heat was also a problem for the first class and other cabin class passengers in their cabins. The impact of excessive heat is illustrated by the following exert from the diary of an intermediate class passenger on a voyage on board the barque *John* in 1839:

"October 20

The weather is excessively hot. We have slept for some time with two sheets on a mattress and can scarcely bear that. Service on deck as usual. Not very well, weak and languid. Read Wesley's sermon on dress."[147]

The matter of adequate illumination was even more problematic. In most ships heavy pieces of glass or bullseyes were set into the ship's deck to shed some light below, but these were inadequate and on many ships the cluttered nature of the deck with its deck cargo meant that these sources of light were often covered. Oil lamps were therefore the main source

---

147. Acher, Elizabeth. Diary kept on voyage from Gravesend to Adelaide 1839/40. As transcribed by Main, Jean. The Barque *John*. A Voyage to the Land of Hope. Aranda, ACT, 1994. p.17.

of illumination below decks. They were hung on a hook located in an overhead beam. The lamps comprised a heavy metal cage with thick glass panes and even under optimal operating conditions they provided very faint light. They had the disadvantage of emitting a pungent smelling vapour, which was not entirely compatible with the nauseated state of many passengers. This odour added to the foul smells below, particularly when hatches had to be battened down and the use of ventilation wind sails was curtailed in rough seas.

There was also the ever-present danger of fire on board these wooden ships. To reduce the risk of fire the use of candles and any other type of open flame was strictly forbidden when the oil lamp came into use. There were also strict rules about the time at which lights had to be extinguished. A member of the crew or an appointed emigrant thus extinguished these lights at a stated time. Frequently this appointed time was 8 pm but sometimes it was as late as 10 pm.

These precautions against fire were necessary because the outbreak of fire on one of those wooden vessels would most likely be devastating to the vessel and those on board. The horror of fire at sea is illustrated in the following extract from a report carried in the *South Australian Register* on 30 March 1850:

> *"The emigrant ship, Caleb Grimshaw, was destroyed by fire on 12 November, sixteen miles S.E. of the island Flores, one of the Azores. The emigrants, 300, with the crew were saved. The fire was discovered abreast of the chain locker, and the immense quantities of water poured on it generated steam to such an extent as rendered the heat insufferable. For five days and nights the boats towed astern were filled with poor emigrants bewailing their unhappy fate, sixty being on a raft, when the barque Sarah, bound for New Brunswick, hove in sight, and descrying the signal of distress approached. Owing to rough weather, but three boatful of passengers could be extricated from their perilous position. The following day 150 more were removed. On the 19th, owing to heavy sea, nothing could be done. On the 20th ten, who had escaped from the burning ship, volunteered to relieve their remaining comrades whose supply of water and provisions was*

exhausted. Fortunately the vessel drifted into smooth water to leeward of Flores, and during the night the remaining passengers were got off. The escape of these persons is all but miraculous. Nothing but constant flooding prevented their vessel being burned to the water's edge; and to prevent this, crew and passengers had to work like horses. Too much praise cannot be accorded to Captain Cook of the Sarah, who for three days and nights hovered around the burning vessel in the midst of tempestuous weather, and whenever there was a lull lowered his boats. The emigrants, who had lost everything, were conveyed to Fayal ...."

The only advantage the emigrant derived from poor lighting was that it offered a degree of privacy in very crowded conditions.

Various individuals and organisations attempted to improve conditions for steerage passengers emigrating to Australia. Dr John Dunmore Lang was one who believed that conditions could be improved. In his drive to attract emigrants to Australia, of the right type, he chartered ships and sought to improve conditions for the voyage. On three of these ships (the **Clifton**, **Larpent** and **Travancore**), he had the steerage quarters fitted with temporary-type cabins on each side of the ship with a passage down the centre.

However, as I outlined in the previous chapter, the person that did most to improve conditions for emigrants was Caroline Chisholm who had worked for some years assisting immigrants arriving in Australia. She gained much from the first-hand experience of those she assisted. Mrs Chisholm was a person of some influence and used this to improve conditions for those who emigrated using her co-operative scheme. She was particularly opposed to the lack of privacy on board emigration ships. The first emigrants to embark for Australia under her scheme did so on 28 June 1850 on the **Slains Castle**. She had chartered this vessel and had it fitted out to her specifications. In the place of bunks between decks there were small cabins of varying sizes, similar to the arrangements organised by Dr Lang. The Family Colonisation Loan Society, established by Chisholm, reached its peak with the building of the **Caroline Chisholm**, which incorporated her requirements into the ship's design.

However, the second half of the century saw a considerable increase in the numbers emigrating, commencing with the sudden increase resulting from the gold rush. Thus schemes like that devised by Caroline Chisholm could not keep up with these vast increases in numbers. Those coming to Australia as part of her co-operative arrangements probably only amounted to some 5000, which is a small proportion of all those who emigrated.

While there were examples of emigration vessels that provided improved comforts and privacy, and there were initiatives by some groups and individuals, it seems that the majority of steerage passengers sailed out with accommodation that lacked basic comforts and privacy. It appears that this situation prevailed until late in the century, as described by Dr R Skirving, recounting his voyage to Sydney on board the ***Ellora*** in 1883:

> "...it was horrid, and even indecent for decent married people to be herded together like beasts, with almost no privacy to dress or undress, and where, in the close and stuffy double bunks they slept in, only a thin board separated each couple from another alongside, another below, and another lot end to end. The ventilation was very poor, and in the tropics with a temperature of 90 degrees, the air was mephitic... The married couples slept in bunches of 16 human beings in two tiers ... the very young children slept with their parents and the older children piled in together somehow in other double bunks.
>
> ... It would not be pretty... to enter into all the adventures, embarrassments and awkward moments of a domestic day and night spent in such conditions of communal crowding, which in happier conditions, are rightly separate, personal or familial."[148]

It's interesting to note these comments about the conditions on the ***Ellora,*** which at 1699 tons was a fairly large vessel compared to many of the emigrant vessels which were often half this size or even smaller.

---

148. Skirving, R Scot. Cited in Charlwood, Don. The Long Farewell. Ringwood, Victoria, 1981. p. 118.

Clearly the scene below decks on most nights must have been dark, pungent and noisy. It is not difficult to imagine the particular environment of the married quarters with crying children, sick people, the pungent smells of food cooking, aftermath of seasickness, the particular and unpleasant smell of the oil lamps and the combination of odours from many bodies. All these and more combining to make an unpleasant cocktail of noise and smell.

It was not uncommon for steerage passengers to complain at the end of a voyage about the conditions during the voyage. Although these complaints were usually investigated they appeared to have had little impact on future accommodation arrangements, persons responsible for any neglect were generally not present and, of course, the complaining emigrant did not benefit from any findings of neglect or ill-treatment (although future emigrants may have been the beneficiaries). An investigation of conditions and passenger treatment was conducted by the Immigration Agent following the arrival in Tasmania on 6 November 1857 of the ***Trade Wind,*** which had brought 294 bounty passengers, sponsored by the Hobart Town Immigration Society and the Launceston Town Aid Immigration Society. The Immigration Agent compiled an 81-page document, which was submitted to the Colonial Secretary detailing conditions on board the ship during the voyage. The ship was carrying more passengers than it was entitled to carry and the Agent reported:

> "....it was found that there was inadequate ventilation throughout the berths, the hospital was ill-placed, the toilet facilities were not sufficient and were a danger to health, and the cooking apparatus for the passengers ... was of an old construction and of the rudest and most imperfect kind being likewise in bad order."[149]

The Agent concluded in his report:

> "It is distressing to reflect upon the injury to health and life, the misery, the waste of money and of time and the ill feeling occasioned by the want of proper arrangement on board ship."[150]

---

149. Quarry, Patricia. Folio Pamphlet. "Trade Wind", February 1958.
150. ibid.

There had been a number of deaths during the voyage caused by typhus fever.

It's difficult to know what the initial reaction of steerage passengers may have been immediately following embarkation. Some apparently expected the accommodation to comprise some kind of cabin arrangement. For others accustomed to sharing a room with family it may have appeared fairly normal or even a little cleaner and more orderly than normal. However, for most the scale of the arrangements and the closeness of the other passengers, who were in most cases complete strangers, must have given rise to second thoughts about the wisdom of the decision to emigrate. Early arrivals on board may have fared slightly better than late arrivals, possibly securing an upper berth nearer a source of light and in a slightly better ventilated area. These advantages would have offered only marginally better conditions on such a long passage.

The steerage passengers would have taken little time to settle in after locating a bunk and depositing the few possessions that the space permitted. The next step would have possibly involved a return to the main deck to see the ship move away as the voyage commenced and possibly to participate in the first muster after the anchor was weighed. At this point there may have been a sudden awareness of the small size of the vessel, particularly the cramped accommodation that would constitute the emigrant's few square feet for the coming months. Standing on deck it would have been difficult not to become conscious of the wind in the billowing sails and the creaking of the ship and its apparatus. These noises would be with the emigrant day and night for the duration of the long passage that lay ahead.

These noises and those associated with the operation of the ship and the large number on board meant that sailing on a nineteenth-century vessel was a noisy affair even for those in cabins. This made it difficult for passengers seeking or needing peace and quiet and interfered greatly with sleep.

> *"...Sleep at night was out of the question. The awful creaking of every part of the vessel, hollering of the sailors and roaring of the sea, with noises of every description completely preventing it".*[151]

---

151. Johnstone, William journal kept on board the *Arab* during a journey to Tasmania in 1841-42. Quoted in Greenhill, Basil and Giffard Ann. Women Under Sail. Newton Abbot 1970.

The constant noise on board these vessels would have no doubt been a greater problem for sick passengers. This is illustrated in the comment below by Francis Taylor, a passenger on board the ***Stag*** during the passage to Adelaide in 1850. Taylor and many of the passengers had been ill for some time during the passage.

> *"Our time for reaching Adelaide is variously calculated at from ten to fourteen days, thank God we are so near as we are, for I want a few days quietness, which I shall never get on board the Stag…"*[152]

While the constant noise was a problem for many passengers it did assist in providing an aid to privacy by masking the sounds coming from adjoining cabins or bunks. The difficulties of living so close to so many people on board such a small vessel for such a long passage would soon become apparent to all passengers.

As the anchor was weighed and the vessel towed out to start its long passage most passengers would have experienced an immense feeling of sadness at leaving family, friends and their old home. An 1851 passenger, J Hindmarsh, sailing on the ***Havering*** from Plymouth to Sydney, expressed his feelings in verse:

> *"Farewell, farewell dear England, the closing shades of night Still linger in the distance, revealing thee to sight. We gaze each one in silence, for tis the last fond view will have of thy fair country; the land we love so true. Tis' now an hour of sorrow: - tis now that each ones heart, Feels, that tis hard to conquer, the pain that tis' to part; To part with loved companions, with friends, both true and kind. To leave our home, our Country, for fortune's smile to find. But while our hopes are kind led by other Countries fame, We ever shall remember, old England's far spread name."*[153]

---

152. Transcribed diary of Francis C Taylor in Limbrick, Doug: The Stag Diary, Passage to Colonial Adelaide 1850. Xlibris Corporation, 2012.
153. Hindmarsh, J H S. Scenes during a passage from England to Australia. 18 November, 1851 to 16 February 1852. National Library of Australia Manuscript MS 4156.

CHAPTER 7

Passage to the Colonies

"The fair breeze blew, the white foam flew,
The furrow followed free;
We were the first that ever burst,
Into that silent sea."[154]

The voyage to the Australian colonies in the nineteenth century did not exactly equate with the imagery of Coleridge's verse (above). There were, in fact many occasions when the breeze for emigrant ships was far from 'fair' and the white foam was replaced with raging seas. At other times during the long passage the 'fair breeze' was almost entirely absent and the vessel was virtually becalmed, this usually occurred in the oppressively hot and humid weather around the equator, which made conditions on board a small crowded and poorly ventilated sailing ship almost unbearable. However, there must have been many times during the long passage, when there was nothing for passengers to see but ocean, and they may have felt they 'were the first to ever burst' into the vast sea that lay before them.

The trip from the British Isles to Australia and New Zealand was the longest regular passage undertaken by sailing ships. The complete voyage back to the home port frequently circled the world. This occurred to enable ships to use the prevailing winds. While the route changed during the era of the sailing ship the original route was over 13,000 nautical

---

154. Coleridge, Samuel Taylor. Rime of the Ancient Mariner.

miles in distance to Sydney. This course followed the route laid down by the Admiralty; a route in general use until the gold rush.

Thus the voyage would start in the British Isles and, using the North Atlantic westerlies and then the northeast trade winds, the captain would seek to navigate the ship across the Bay of Biscay into the South Atlantic Ocean, where he would look for the South East trade winds. These winds would carry the ship south towards the Roaring Forties, where the westerlies would speed the ship towards Australia. The return trip would use the easterlies to Cape Horn and, after rounding the Cape, would move north through the South and then the North Atlantic Oceans to complete the circumnavigation.

However, the winds could not always be relied upon to arrive at the right time, from the right direction and in the right strength. It was not uncommon for vessels to spend weeks in the Channel. They would often anchor waiting for a change of wind or in case of too much wind, shelter at places like Plymouth.

Having at last departed from shore, ships often had considerable difficulty in crossing the Bay of Biscay. The weather in the Bay can be very difficult for a modern liner to navigate, let alone a small timber vessel of less than 1000 tons. A different problem was encountered when ships approached the equator, where light winds could be expected. This was referred to as the doldrums and progress would be slow until the southeast trade winds were encountered. In fact some vessels were becalmed, which frustrated a speedy voyage but offered opportunities for new experiences.

> *"....no wind, finished bending the old sails, on the look out for Turtle, Captain had one of the quarter boats out and all of the saloon passengers who liked went we had a boatful the male fraction taking the oars one steering and the Captain in the bow none of the sailors on board we rowed about some time looking for Turtle after some time we came across one and crept up to him very quietly the Captain reached out and secured it by the hind flippers and dragged it in catching another one*

soon after in the same manner and after being out about two hours pulled in to lunch, went out again after lunch, and caught two more ...... went out again after dinner and caught two more making six in all averaging about 25 lbs a piece ..... went out again in evening as it was getting dusk a little air getting up the ship began to move slightly and we had a sharp pull to get alongside..."[155]

Sketches on Board an Emigrant Ship[156]
(State Library of Victoria)

Many ships called at Madeira, Rio de Janeiro or Cape Town to repair storm damage and rest the crew. These stops also enabled passengers to recover and regain strength for the remainder of the passage. The captain also used these stopovers to replenish stores and water. However, for some ships there were no stops on the way to the colonies and it was thus straight into the Roaring Forties. These stopovers were common prior to the 1850s, but for the majority who

---
155. EL. Diary kept on board the Hesperus on voyage to Adelaide, 7 August to 31 October 1879. National Library of Australia Manuscript MS 4056.
156. Illustrated Australian News, 24 March 1875.

came in the mass migration period after the 1850s the passage was made non-stop.

Until about the time of the gold rush, the vessel on reaching Cape Town (the approximate mid-point of the passage) would then proceed to cross the southern Indian Ocean. The some 7000 miles of ocean that lay ahead was devoid of any landmass, with nothing closer than India in the north and Antarctica in the south. While this part of the passage could be more difficult than the part that lay behind, the conditions encountered were relatively mild compared to the southern route in later use.

In 1847 John Towson's book, *Tables to Facilitate the Practice of Great Circle Sailing*, was published by the Admiralty. Towson presented his calculations for sailing on a curved route, which was broken up into a series of chords or rhumbs. To follow this route would involve sailing as far south as ice would permit and would cut out Cape Town completely. Three years went past before a ship's master dared to follow Towson's calculations. The reluctance to adopt this new route was based on the fact that it would lead into hazardous waters and would necessitate a high proficiency in seamanship, particularly in the use of the sextant and the chronometer. This degree of proficiency was necessary so the masters would know exactly when to change course onto a new chord. The first to try the new route was Captain Godfrey, sailing in the **Constance** in 1850. Following the discovery of gold in the colonies there was a sense of urgency about getting to the colonies by many prospective passengers. Hence, a speedier passage to the colonies was needed and a number of ship's masters were motivated to follow Towson's route.

The ships that followed Towson's route would thus swing in a southerly direction in the latitude of Rio de Janeiro in search of westerly winds that would carry them in a huge arc. This arc would carry them towards the Antarctic and eventually back towards Australia. Thus this route exploited the earth's round shape, rather than following the line of latitude as if the earth was flat. This became known as the Great Circle route.

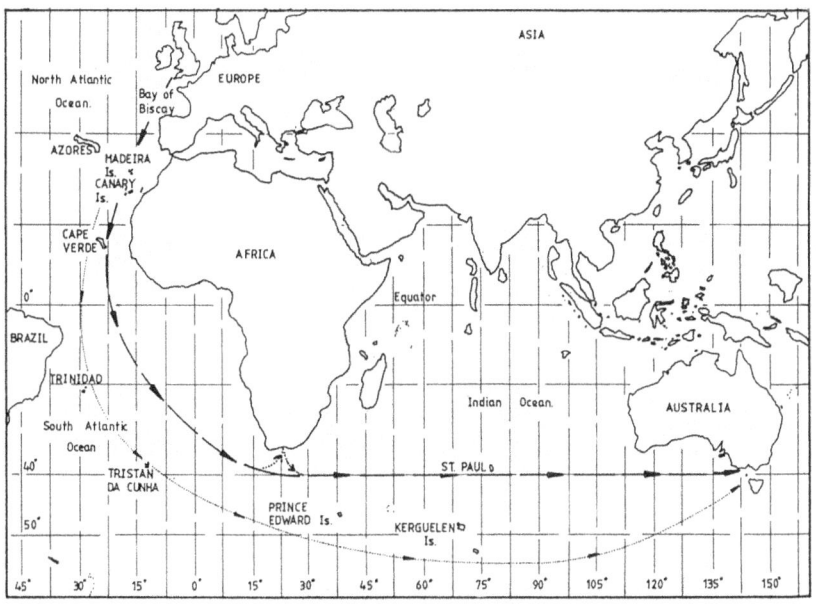

Map showing the Two Routes used by Vessels Sailing to the Colonies in the Nineteenth Century

The journey south towards the Antarctic meant that ships passed several hundred miles south of the Cape of Good Hope into seas that were frequented by icebergs. The small wooden square-riggers could easily be demolished by collision with an iceberg. Even the much larger composite or steel hull sailing vessels faced damage or destruction if collision occurred. On this route skilful sailing was not only necessary because of the possibility of encountering icebergs, but also because the weather frequently produced extreme conditions, including gale force winds and gigantic seas. Unlike travelling on a modern aircraft, where the captain can usually vary altitude to secure greater comfort for passengers, the captain of the sailing ship could do little to avoid bad weather and thus passenger discomfort was frequently extremely high in these southern waters. It was possible to encounter snow and crew often had to contend with ice on the deck, sails and rigging. The more southerly route usually meant sleepless nights for passengers, seasickness and a heightened fear of perishing at the hands of the sea.

Vessel in Big Seas, Seamen Aloft
(State Library of Victoria)

An 1851 passenger recorded in verse the scene on board as a storm arrived:

"Hush! tis the hour of Midnight, methinks a Storm spreads round. The wind is howling fearful - a dread and mournful sound - "All hands on deck, 'reef Topsails" the Boatswain's heard to cry. And o'er our bosom flashes, the truth a storm is nigh. And now above the Tempest, is heard the Seaman's strain, Cheering his fellow comrades, amid the cold and rain."[157]

An 1879 passenger travelling on the **Hesperus** reported:

"15th October (Wednesday) Gale continues still driving south with hardly any sail set constantly shipping water over the quarter and poop..... it is quite a labour of love to eat ones meals, went on the Poop this evening for a few minutes it being very hot below, before I had been there many minutes she shipped the heaviest sea she had taken yet over the Poop knocked me down and drenched me and while I was down gave me another one ..... also lifted the top of the after sky light and knocked open the Companion doors and popped about a ton of water into the Saloon the man at the wheel was knocked down only saved himself by hanging on to the wheel ..."[158]

The *South Australian Register* reported on 18 June 1850 on 'The Quickest Voyage to Australia - Great Circle Sailing':

"Our accounts of Capt. Godfrey's unprecedented short voyage to South Australia, in the emigrant ship Constance, having produced a greater sensation among those interested in Australia and New Zealand than any voyage ever before made, we are induced to publish the following additional details of the track Captain Goodfrey pursued by the aid of Mr Towson's tables.

---

157. Hindmarsh, J H S. Scenes During a Passage from England to Australia, 1851. National Library of Australia, Manuscript MS 4156.
158. E L. Journal of voyage to Adelaide on the *Hesperus*, 7 August to 31 October, 1879. National Library of Australia, Manuscript MS 4056.

The *Torrens*, Composite 1276 Tons, on arrival in Port Adelaide after striking an iceberg in the Southern Ocean, 11 January, 1899.
(State Library of South Australia)

...He immediately resolved to make what the author of the tables has termed the composite track, which is thus described in the work alluded to:-

'To follow the great circle track rigidly would sometimes lead through latitudes so high as to be impracticable. This generally happens, too, when the greatest amount of distance would be saved; but though in such cases it would be unwise to attempt the great circle, yet there is a very simple application of these tables, which will give the shortest possible route consistent with a restricted maximum latitude'

The composite route to Australia does not differ from other voyages until the mariner has reached about the latitude 24° S. Having cleared the trade winds, he then shapes his route on the arc of the great circle, varying his course by compass according as the latitude of the ship varies..."

Constance on her Passage from Plymouth to Adelaide 1849 by T.G. Dutton
(Rex Nan Kivell Collection NK529, National Library of Australia)

Despite the excitement about the quick passage by the **Constance** it was not an uneventful passage for most of the emigrants. Within four days of departing Plymouth in August 1849 sickness broke out amongst the passengers, followed by diarrhoea, cholera and other health problems. The vessel had departed at a time when an epidemic of cholera was ravaging Britain and Ireland. The sickness on board quickly reached epidemic proportions. The emigrants had to endure seasickness in the Bay of Biscay, followed by extreme heat in the tropics and freezing conditions in the high southern latitudes (including dodging icebergs). It was a tribute to the surgeon that under these conditions he was able to contain the epidemic and limit the number of deaths to 28.

As a result of the experience of the **Constance** and other vessels following the Great Circle route, the Commissioners attempted to force masters to avoid the high southern latitudes. A modified Great Circle route was devised for government-chartered vessels, which was intended to prevent emigrants from having to endure the hardships encountered on the ***Constance*** in the icy parts of the Great Southern Ocean where vessels met with hazardous Antarctic pack ice. It's clear that many masters ignored this direction and continued to sail further south to pick up favourable westerly winds. As a result Commissioners placed a new clause in the charter for each vessel. This was impossible to enforce and so was dropped by the Commissioners. Thus emigrants on some vessels had to endure considerable discomfort, extreme cold and possible fear and distress when the master decided to follow the extreme Great circle route.

While the most difficult conditions encountered during the long passage to the colonies were usually found in the far southern waters sailing conditions could be very difficult at many points during the passage, including during the early part of the passage in the English Channel. Most passengers thus encountered conditions never before experienced at some point during the passage:

> "*Monday 1st January 1838*
>
> *The whole of the 24 hours alternate calms and squalls, attended with very heavy rain - Made a shortened sail, and tacked ship as requisite - During the night we had a great deal of Thunder and Lightning - the slashes of Lightning were the most vivid and the Thunder the loudest and most prolonged of any I ever experienced.*"[159]

Most of the ships' masters had gained their sailing experience on the Atlantic. The much longer journey to Australia, including the long easterly run across the southern Indian Ocean presented a problem that many had previously not encountered (i.e. the need to determine longitude). In order to avoid the problem of not knowing the position of the vessel accurately navigators had, where possible, relied on taking advantage of their knowledge of latitude. They would sail to the latitude of their destination, turn towards the destination and follow a

---

159. Mr A. Journal of Voyage to Van Diemen's Land on Board the *Clifton* 1837-38. National Library of Australia, Manuscript MS 4058.

line of constant latitude. This was known as 'running down a westing' (if westward, otherwise easting). This prevented a vessel from taking the most direct route or a route with the most favourable winds and currents, which could extend a passage by days or even weeks. Improving navigation relied on finding a way to measure longitude.

The problem of measuring longitude engaged astronomers, navigators and clock makers for some two hundred and fifty years. There was a considerable amount of activity in most seafaring countries to find a solution. The British Government established the Board of Longitude in 1714 and in the same year offered £20,000 for a solution, which could provide longitude to within half-a-degree (2 minutes of time). The methods proposed had to demonstrate that they were capable of determining longitude of a vessel at sea.

In theory, the determination of longitude was a relatively simple matter. Since the earth rotates at a steady rate of 360 degrees per day (or 15 per hour), there is a direct relationship between time and longitude. If a navigator knew the time at a fixed reference point and the local time at the vessels location the difference between the two would give the vessels position relative to the fixed location. Determining local time was relatively easy. The problem ultimately was how to determine the time at a distant reference point while on a vessel.

A number of astronomers worked on developing a lunar distance method. This involved the measurement of the angular distance between the moon and a star or the sun using a sextant. A series of complex calculations using logarithms was then required. The complexity of these calculations was a barrier for navigators. However, a series of tables (Nautical Almanac) was published with data for 1767. The Almanac included daily tables for the positions of the sun, moon and planets, and tables giving the distance of the moon from the sun and a number of stars. This became the standard almanac for mariners worldwide, and since it was based on the Royal Observatory, it led to the international adoption of Greenwich Mean Time as an international standard.

Others felt the answer to determining longitude lay in chronometry, that is, in developing an improved timepiece that would work on extended voyages at sea. A suitable timepiece was eventually built by John Harrison, a Yorkshire carpenter. He went on to build further versions and the last one (known as H-4) was tried at sea and met all the requirements set down by the British Government. However, because chronometers were very expensive the lunar distance method was widely used at sea from 1776 to about 1850. Between 1800 and 1850 affordable, reliable marine chronometers gradually became available. As they reached the market in large numbers the lunar distance method progressively lost favour as the preferred way of determining longitude. By 1850 the vast majority of ocean-going navigators worldwide had ceased using the lunar distances method.

Noon was an important time in the routine of shipboard life. It was at noon that the ship's time and position were fixed. In fact the ship's day started at noon rather than at midnight. Prior to the use of chronometers the early vessels used a sandglass to measure time. It took half an hour for the sand to run through and this was marked by the ringing of the ship's bell.

The speed of the ship was determined using a 'log'. The log was dropped overboard to float with a line attached, which ran out over the stern of the ship as it sailed. The line had a number of knots at intervals along it. The number of knots passing over the stern were timed using a sandglass and this gave the ship's speed.

Even with these instruments much of the navigation involved a calculated guess by the master. This was referred to as 'dead reckoning'. The instruments available to the master of a sailing ship were fine in ideal conditions. Unfortunately, conditions at sea were rarely ideal. Following some weeks at sea the chronometer could become inaccurate. Cloudy or overcast skies could prevent a master from taking sun or star sights with the sextant. The captain could never be certain as to how much sideways drift had occurred because of unknown currents.

The weather was not always the destroyer of these sailing ships. There were many other hazards. Some often only became apparent towards the end of the journey when land was finally in sight. The Australian coasts, for example, were potentially treacherous to sailing ships. It was easy to become caught in strong currents or rips, especially in a light breeze. Charts were not always accurate and an uncharted reef could be encountered, even in fair weather.

Thus the safe arrival of a vessel was in no small part due to the skill and experience of the master, backed by a good crew. If a master miscalculated or the lookouts were distracted (possibly tired from a long night of work in heavy seas) then the ship could easily come to grief. All factors considered, it is amazing that so many of these small sailing ships successfully made the passage from the British Isles to the Australian colonies.

In addition to being a long and difficult passage, from a navigational view point the journey to the Australian colonies in a small sailing ship of less than 1000 tons was no picnic for passengers and crew. Ships were often lost at sea and injury to the crew was not uncommon, with many losing their life by drowning. In the southern part of the voyage crewmen often had to battle their way across decks swept by icy seas. Handling ice covered sails high above the deck in a gale force wind with high seas tossing the small ship around provided extremely dangerous working conditions for the crew. And on top of all this, the living quarters for the crew on a small sailing ship were spartan. The eighteenth-century writer Dr Samuel Johnson wrote:

> *"No man will be a sailor who has contrivance enough to get himself into jail; for being in a ship is being in a jail, with the chance of being drowned .... A man in jail has more room, better food and commonly better company."*[160]

It was not uncommon for sailors to perish at sea. During the Napoleonic Wars the British Navy assumed that one sailor in thirty would die of disease or accident at sea (excluding casualties that occurred in battle) and one in six would always be ill.[161] In the early part of the nineteenth century the Royal Navy began recruiting young men trained and examined in medicine. Hence it's clear that doctors on Royal Navy vessels would have been more competent than the average doctor on an emigrant vessel. Thus it might be expected that

---

160. Cited in Noble, John. The Golden Age of Sail. South Australia, 1985. p. 1.
161. Hughes, Robert. The Fatal Shore. Vintage 2003, p144.

the death rate of sailors on emigrant vessels would be higher than the rates for naval vessels.

Some Captains had difficulty in maintaining commitment by the crew on such a long voyage under difficult and demanding conditions. There are references to problems of discipline in passenger diaries and ship logs and of Captains resorting to harsh measures to restore order. The Captain of the ***Clifton***, on a 1837-38 passage to Launceston appeared to have encountered crew dissatisfaction on several occasions during the latter part of the passage. For example, some four months into the voyage:

> *"Tuesday 13th March 1838*
>
> *...Increased symptoms of insubordination amongst the Crew, one watch having refused to do its duty..."*[162]

Furling the Foresail, Ship *Discovery*
(Malcolm Brodie Shipping Collection, State Library of Victoria)

---

162. Mr A. diary of voyage from Liverpool to Launceston, November 1837 to April 1838. National Library of Australia MS 4058.

However, despite the hardship, danger and deprivation, there were always plenty of new recruits seeking adventure at sea. It is possible that recruits were readily available for the same or similar reasons that drove people to emigrate.

For the passengers the journey was sometimes an adventure, frequently a challenge and often an ordeal. At times the passage was also shear boredom, with little to do in between the routine of ship life. As with the conditions on board for crew, shipboard life for the majority of passengers was also equally spartan. Most of those who came to the Australian colonies travelled as steerage-class passengers, where there was little space and privacy. On some of the earlier passages to the colonies emigrants were exploited and subject to extremely primitive and unhealthy conditions. For example, in 1835 the **John Barry** had one bathtub and two privies for 400 emigrants and in 1836 the **Lady Mc Naghten** carried 50 bunks for 100 men and boys and 106 small berths and 6 hospital berths for 185 women.[163] While the conditions on these vessels may have been of an extreme kind, conditions were nevertheless not significantly better for the majority of steerage passengers travelling between decks on nineteenth-century sailing vessels. The sanitary conditions were generally austere and privies were frequently only provided for first and cabin class passengers. In many vessels the steerage passengers were provided with buckets, which were screened and sometimes fitted with a seat. There were generally no special washing places and water was rationed. Even for first and cabin passengers the sanitary arrangements were primitive. For example, a privy usually consisted of a seat with a hole opening straight down to the sea below. They possibly had a flap of leather fitted to lessen the likelihood of a wet backside from water thrown up by the vessel's wake in bad weather. Most vessels carried livestock (sheep, pigs, poultry and cows) to provide fresh food for paying passengers and the captain. The livestock was housed on the deck of the vessel and generated smells, which permeated much of the vessel. The smells of the vessel and of unwashed humanity in very crowded spaces must have been appalling. It is clear from many accounts of passages to the colonies that the smells generated during a long voyage on a nineteenth-century sailing vessel was an aspect of shipboard life that was long remembered. The fresh smell of the air on arrival was

---

163. Clark, C M H. A History of Australia, Part III. Melbourne University Press, 1979. pp. 228-229.

absolutely wonderful according to the records of a number of emigrants. The record of the arrival of the **Mona** in Portland Bay on 13 October 1843 provides an example:

> *"....by 9 am we were at anchor in Portland Bay about half a mile from shore........The bay is both spacious and beautiful.....The grass looks green, the trees are plentiful and truly it is refreshing to the eyes to have such a pleasant prospect and to the nose to enjoy such desirable fragrance, as greeted us when we went on Deck this morning."*[164]

Emigrants at Dinner – Typical Scene of Steerage Class Emigrants[165]
(National Library of Australia, NL 3428)

There were also a large number of deaths on board some emigrant ships during this period. For example, the **Layton** sailed from Bristol in September 1837 and, of the 178 children on board, 70 died during the passage. It appears that the major cause of death was measles. There were also large numbers of deaths on board passages made by the **Palimira**, the **William Rogers** and the **Maitland**. Scarlet fever was thought to have been the cause of death on these passages. A board of inquiry appointed in December 1838 found that there were too many children on board,

---
164. Wood, Mr. Journal of voyage from London to Launceston on the Mona 1843. National Library of Australia MS 9113.
165. Illustrated London News, 13 April 1844.

supplies of clothing were inadequate and the food was not 'consistent with the previous habits of the people'.[166]

Where there was considerable sickness on a passage it was usually due to an epidemic of one or more of the contagious diseases prevalent in the nineteenth century (measles, scarlet fever, whooping cough). Even in a vessel with an excellent housekeeping record it was difficult to prevent the spread of these airborne infectious diseases amongst the steerage passengers who were accommodated in such confined and closed quarters. Diarrhoea was also a problem on some vessels and in some cases reached epidemic proportions. It lowered the resistance of those affected and so made them more susceptible to infectious diseases. This combination of diseases had a bigger impact on children and often resulted in death. Some surgeons believed that diarrhoea was often caused by contaminated drinking water and a change of drinking water when possible led to the cessation of diarrhoea. A number of the surgeons believed that improving ventilation in the steerage area and improving the quality of drinking water would lead to improved health of emigrants, especially the health of children. There were some advances in ventilation technology during the century, which were incorporated in some emigrant vessels. From the middle of the century there were improvements in distillation (using sea water) which meant that where these methods were employed the vessels had better quality water that was free from contamination and the foul taste of barrel water.

While on some passages a number of deaths occurred, it was nevertheless disturbing, distressing and deeply felt by most passengers each time it happened. For many of the passengers the burial ceremony was confronting. This can be seen from the following account by passenger Francis Taylor on board the ***Stag*** in 1850:

> *"We have received the news that a child of 10 months old, has expired below, it has been ill some time, its body is to be committed to the DEEP as soon as possible, dead bodies are not*

---

166. Report of Board Appointed on 5th December 1838 to Inquire into and report on, the possible causes which have produced during the previous year a greater degree of sickness on board Immigrant Ships, Chartered by Government, than those fitted out under the Bounty System. Immigration Office, 15 January 1839. p. 8.

allowed to be kept no longer than they can possibly be enwrapped, etc. Every one ordered on deck except surgeon, First and Second Mate who are preparing the body for committal to the waves. 5 o'clock body brought upon deck folded in canvas wrapping in which are also enclosed four iron bolts, about 56 lbs in weight to cause it to sink immediately. 6 o'clock Minister and Surgeon came on deck and commenced the funeral service, The First and Second Mate supporting the body on the Bulwark until the words: 'We therefore commit his body to the deep' are pronounced, when they instantly drop it and it is seen no more, although it matters not what becomes of the perishable body still the horror fills the hearts at the thought of a human creature being undoubtedly devoured by some of the innumerable inhabitants of the Ocean. God preserve us from another such scene." [167]

The passengers on board the **Stag** were to witness a further seven burials before reaching their destination at Adelaide.

A Burial at Sea, 1880 **(Illustrated Australian News, November 1880)**
(State Library of Victoria)

---

167. Transcribed diary of Francis C Taylor in Limbrick, Doug. The Stag Diary Passage to Colonial Adelaide 1850. Xlibris Corporation, 2012, p.68.

A Parliamentary Enquiry in 1844 was told that conditions for steerage passengers on emigrant ships, during the long passage to the colonies, were frequently every bit as hard and revolting as those experienced on board convict ships. The report commented on steerage passenger conditions:

> "It was scarcely possible to induce passengers to sweep the decks after their meals or be decent in respect to the common wants of nature; in many cases in bad weather, they would not go on deck, their health suffered so much that their strength was gone, and they had not the power to help themselves. Hence the between decks were like a loathsome dungeon. When hatchways were opened, under which the people were stowed, the steam rose and the stench was like that from a pen of pigs. The few beds they had were in a dreadful state, for the straw, once wet with sea water, soon rotted, besides which they used the between decks for all sorts of filthy purposes ... the first days were those in which the people suffered most from sea-sickness and under the prostration of body thereby induced were wholly incapacitated from cooking. Thus though provisions might be abundant enough, the passengers would be half-starved." [168]

These difficulties and the exploitation that occurred on some voyages led the British Government to take steps to protect those emigrating to the Australian colonies. Regulations were gazetted and from around the 1840s greater protection was provided to passengers on the Australian route. While protection was offered to passengers coming to the Australian colonies, those emigrating to North America remained unprotected by Government regulation. These regulations led to a lengthy set of rules and practices that had to be observed by all parties sailing to the Australian colonies.

One of the changes involved the appointment of a Surgeon-Superintendent for each voyage. It was the occupant of this position that was charged with the responsibility for taking care of passenger welfare, providing for spiritual well-being, setting and upholding

---

168. Lubbock, Basil. The Colonial Clippers. Glasgow, 1924. pp. 3 and 4.

the rules for the passage and as necessary act as the disciplinarian. The Surgeon-Superintendent, however, was not necessarily a person with any special medical qualifications and certainly was not a person with surgical qualifications in the modern sense. Some Surgeons were less than competent and accepted the post to obtain free passage to the colonies. For some this was a way of escaping financial or other problems at home. Others were efficient and regulated life on board ship, particularly when conditions were difficult, discomfort high and sickness was prevalent. However, medical knowledge was such that little was known about the causes of the diseases that were prevalent on sailing ships during this period. Even in those instances where he had some understanding of the cause of an illness it was impossible to materially change the conditions on board these small sailing vessels. Thus illness and death continued to be present on board emigration ships to the colonies.

The rules developed to regulate shipping to the Australian colonies were translated into a comprehensive set of instructions, which were issued to Surgeons travelling on board emigration ships. The instructions included the following:

> "XI - He will insist on passengers not being molested on crossing the Line. The entire management, as well as the medical treatment, of the emigrants being entrusted to him, he is to see that they have their due rations of provisions without any deductions whatever; that their victuals are properly cooked, and served to them regularly at the usual meal times; and that they have a sufficient allowance of water. For the convenience of order, he will divide the emigrants into messes as he shall see fit. Two emigrants (one from each of two messes on rotation) are to be present when the provisions are issued.
>
> XII - He is not in any way to interfere in the navigation of the ship.
>
> XVII - He is to take care that the greatest cleanliness be observed among the emigrants.
>
> XIX - One day in the week to be appointed a washing day for clothes...

XXI -	He is, on all occasions when the weather permits, to read church services to the emigrants upon Sunday, and prayers upon other days...
XVIII -	No spirits are to be allowed to be used. No gambling. No smoking between decks.
XXVI -	He will keep a journal of his proceedings..." [169]

These instructions led to closely regulated life on board emigrant ships, with a well-ordered daily and weekly routine. For example, on board government ships passengers were to be up by 7 am and before breakfast at 8 am, the children were to be washed and dressed, the decks swept, the beds rolled and carried on deck (weather permitting) and the berths brushed out; dinner was at 1 pm and tea at 6 pm. To ensure that passengers were personally clean the Surgeon-Superintendent conducted a muster at 10.30 am each Sunday, after which divine service was performed. Similar regulations were in place to ensure cleanliness, comfort and safety on board bounty ships.

A key to the successful application of the rules and regulations during the long passage to the colonies was the fact that the Surgeon-Superintendent was given the authority to implement them. It seems that a large part of the role of the surgeon was maintaining discipline. If a vessel arrived in a dirty or disordered state this was usually considered to be because the surgeon failed to maintain the rules and standards set by the colonial and imperial authorities. This was usually caused by a breakdown in his authority due to lack of experience, incompetence, laziness and, occasionally, drunkenness. The surgeon was required to keep a journal, which had to be submitted to colonial authorities on arrival for examination and subsequently forwarding to British authorities for inspection and auditing. These documents were usually delivered to the Colonial Secretary via the Immigration Agent and sometimes were available for newspaper reporters to read. This often resulted in detailed reports being published in the press the day after a vessel arrived. These reports were often reprinted in British newspapers, thus any irregularities on a passage were known by the Emigration Commissioners before

---

169. Detailed Instructions Issued to Surgeons Superintendent on Board Emigrant Ships Proceeding to New South Wales and Van Diemen's Land, 1838.

the report arrived in England. The surgeon also submitted a summary report, which remained in the colony. The information contained in these reports led to the ongoing adjustment of the rules and regulations relating to emigration to the colonies.

From 1849 owners of all British emigrant vessels carrying 300 or more passengers were required under the Passenger Acts to provide a surgeon and he was to be given the authority to enforce regulations necessary for the maintenance of health.

However, even with these new requirements and the changes to shipboard life that they brought, there were continuing examples of inappropriate appointments to the position of surgeon, leading to misconduct and ill-treatment of passengers on emigrant ships. A Blue Book on Emigration, ordered by the House of Commons in July 1849, included a number of comments about the surgeons on particular vessels. For example;

> *'The Surgeon of the **Canton** is pronounced not qualified for his office.'*
>
> *'**Equestrian** - Surgeon not sufficient energy or activity.'*
>
> *'**Fairlie** - Deficient in energy and principles bad.'*
>
> *'**Charlotte Jane** - Surgeon, bad habits; intoxication, undesirable that he should be employed again.'*
>
> *'**Lady Peel** - Total unfitness of Surgeon for his duties.'*
>
> *'**Hyderabad** - Duties of Surgeon Superintendent not performed in a satisfactory manner, and should not be employed again.'*[170]

It appears that in the twelve-month period investigated for the Blue Book, out of the twenty surgeon Superintendents selected by the Emigration Commissioners, eleven were reported by the colonial authorities as more or less unfit for their responsible duties.

---

170. Sidney, Samuel. Female Emigration, As it is, as it may be. A letter to the Right Hon. Sidney Herbert, MP. London, 1850. p.9.

Given the deficiencies in the selection of the doctors for emigration ships it is not surprising that some were unable to perform the duties expected on the long passage to the colonies. On 7 January 1850 the *South Australian Register* reported the arrival of the **Brightman** and commented on the performance of the ship's doctor:

> *"The Brightman, from Plymouth 17th September, with 120 passengers, beside cargo, arrived at the Lightship on Saturday morning after a fine but lengthy passage of 110 days from the port of final departure... The passengers speak in highest terms of the Captain and the general arrangements on board the Brightman, with one exception. The solitary exception alluded to, is the Doctor, whose conduct upon the voyage was anything but 'uniformly satisfactory'. We forbear, at present, to publish the precise report as it has reached us, but seeing, as we have done, so many instances of very questionable appointment to the serious and important office of surgeon and surgeon superintendent, we cannot forego, the duty of advising those intending emigrants and confidential agents in England, who may read this announcement, to make every possible enquiry..."*

This report on the inadequacy of the doctor who sailed on the **Brightman** led to some rather vitriolic letters from the doctor in question, including one which was printed on 9 January 1850, and caused the paper to question the doctor's sanity:

> *"We have received a letter from one Dr Groves, of the barque Brightman, complaining of the few gentle remarks made by us in our impressions Monday last. If we had nothing else to convince us of the terrible laxity of the responsible parties in England, in the selection of medical men for emigrant ships, the letter of this blasphemous madman would be quite sufficient..."*

[Then followed extracts from the letter that were difficult to comprehend, concluding with the signature: 'Ellison Spencer Douglas Groves, Surgeon to the *Brightman* and first of the English Bards; God the Holy Ghost; or Christ 2nd'.]

While there were accounts of incompetent surgeons it is clear that there were also many positive experiences with very competent and compassionate doctors on emigration ships. Diarist, Francis Taylor, who travelled steerage during the 1850 passage to South Australia, held the doctor on the *Stag*, William Thompson, in high regard:

> "...the surgeon ... who is to every orderly passenger on board all that they could wish for, he truly spares no pains night or day in attending those who may require him professionally, whilst the healthy are treated more like brothers and sisters than total strangers..."[171]

Despite the problems encountered on some emigrant vessels because of an ineffective Surgeon-Superintendent, the experience on most vessels was very positive. In fact, the decision by British authorities to appoint a Surgeon-Superintendent with clearly defined duties and the authority to carry them out was instrumental in achieving the successful landing of so many emigrants in relatively good health and ready to disembark and start a new life. These procedures had reduced mortality on convict vessels from about 1815 and their adaption and adoption for government emigrant vessels was important to fulfilling a key objective of emigration officials, which was to deliver healthy emigrant workers to the colonies. Surgeons who had a good record were often consulted on their return to London and utilised for further passages to the colonies. Some surgeons made only the one passage settling in Australia, while others remained in service for many years making many voyages. The close monitoring of passenger conditions, the health of emigrants and the performance of the surgeons over the course of the century by the British and colonial governments enabled change, adjustment and upgrading of the emigration processes and practices. This was clearly important in achieving declining mortality on the emigration vessels that carried so many people during the nineteenth century some 14,000 miles and successfully delivered them at their destination. Despite a lack of sophistication in medical science, close attention to clean water and diet, sanitation and hygiene proved to be the answer to low mortality. These lessons in reducing mortality at sea led to changes in practice on land.

---

171. Transcribed diary of Francis C Taylor in Limbrick, Doug: The Stag Diary – Passage to Colonial Adelaide. Xlibris Corp. 2012.

In August 1842 the Carriage of Passengers in Merchant Vessels Act prescribed conditions to ensure seaworthiness of ships, the height between decks, the dimensions of sleeping berths and the quantities of food and water to be issued to each passenger. Thus, by the early 1840s the tales of horror which were evident from some of the early passages were to progressively become a thing of the past. However, while these requirements led to safer and cleaner conditions on board emigrant vessels, the physical environment produced by the weather and the state of development in sailing vessels meant that emigration to the colonies under sail would continue to be a difficult and largely uncomfortable passage.

Seasickness was ever present on passages to the colonies. It usually affected most passengers at some time during the passage. For some passengers it was a significant problem for most of the passage, and for those that it afflicted the debilitation that it caused was often very distressing. Some passengers were victims of seasickness as soon as the ship sailed. One captain of a square-rigger reported on the sight that greeted him after the first night out from port:

> *"...I slept well, and was quite refreshed when I was called soon after dawn ... the frightful aroma which filled the area assailed my nostrils... I realised that the crowd around me was vainly trying to cleanse itself ... everybody and everything appeared to be permeated with the awful product of sea sickness. No one had been able to remain on deck during the night, as heavy sprays and occasional seas had apparently swept over the vessel, and the great conglomeration of people had all been herded close together in the crowded saloons. Some, by the very nature of things, had been sick, and the effect of these, in that confined space, had made everybody else follow suit. Never had I beheld so revolting a spectacle."*[172]

While this may have depicted an extreme case of seasickness, there were many instances where victims were forced to remain under deck because of the conditions on board caused by the weather and a rough sea. In these instances those debilitated by periods of seasickness would emerge on deck from time to time, conditions and strength permitting. The debilitating

---

172. Hurst, A A. The Call of High Canvas. London, 1958. p. 52.

effect of seasickness is illustrated in the following extract from the diary of Joseph Jennison on his voyage to Portland, Victoria, on board the ***Marmion***:

> *"We have had some dreadful weather since I wrote last. Sea sickness is past description. We are ready to drop through want of food on the one hand and exertion of vomiting on the other. Five out of six in our mess have generally been sick at one time, so that even the few things we have brought with us we cannot get them cooked. Putting our clothes on or carrying a little tub of water on deck when we are sick and the ship is rocking as though she were trying to go over, are undertakings of no mean importance, and more than once I have sat for an hour meditating the best way of performing these feats before I have begun."*[173]

It was common for at least one member of a family to be seasick and for many this lasted for many days, while for others it reoccurred periodically during the passage. A diarist travelling on the ***Clifton*** to Launceston in 1837-38 wrote:

> *"Saturday 18 November 1837*
>
> *Mrs A and the family still continue very sick...*
>
> *Wednesday 22nd November*
>
> *The children somewhat better today but Mrs A still continues very ill - Got Edward on deck for a little while but was obliged to go below again ...*
>
> *Sunday 26th November*
>
> *Devine Service was read for the first time. Mrs A being nearly recovered from her sea sickness was able to attend - the Children and Servant are all quite well..."*[174]

---

173. Diary of Joseph Jennison passenger on Marmion, 1853. in Morgan, Dalma and Poole, Harry. Voyage of a Lifetime. Adelaide, 1978. p. 56.
174. Journal of Mr A on voyage to Launceston from Liverpool, 15 November 1837 to 4 April 1838 on board the Clifton. National Library of Australia MS 4058.

Most emigrating vessels included among their passengers a number of children. In fact on some of the earlier voyages there were significantly more children than adults (see also the discussion on children in Chapter 4). Following a large number of deaths on some of these early passages an inquiry recommended limiting the number of children, including excluding completely the very young. However, despite these regulations it was commonplace for large numbers of children and for pregnant women to undertake the passage to the colonies and for childbirth to take place. Advice was given to intending emigrants recommending against pregnant women undertaking the journey to the colonies.

One publication included in its hints for emigrants:

> *"No woman would be received on board who is so far advanced in pregnancy as to render it probable that she might be confined before termination on the voyage."*[175]

However, many pregnant women undertook the journey in the knowledge that childbirth would occur during a passage, which lasted 100 days or longer.

The birth of a child on land was a considerable risk at that time. Hence, the risks to mother and child on board ship at sea were increased considerably. Although midwives were not employed on board emigrant ships it was usual to find someone who had been present in a past confinement. For example, most of the wives of labourers and farm workers were as experienced and capable as anyone else to attend childbirth in those times. The surgeon would generally not be summoned unless there were problems.

When the surgeon was finally notified of a birth he would usually pay a visit to the mother and newborn child and may have ordered for the mother a bottle of porter (a style of dark beer like stout) or some other item from his medical store.

---

175. J B W. Emigration its Necessity and Advantages. 2nd Edition, London, 1841. p. 23.

Privacy during childbirth was not always easy to find in the steerage part of the vessel. This was usually achieved by draping a lower berth with old blankets or canvas. Weather permitting other passengers would be sent up on deck. Failing this they would be moved to one end of the accommodation. Frequently mothers of newborn children suffered from seasickness, which could be enormously debilitating and they thus had difficulty caring for and feeding the infant. It's also likely that many infants were delivered prematurely. There were also reports by surgeons of parents neglecting children by not providing adequate food or by refusing medication. Some emigrants were not familiar with medical treatment and had little experience with doctors and were suspicious of advice provided by the surgeon. The chance of survival for the newborn child at sea was apparently less than fifty-fifty.

Despite the hardship involved in the long passage to the colonies, including the health risks, it's interesting to observe that during the nineteenth century over ninety-eight per cent of assisted emigrants who boarded vessels at ports in the United Kingdom arrived in the colonies in reasonably good health ready to start a new life.[176] Clearly there were examples of passages to the colonies that involved high mortality rates because of an epidemic during the passage. While these passages are remembered because of the distress and horror associated with the very high death rates they were nonetheless very much the exception during nineteenth-century emigration to the colonies. A distressing aspect regarding the some two per cent that died at sea is that most of those who died were children. There seems to be consensus that the relatively low death rate on vessels that brought emigrants to Australia related to the concern for the safety, welfare and wellbeing of emigrants which was particularly evident from the beginning of assisted passage in 1831 and found expression in the tight regulations incorporated in the Passenger Acts.

Apart from coping with a variety of sailing conditions, ranging from the doldrums to the gales of the South Ocean, complying with the rules set by the Surgeon-Superintendent, including the ships routine set by the daily and weekly time table, the illness, seasickness, death and burials at sea and the occasional childbirth the passengers to Australia

---

176. Haines, Robin. Doctors at Sea. Palgrave Macmillan, 2005, p.7.

had a considerable amount of spare time on the long passage to the colonies. For many passengers this meant long periods of boredom and some captains recognised the need to encourage activities to occupy the attention of passengers. The passage of the **Superb** to Tasmania in 1879 incorporated the production of a newspaper, the *Superb Gazette*, which aided in creating a sense activity on board. The first issue recognised the need for amusement and indicated the start of a number of activities:

> *"To relieve the tedium and monotony, all kinds of amusements were talked of. To begin with, a choir for Sunday services has been organised..."*[177]

On many vessels the crew organised activities to occupy the passengers. This activity often coincided with traditions associated with sea travel. For example sailors 'buried the dead horse' to mark an era of returning prosperity having received their wages in advance before sailing:

> *"...The performance commenced at 7 pm, at which time the procession bringing the horse started from the fo'castle. The horse, a capital imitation of a full-grown animal, made of canvas and well-stuffed, was mounted, as if at full gallop, upon a cask lashed upon a ship's ladder. Its flowing mane and tail, and sparkling eyes, were perfection. Upon it was mounted one of the sailors (Hardbread), who bestowed his charger like a professional, and whose fantastic and cavalier dress came to full advantage... Everybody was, of course, on deck ... and when the horse arrived at the main mast, one of the sailors (Spence) officiated as auctioneer, putting the animal and trappings up to the highest bidder. A very animated and excited bidding followed ... it was knocked down to a gentleman ... for £ 3 5s ... the horse was bound and swung up to the end of the mainyard ... a number of blue lights and fireworks were burnt at different parts of the rigging. While the last light was still burning, the rider deftly cut away the lashing by which the horse was suspended, and amid*

---

177. Superb Gazette (W Barringer) June 1879 to November 1879. National Library of Australia Manuscript MS 1105.

loud hurrahs from the sailors, joined by everyone, the "dead horse" went plunging down into the seas, and was soon lost to view..." [178]

Another activity was an enactment of the arrival of Neptune on crossing the line:

"...Mr and Mrs Neptune came on board no carriage could be drawn but they were proceeded by four sailors in rope harness all four dressed up in sacking with big sheepskin tails driven by another with a red turban and shirt and high boots along with Mr Neptune came his Secretary, Doctor, Barber, Body Guard and one or two more all got up very well..." [179]

Montage of Emigrants Going to Australia
(National Library of Australia, Bib ID 1574674)

Women were encouraged to bring with them a supply of material to occupy themselves in making clothing during the voyage. On this point

---

178. ibid. p. 6. National Library of Australia Manuscript MS 1105.
179. EL. Diary kept on voyage to Adelaide on board the Hesperus 7 August to 31 October 1879. National Library of Australia Manuscript MS 4056.

Capper in his book, which was published to inform emigrants, said that a stock of material:

> "*would help dispel the sameness and languor consequently attending their passage to the country of their adoption*"[180]

Passengers were frequently forced to make up their own entertainment to relieve the boredom. Card playing was a popular pastime and could take place under most conditions during the passage. When weather was favourable passengers often attempted to catch fish or even dolphins. Encouraged by the sailors passengers also undertook bird 'fishing', using lines and hooks. A variety of birds followed the ships at various points during the passage to the colonies. The largest of those birds was the albatross, which could follow ships for weeks during the passage through the southern hemisphere. According to tradition it was bad luck to kill an albatross. However, many sailors ignored this and sought this big bird to make tobacco pouches from its big webbed feet and pipestems from leg bones. A passenger on board the **Clifton** in 1838 from Liverpool to Launceston reported:

> *'Friday 23rd February 1838*
>
> *We this day succeeded in catching an Albatross and when we hauled it on deck I was much surprised at it being so much larger than it appeared to be when on the wing - it measured 9 feet 6 inches from tip to tip of the Wings...*
>
> *Saturday 24 February 1838*
>
> *...We this day caught another Albatross which measured 10 feet from tip to tip...*"[181]

Passengers were encouraged to bring books for the passage. However, books were generally at a premium and occasionally the Surgeon-

---

180. Capper, Henry. South Australia. London, 1938, in Morgan, Dalma and Poole, Henry. Voyage of a Lifetime. Adelaide, 1978. p. 53.
181. Mr A. Voyage to Van Diemen's Land 1837-38. National Library of Australia, Manuscript MS 4058.

Superintendent had a small number, which were lent to selected passengers. On some passages the Bible was provided for the edification of passengers. In some instances there were also Bible studies or Bible classes. For many of the passengers reading was not an option because of illiteracy and for those with books reading conditions were in any case often difficult underdeck. Sometimes there were public readings of the popular books of the day.

In the case of some high-spirited passengers boredom sometimes led to conduct that earned a reprimand or worse, from those in charge. One such activity occasionally pursued by the younger men on these long voyages was to climb the ship's rigging. This was a practice strictly forbidden and quickly dealt with. Behaviour of this kind was witnessed on the **Marco Polo** voyage from Liverpool to Australia in 1854:

> *"The sailors of the ship have been doing a great stroke of business during the voyage, in consequence of the number of amateurs who mount the rigging, and relieve themselves from punishment usually inflicted for the offence by the payment of a fee to their capturers. If no payment is immediately made, the gentlemen are bound hand and foot to the rigging, which soon produces the desired effect."*[182]

On some vessels, where there were significant numbers of children, the Surgeon-Superintendent would appoint an appropriate person to teach reading, writing and basic arithmetic.

Where a vessel was fortunate enough to have among its passengers two or three musicians, then this generally meant that the passage would pass a little quicker because of the concerts and dances that would be organised upon deck. The organisation of these gatherings of course depended very much on the right weather.

There were also a number of songs composed for and by emigrants. Many were composed aboard the emigrant vessel as it sailed to foreign

---

182. Extract from a report in the *Marco Polo Chronicles* (a weekly journal produced during the 4th voyage to Australia, 29 July to 16 September 1854). National Library of Australia Manuscript MS 6174.

shores. Some of these songs and poems were laments about leaving home while others were happy, cheerful and optimistic about the anticipated opportunity and life in a new country. The Scots wrote a number of songs and poems about having to leave because of the clearances of crofters from the land. Likewise, in Ireland's rich tradition of music and song, emigration is one of the big themes. A large body of material exists, in English and Irish, both in Ireland itself and throughout the Irish diaspora.

On some passages the entertainment was well organised, particularly for the 'paying passengers'. Passengers on some passages delivered lectures; a popular subject at the time was temperance. Another activity to engage the passengers involved the formation of debating teams. There were also instances of special activities being organised during the voyage. They were usually reserved for first-class and possibly cabin-class passengers. For example, during an 1854 passage of the **Marco Polo,** a 'Grand Fancy Dress Ball' was organised for first-class passengers, complete with printed invitations and the decoration of the poop deck as the 'ball room'. However, for the bulk of passengers travelling steerage class, entertainment was generally much more mundane.

Some passengers used their free time writing letters and thinking about family and friends they had left behind. For a small number this also involved keeping a diary of the voyage; usually intended as a means of letting family and friends know the details of their experience during the passage. After many days at sea with only water in view the sight of another vessel was cause for excitement, as it broke the routine of the day and when the other vessel was travelling in the opposite direction there was a possibility that mail could be sent home. When the other vessel was travelling in the same direction there was nonetheless the possibility for an exchange of greetings and information. Conditions permitting there was sometimes an opportunity to visit the other vessel:

> "*Thursday 4 January 1838*
>
> *…The Brig we signalled yesterday still in sight and as the day was so calm the Quarter Boat was lowered down, and the Mate and*

several of the passengers boarded the Brig, which proved to be the Southampton from Plymouth to Lima out 35 days ..."[183]

A passage to the Australian colonies in the nineteenth century was in many respects not a predictable proposition. The passage involved embarkation on a journey involving a vessel that was small and uncomfortable, where there were considerable risks to passengers and crew, with weather that was unpredictable, where there were many unknowns, communications were primitive, the passage was long and at times boring, many would be seasick and/or ill and some would die. Despite these factors many departed the British Isles during the nineteenth century for the colonies. While some were apprehensive about the prospect of a long passage on a sailing vessel, others had mixed feelings about leaving home and there were those who were excited and enthusiastic about the prospect of an adventure and new life. However, it is clear that what lay ahead on the passage was largely a mystery to the majority of those who emigrated to the colonies in the nineteenth century. Most would have had some idea of how long the passage might take, possibly some idea that there might be a problem for some with sea-sickness and they may have known that the weather would be likely to be variable during the long passage. However, for most passengers this would have been their first sea voyage and hence the realities of life at sea in a nineteenth-century vessel would have been a complete mystery and hence much of what unfolded during the passage would have come as a surprise and possibly a shock. Some of the emigrants may have been depressed by what unfolded and in some cases it's not hard to imagine that some would have been traumatised by the experience and the events that took place.

Diarist William Howitt summarised his impressions of the passage for the some three hundred passengers that made the voyage to Australia on the **Kent** in 1852:

> *"Imagine 300 people, for the most part unaccustomed to the sea - imagine these people in their little crowded cabins overtaken [by] an earthquake, everything tossing and rolling around them,*

---

183. Mr A. Voyage to Van Diemen's Land 1837-38 on board the **Clifton**. National Library of Australia, Manuscript MS 4058.

tins, clothes, boxes and pots ... Overhead a thunder of waves, shouting, and bawling and shrieking as if the vessel was going down ... Imagine amid all this a mass of human beings thrown in unusual, weltering confusion, sick to death and no one capable of helping another."[184]

This story of a journey on board a nineteenth-century emigrant vessel, as told by Howitt, portrays a very bleak picture. While it is clear from what other emigrants have written there were those who found the experience to be more of an adventure with some ups and downs, there were nevertheless many emigrants (particularly those travelling steerage class) whose experience was similar to that described by Howitt. It's thus not difficult to conclude that for most of the nineteenth-century emigrants the desire to arrive (as soon as possible) would have been the thought uppermost in their minds.

---

184. Diary of William Howitt written in 1852 onboard the *Kent*. Quoted in Walker, Mary Howitt. Come Wind, Come Weather. A Biography of Alfred Howitt. Netley, South Australia 1971. p.26.

CHAPTER 8

Arriving

"..And on the coming morrow, we scan the misty dew
But could no land discover, no shore was yet in view
Till after anxious moments, at Noon it cleared away
And there towards the Westward the Sydney Headlands lay"[185]

As the emigrant ships neared their final destination excitement grew among the passengers. Word spread quickly on board these small vessels when land was near. Weather permitting, they would gather on the deck and peer into the distance hoping to glimpse a sight of land. The passengers on these emigrant ships had every right to be excited, after all they had survived a voyage of some 13,000 nautical miles, lasting many weeks, on board a small, cramped vessel. By this stage all on board, including the crew, were eager for the passage to end. This would also be their first sight of their new home, a place that for most emigrants was largely a mystery. For many it also signified a new start and hope of possible wealth and prosperity. Thus any sight of land, no matter how faint or how distant, would be significant. This search for land was frequently frustrated by poor visibility, which left passengers straining their eyes hoping for the sudden appearance of land. Following such a long and frequently hazardous passage, involving uncertainty, death, danger and discomfort, the sudden cry of land ahead would bring to the emigrants an overwhelming sense of happiness, relief and safety. Diarist Francis Taylor reported that the passengers on board the **Stag** were smitten by the first sight of land on their 1850 passage to Adelaide:

---

185. Hindmarsh, J H S. Scenes during a Passage from England to Australia. p. 26. National Library of Australia Manuscript MS 4156.

"12 o'clock Kangaroo Island about which there has been so much talk is at length seen but it requires every keen eye to discern it, as it appears like a dark spot arising out of the ocean. 2 o'clock we are now approached within about six miles of it, which is the nearest we shall be, it is surprising how we are all smitten by the sight of land ..."[186]

The Emigrants, 1852[187]
(National library of Australia, NK10873)

However, this sense of safety was often premature, as the sight of land did not mark the journey's end. The vessel had yet to navigate a safe passage along the long Australian coastline and into port, before the passage had concluded and disembarkation could take place.

Danger was an integral part of life on board a square-rigger as she negotiated the vast oceans, but it is ironic that the vessel was often in

---
186. Transcribed Diary of Francis Taylor in Limbrick, Doug. The Stag Diary. Passage to Colonial Adelaide 1850. Xlibris Corporation, 2012, p.107.
187. Illustrated London News, Musical Supplement. 19 June, 1852.

greatest danger when it had passed through the great storms and gales of the southern ocean and was within miles of its destination.

After safely navigating the long passage to the colonies, involving for many vessels the survival of extreme conditions of weather and enormous seas, avoiding icebergs, and coping with the imprecise nature of navigation equipment, it could be expected that the last few miles would surely be the simplest part of the passage. However, this was usually not the case and ships could easily founder in this final part of this long passage because of uncharted hazards, sketchy charting of the coastline, poor equipment and the nature of the sailing ships of that time, which were generally difficult to manoeuvre quickly under certain conditions. While the master would look for familiar landmarks, their appearance could sometimes signal new problems. The captain of these emigrant vessels had to sail along some of the most exposed and inhospitable coastline in the world. There were very few lighthouses or navigation aids along the 2500 miles of coast from Cape Leeuwin in Western Australia to Sydney in New South Wales. As a result a number of emigrant ships came to grief around the Australian coast.

There were many pitfalls for inexperienced shipmasters that could result in grief for a vessel along the Australian coast. Vessels were sometimes moved off course by the action of strong currents, which caused sideways drift. Even if the captain was aware of this he could never be sure of the exact extent of the movement. Large cliffs and curving coastline were a potential problem, testing the skill and judgement of the captain and crew. In these circumstances ships often found that they could only make headway by tacking (i.e. by sailing zigzag across a contrary wind). If the captain failed to tack then the vessel would be driven into the cliffs. Even when the vessel was tacked there was still a danger in miscalculating a tack and so coming too close to shore. This was easier to do if the shore curved. Thus a flaw in the wind, a slight miscalculation, a problem with equipment or a mistake by a crewmember could mean disaster.

There were a series of traps along the rugged southern coast. Ships that safely navigated Cape Leeuwin then had a relatively easy passage until arriving at Eyre Peninsula. This was followed by the rocky islands of Spencer Gulf, the long and difficult coast of Kangaroo Island and then the 200 miles of exposed beach stretching from the Murray mouth along the Coorong to Robe. A vessel driven into the sand barriers had little chance of surviving and the crew and passengers would be lucky to get to shore through the rollers breaking on the offshore shoals.

The confined waters, between the mainland and Tasmania were the most hazardous stretch along the whole coastline. The configuration of the land caused strong rips, the area is studded with islands surrounded by reefs and there are prevailing winds channelled through the funnel between the two landmasses. In addition there are very large cliffs running along the Victorian coast to Cape Otway and vessels had to manoeuvre close to them as they entered Bass Strait. To avoid this area many shipmasters heading for the east coast preferred to sail south of Tasmania. However, those heading for Portland, Melbourne or Launceston were forced to negotiate Bass Strait. Many ships came to grief on the rocks and reefs of King Island in the centre of the approaches to the narrow section of the strait. Between 1835 and 1877 twenty-three ships were wrecked on King Island, with a loss of more than 800 lives.

At the eastern end of Bass Strait, between Victoria and Tasmania, there lies the Furneaux Group of islands, rocks and shoals. This group includes 52 islands. The islands were named after British navigator Tobias Furneaux, who sighted the eastern side of them after leaving Adventure Bay (eastern side of Bruny Island, Tasmania, named by Furneaux after his vessel **HMS Adventure**) in 1773 on his way to New Zealand to re-join Captain James Cook. The largest islands in the group are Flinders Island, Cape Barren Island and Clark Island. This is an area associated with some 200 shipwrecks.

To add to these difficulties some unscrupulous shipowners overloaded and over-insured their vessels. Thus if a vessel came to grief the owners were amply compensated for the loss of the ship and the cargo. However, they did not have to account for the loss of life of crew or passengers.

In 1873 Samuel Plimsoll helped to rectify this by producing a booklet entitled: *Our Seamen*. A subsequent Royal Commission recommended action and in 1876 the Merchant Shipping Act was amended to require that a load line be painted on the side of every vessel. This line became known as the Plimsoll line. However, by this time the century was three quarters over and the era of the sailing ship as the major form of emigrant transport was starting its decline.

The state of navigational technology at that time meant that a captain would be unable to exactly plot the position of his ship. This often resulted in a vessel being several miles from its intended location. These few miles could be significant to the safety of the vessel. An example of the consequences of this can be found in the demise of the ***Dunbar*** on 20 August 1857, with the loss of 121 passengers and crew, as a result of the vessel being dashed into pieces within minutes against the cliffs at the base of the Gap, near South Head, at the entrance to Sydney Harbour. The vessel had departed England on 31 May and at about 11.30 pm on the 20 August the captain reckoned the ***Dunbar*** to be about six miles from land. However, she was only about two miles off shore. In extremely bad weather this was an understandable error. The error was compounded because the captain also believed that the vessel was immediately opposite the harbour entrance.

Ship *Dunbar*
(Brodie Collection, La Trobe Picture Collection State Library of Victoria)

In fact he was out in his estimate by about a mile and, as a consequence, within minutes breakers were observed straight ahead. The captain ordered the ship to be put hard a-port. However, the ship carried too little sail to respond and, with the wind and sea still setting her leeward, she struck about two minutes later. At once heavy seas began to pound the ship. Boats, bulwark, masts, passengers and crew were swept into the seething water as each wave struck and within minutes the ship had begun to disintegrate. There was only one survivor, James Johnson, who had found refuge on a ledge and was subsequently able to give precise details of what had occurred.

Even relatively large vessels came to grief on the Australia run. As reported in a previous chapter, the 1600 registered tons, **Schomberg**, ran aground on her maiden voyage on 26 December 1855, some thirty-five miles off Cape Otway in Western Victoria. On that occasion all 430 passengers were saved, due to the timely arrival of a steamer operating between Portland and Melbourne.

The difficulties that a captain had in quickly manoeuvring a square-rigger, of avoiding dangerous areas and of working against the forces of nature are illustrated in the demise of the **Loch Ard.** This was an example of a vessel, which by some combination of wind, sea and tide was driven remorselessly towards a lee shore. Vessels caught in this combination of conditions had no reserve of power to call upon, as would be the case with a steamer. An iron, three masted, 1693 tons, full-rigged ship, some 90 days out from Gravesend, sailing in conditions of poor visibility, the **Loch Ard** ran into trouble on 1 June 1878. When the haze lifted at about 4 am cliffs were visible about one nautical mile ahead. Readings taken the previous day in conditions of poor visibility were partly responsible for the navigational error that placed the vessel so close to the shore. The ship was sailing under just topsails, jib and spanker. The captain immediately ordered the sails set and attempted to go about. The vessel did not have enough weight to pass through the eye of the wind and slipped back to port with sails luffing. As a last desperate effort to save the ship the captain ordered the yards to be braced around to the port tack. However, there had only been time for the mainsail to be tacked when she struck the reef running out from Mutton Bird Island, off Cape Otway. Only two of the fifty-four on board survived. The other fifty-two **Loch Ard** passengers were the last emigrants to perish under sail on the Australia run.[188]

The demise of the **Loch Ard** was recorded in verse:

> *"Another victim of the ocean's spite,*
> *Loch Ard was wrecked and done for at the gorge*
> *Now named for her, short of Cape Otway's light*
> *Which saved her not; nor those, save two, on board."*[189]

The *Loch Ard* Sinking[190]
(State Library of Victoria)

There were many other shipping disasters and possibly the worst one in Australian maritime history was the loss of the ***Cataraqui*** in 1845. The ***Cataraqui*** set sail on 20 April 1845 bound for Port Phillip with 367 bounty passengers and 46 crew. The journey was uneventful until the vessel departed Cape Town when she was hit by gale-force winds and constant rain, which forced the passengers to remain below deck for several weeks. During this period six babies and young children died.

---

188. Castleton, Phillip. GEO. No. 14, Vol. 2, May-July 1992. p.82.
189. Smyth, Dacre. Emigrant Ships to Australia. 1992. p. 61.
190. Illustrated Australian News. 8 July 1878.

In early August the captain calculated that the vessel was only a short distance from the entrance to Port Phillip Bay. However, for two weeks he had been unable to make reliable readings because of the storms and the vessel was in fact some 100 miles south of Port Phillip. On the 4th August there was a lull in the storm and the captain decided to make for land. The chief officer, Thomas Guthrey, told the story of what occurred:

> "At half past 4, it being quite dark and raining hard, blowing a fearful gale, and the sea running mountains high, the ship struck a reef situate on the west coast of Kink Island... The scene of confusion and misery that ensued at this awful period it is impossible to describe. All the passengers attempted to rush on deck, and many succeeded in doing so, until the ladders were knocked away by the workings of the vessel ... As the day broke we found the stern of the vessel washed in, and numerous dead bodies floating around the ship - some hanging upon the rocks. Several of the passengers and crew (about two hundred altogether) were still holding onto the vessel - the sea breaking over, and every wave washing some of them away ...The buoy rope was then hauled on board to rig life lines and lash the survivors, who were then clinging to the wreck... Numerous died and fell overboard or sank, and were drowned at the places where they were lashed. As day broke the following morning it discovered only about thirty left alive - the survivors mostly dead through exhaustion and hanging where they were lashed. During the previous evening the quarter boat (the only remaining one) was attempted to be launched, into which the boatswain and doctor (Charles Carpenter) with four of the crew got, but she immediately capsized and al were drowned.
>
> ...The lashings of the survivors were now undone, in order to give them the last chance of life... [I] soon found it was impossible to live with such sea breaking over, sized a piece of plank under his arm, and leaping into the water, was carried over the reef, and thus got on shore."[191]

---

191. Sydney Morning Herald, Supplement, 27 September 1845.

Only nine people survived: one emigrant and eight crew. They were found on the island by a sealer who had also lost his boat in the storm. However, he was able to provide food and shelter until rescue arrived in the form of the cutter **Midge,** which took the survivors to Melbourne.

A number of convict ships also came to grief off the Australian coast. As a consequence, over 500 convicts perished as a result of shipwreck during the eighty years of transportation.

The last few miles of the passage often involved a mixture of emotions for the emigrants: excitement at being so near and yet frustration at the time taken to complete the last part of the passage. As a result of these mixed feelings tension often mounted, particularly if there were delays or apparent delays in bringing the passage to an end. At this time the difficulties of the journey, including the cramped conditions below deck, the smells, the tensions with close neighbours, the lack of fresh water and food and many other little problems would suddenly assume greater significance and almost become intolerable. While some vessels met bad weather in this last part of the passage others met light winds and so their progress was slow. The feelings of passengers experiencing these difficulties were captured by William Johnstone, on board the **Arab** in March 1842, as they neared their destination of Van Diemen's Land:

> "This was perhaps the most wretched part of the voyage - all had been looking forward to landing ere this that they were getting quite worn out with expectation - hope deferred sickening hearts in proportion etc, etc. When some weeks' sail from port a day's delay seems to be of no consequence, but with the wave worn traveller approaching so nearly his future home, the case is different - an hour's illness appears an age..."

Then notice the difference in reporting some four days later:

> "...At breakfast the Captain informed us that at about 10 (if his Chronometers were correct) we should first catch a glimpse of terra firma. As may be supposed all were on the qui vive - telescope was mounted and brought up and a lookout sent aloft. A few minutes before 11 we heard the Mate's joyful cry 'Land ahead

on the Larboard Bow', and true enough a dim mist could just be discerned rising out of the water in the distance - the old boy was quite cranky with delight. Another hour and the coast was quite distinct. The Capt frisked about the deck and rubbed his hands with all the glee of a schoolboy returning home for the holidays - 'Ah sir', he said to me, 'what a wonderful science is navigation. To think of having come 20,000 miles over the trackless ocean and yet to be enabled to name an hour and almost to the minute when we should again discover land, is indeed most astounding'..."[192]

One cannot help but wonder about the captain's comments and think that no matter how good his navigational skills might have been, that the precision he boasted was not possible at that time given the state of navigation equipment, the charts and the vessels in 1842 and the safe arrival involved a considerable measure of luck. It is also worth noting that the ***Arab*** was only a small vessel of 300 tons.

For those emigrants that arrived safely there was considerable excitement and so passengers crowded on deck hoping for the first glimpse of their new home. It seems from many accounts of emigrant arrivals that for most the first view brought a positive response. The excitement of that first sight of land was captured in 1842 by a diarist on board the ***Caledonia***:

"Sunday 7th. Fair wind - showery day - passed Cape ... at entrance of Bass's Straits about 8 o'clock in the morning - every body's countenance radiant with smiles as they watched the approach of land."[193]

It appears that colonial governors were equally curious, as seen from the record of arrival of the first governor of the new colony of South Australia, Captain John Hindmarsh. In his case they had been at sea for nearly six months, arriving just before Christmas Day in 1836. Their vessel, the ***Buffalo***, came to anchor in Holdfast Bay, due west of Mount Lofty, and

---

192. Cited in Greenhill, Basil and Giffard, Ann. Women Under Sail. Newton Abbott, Great Britain, 1970. pp. 90-91.

193. Meade, Susan. Journal of journey to Melbourne on board the *Caledonia*, 12 April to 10 August, 1842. National Library of Australia, Manuscript MS 4053.

about thirteen miles to the southward of the intended harbour. Hindmarsh's nephew, HT Morris, recorded his first impressions some years later:

> *"I remember my uncle saying to me: 'Harry, run up the main rigging and tell me what you think of the country'. I went up obediently and had a good look. When I came down, I told him ashore it looked quite like the Old Country. It looked as if it were covered with wheat fields, whose fences were dark shadows made by gullies in the hills."*[194]

I suspect that many of the new emigrants hoped that their first sight of their new country would reveal a land much like the one they left behind. Clearly for some the landscape was a wonderful sight and for others it was a disappointment. An 1842 emigrant sailing on the **Mona** made the following observation about the new country:

> *"Tuesday 17 October*
>
> *This morning at six o'clock we entered the River Tamar. Between 7 and 8 Mr Dryburgh Custom House Officer at George Town came on board... The sail up we enjoyed much. The beauties of the scenery formed a fertile topic of conversation reminding us as they did of our Native land of mountains and flora. The principal drawback we found to be the sombre hue of the trees..."*[195]

An 1842 passenger on the **Caledonia** was even more overcome with praise for the new country:

> *"Wednesday 10 August - Fine day - all bustle to leave the Caledonia - About 10 o'clock got on board the Governor Arthur Steamer to proceed on our way to Melbourne 9 miles up the Yarra Yarra - This is the most beautiful river I have ever seen, even the winding graceful Wye with all its natural attractions sinks into insignificance compared with it - As the*

---

194. Vincent, Mary. Sunny South Australia. Adelaide, 1908. Cited in Hindmarsh, F. Stewart. From Powder Monkey to Governor. Northbridge, W.A., 1995. p. 102.

195. Wood. Journal of voyage from London to Launceston on the *Mona*, 1843. National Library of Australia, Manuscript MS 9113.

bay disappeared I became transfixed with admiration for the transcendent beauty of this highly favoured land - No language can convey a correct idea of its loveliness ..."[196]

Not all passengers were impressed by what they first saw on arrival. A diarist on arriving at Holdfast Bay on a passage to Adelaide commented:

"February 5

All morning sailing near Kangaroo Island. At 1 in the afternoon in Holdfast Bay four miles from shore. Dismay and disappointment at the dreary, melancholy appearance of the place, threw a great damp on our arrival. Some passengers wept bitterly."

However, the impression and hence the mood changed on approaching the Port:

"At noon a Pilot came on board but the tide did not serve for going up the river so we had to wait till three in the afternoon. We could just clear the bar. It was an anxious moment. As soon as we entered the face of the country was indeed changed. Beautiful green trees and shrubs with mountains behind were seen on both sides. We had to beat up the river. Sometimes we were nearly amongst the shrubs. It is really a beautiful sail."[197]

Having reached the safety of harbour it was not uncommon, at least from the 1840s onward, for emigrants to see many vessels at anchor. For example, by 1840 there could be up to 100 vessels riding at anchor in Sydney Harbour. Some would be unloading cargo, while others would be loading in preparation for the return passage. Vessels were often in port for several months undergoing a refit and repairs to damage caused on the outward passage. This was usually a period of rest, recreation and recovery for the crew in preparation for the return. However for the captain it was often time to think about the return passage. It was important for

---

196. Meade, Susan. Journal of voyage to Melbourne on board the *Caledonia*, April 12 to August 10, 1842. National Library of Australia, Manuscript MS 4053.
197. Archer, Elizabeth. Diary kept during a voyage from Gravesend to Adelaide 1839-40. Transcribed by Main, Jean. The Barque John.

economic reasons for the vessel to return to the homeport with as much cargo as possible. Often the master was responsible for ensuring that the vessel had a return cargo. Some masters were sold a small share in the vessel as an incentive to try to maximise the profit generated by the vessel. In the Australian context freight was often a highly seasonal commodity. This sometimes meant that vessels sought employment in the coastal trade or made short runs to Cape Town, Singapore or Mauritius while waiting for a cargo back to the United Kingdom or Europe. For example those able to take a cargo to Mauritius could usually be assured of a return cargo to the colonies of sugar and molasses.

Once the vessel had arrived safely the ship-weary emigrant eager to disembark as quickly as possible was forced to remain on board until clearance was provided by the government officials. The vessel had to pass through customs and health inspection. On some occasions this process did not take place immediately and passengers could be forced to remain on board for several days. For some emigrants safe arrival and good treatment during the passage was reason for thanks. It was not uncommon for passengers to publicly announce this and give thanks to the captain in the local press. An example of this is the following announcement to the people of Melbourne:

> *"**SHIP NUGGET, Port Phillip, October, 1855**. To Captain James Renton - Dear Sir. Having now arrived at our destination we wish, before leaving the ship, to express our thanks to you for your kindness to us during the voyage. It is with feelings of gratitude we remember that you have at all times been ready to promote our amusements, attend to our grievances, or join our conversations and comfort, and attend those amongst us who have been temporarily ill. Your name, therefore, and, let us add, the names of your officers, will always be associated in our minds with pleasing recollections; and if any of us should ever have occasion again to cross the seas and the opportunity offered to sail with you, we should be well pleased to avail ourselves of it.*
>
> *That you may have a pleasant voyage back to England, and that success may attend you wherever you go, and in whatever you undertake, is the sincere wish of*

Dear Sir, your faithful friends,
    E.S. Andrews
    Geo. W Bartholomew
    Silvester Butler
    John Floates (for self, wife and family)
    G. Ellis (for self and wife)
    E. Esquilant (for self and wife)
    Luke Gray
    George Harrison (for self and wife)
    William Howatt
    A.H. Lewis
    Eliza Rees
    Ellen Rees
    John Sawden
    Joseph Tarrant (for self and wife)
    Angela Taverner
    G.R. Tibbits
    Frank Ritton (for self and wife)
    Henry G. Ainslie Young."[198]

Some passengers were moved to mark their arrival in verse like passenger JHS Hindmarsh after arriving safely on board the ***Havering*** in February 1852:

"And now with in Port Jackson, our Ship at anchor lays
After a prosperous Passage, a run of Ninety days -
And now our journey, ended to all we bid adieu
Our Voyage; our noble Vessel, the Scenes she's brought us through
And oft shall we with pleasure when years have rolled away
Recall our prosperous journey the Scenes upon its way
The bright days, clad in beauty the Storms arrayed in might
Shall live, within remembrance, be dear to Memory's sight."[199]

Disembarking after a safe arrival was not always an easy process, particularly in the early part of the century. In most places the port

---

198. Melbourne Argus. 6 October, 1855.
199. Hindmarsh J H S. Scenes During a Passage from England to Australia 1851-52. National Library of Australia, Manuscript MS 4156.

facilities were very rudimentary and passengers were sometimes taken to shore in small boats, with the last part of the journey being made by foot or, alternatively, on someone's back or in the arms of several sailors. This type of landing was recorded in verse by Charles Newman, founder of the township of Charleston in South Australia. He recorded his experience of landing thus:

> *"No wharf or jetty could be seen*
> *Along that desert strand;*
> *The tents were few and far between*
> *Among those hills of sand.*
>
> *The men, with wives upon their backs*
> *Made for the distant shore,*
> *Like donkeys with their heavy packs*
> *I'd often seen before."*[200]

Landing Passengers from Immigrant Ship *Jerusalem*
(State Library of Victoria)

---

200. Newman, Charles. Cited in Parsons, Ronald. Port Misery and New Port. Magill, S.A., 1982. p.269.

For other emigrants the trip to land was made by boat but the vessel had to be shared with some of the four-legged passengers:

"February 10

This afternoon I was lowered into a lighter containing the Bull, Cow, three Rams, Susan's and my cabin goods, James, John [Harris], George Clark, Mr Lyons [an ordinary seaman] and Susan completed the load. We were towed up to the Port by small boat. It was therefore some time ere we reached the landing place. We all assisted in getting the goods on shore with much difficulty..."[201]

In some instances the tide was deployed to float luggage and cargo to shore. This method was used to aid in unloading the **Brightman** after she arrived in Holdfast Bay, South Australia, in December 1840. The passengers also experienced a strange and frightening event while awaiting disembarkation as the following account reveals:

"From the time of anchoring to the time of departure from the ship, there was a delay of seven days for some passengers. Boats transported the passengers and their luggage to land. Many floatable articles, such as wooden framed houses manufactured and packed in England for immediate erection on landing in Australia, were simply tossed overboard and then tided into shore. All this took time and meant a long and tedious wait for many passengers. When not concerned with the activity going on around them, those on board found themselves preoccupied with thoughts of what awaited them beyond the shores amid dense forest of trees and scrub with surrounding hills in the background. As it was they could see hundreds of natives moving along the shoreline. More than once they had been startled by noise of a corroboree; one of which had been followed by fierce fighting resulting in many naked warriors being speared to death. Even at a distance it

---

201. Archer, Elizabeth. Diary kept on voyage from Gravesend to Adelaide. As transcribed by Main, Jean. *The Barque John*. A Voyage to the Land of Hope 1939/40. Aranda, ACT, 1994. pp. 59-60.

was somewhat frightening, but still more unnerving had been the screaming and yelling of the lubras as they mourned their dead."[202]

Having successfully negotiated all arrival formalities and overcome any landing problems most emigrants were keen to experience as quickly as possible the comforts of life on land:

"Tuesday 23rd September

At about 8.30 pm we cast anchor about two miles off Sandridge pier and several boats rowed out to us to take any of us ashore as might like to go. Fred Martin, myself and one other passenger named W. A. Gordon, were the only ones who availed themselves of the opportunity the remainder preferring to remain on board until next morning... We all went ashore together at Sandridge Railway Pier and proceeded by train to Melbourne a distance of 3 miles. I went straight to the White Hart Hotel where after indulging in roast beef and salad (two luxuries after a long voyage) I turned into a bed for the first time for fourteen weeks.

Wednesday September 24th

...had another experience of the blessings of Terra Firma in the shape of a new laid eggs for breakfast, then repaired to the Post Office ..."[203]

The locals, at least in the first part of the century, did not always greet arriving free emigrants warmly. Many emancipists regarded free emigrants as intruders and told them so. On arrival as an emigrant in 1825 Alexander Harris recalls being called "one of the free objects - bad luck to 'em! What business have they here in the prisoners' country?"[204]

---

202. Hannaford, Ronda. Susannah Hannaford and Her Family. Gumeracha, South Australia. 1988. p 20.
203. Barringer, William. Diary of Voyage to Victoria and Tasmania on Board the *Superb* 4 July to 6 November 1879. National Library of Australia, Manuscript MS 1105.
204. An Emigrant Mechanic (Harris, A). Settlers and Convicts or Recollections of Sixteen Years Labour in the Australian Backwoods. Melbourne, 1833. p. 34.

A shipload of artisans from Scotland reached Sydney in 1831 and as they passed along the streets they heard from almost every cottage they passed: "There are these bloody emigrants come to take the country from us".[205]

The emancipists felt that they had built Australia. They had done the hard work and now the assisted immigrants were benefiting from their labours. This is reflected in the following poem:

> *"I was a convict*
> *Sent to hell,*
> *To make in the desert*
> *The living well:*
>
> *I split the rock,*
> *I felled the tree –*
> *The nation was*
> *Because of me"* [206]

For some the reception on landing involved more than a few remarks and included threats and some attempts at intimidation. This was to be the experience of a large number of free female emigrants who were landed in Hobart in August 1834 from the **Strathfieldsaye.** *The Colonial Times* provided a graphic account of their disembarkation and reception:

> *"On Saturday, the free females were landed from the Strathfieldsaye. Of all the disgusting, abominable sights we ever witnessed, nothing ever equalled the scene which took place on that occasion. It is well known that the females of the Strathfieldsaye, are of a superior order to those hitherto sent us by the Home Government - poverty being the greatest crime of the greatest part of the number... Early on Saturday morning, it was known all over the Town, that the free women were to be landed at mid-day. The Strathfieldsaye was bedecked with all the colours on board, and great was preparation. About eleven o'clock, some were stowed in one of the ship's boats, and then another boat went alongside, and was filled - and others followed in succession. Those that had first left the vessel, had to remain on the water*

---

205. ibid.
206. Gilmore, Mary. Old Botany Bay. 1918.

upwards of an hour, before all the boats were stowed, when they were all towed together towards the New Jetty. At this time the mob waiting to witness the landing of the women, could not be less in number than a couple of thousand. As soon as the first boat reached the shore, there was a regular rush towards the spot, and the half dozen constables present, could scarcely open a passage, sufficient to allow the females to pass from the boats; and now the most unheard of, disgusting scene ensured - the avenue opened through the crowd a considerable length, and as each female passed on, she was jeered by the blackguards who stationed themselves, as it were, purposely to insult. The most vile brutal language was addressed to every woman as she passed along - some brutes, more brutal than others, even took still further insulting liberties, and stopped the women by force, and addressed them, pointedly, in the most obscene manner. Any women, with one spark of the feeling of modesty, must have felt this degradation of the most terrible kind, and the consequence was, that by far the greater portion could bear the insults no longer - scarcely a female was there, but who wept, and that most bitterly; but this again, was made the subject of mirth, by the brutes who were present. One of the poor creatures was so overcome, that she absolutely fainted - but there was no hand to assist - no one present who appeared to have any power in preventing these disgraceful scenes. After the females had passed through the long passage, the ordeal was not over; for men singled out the girls they fancied, and went in pursuit of them, annoying them, till they arrived at the door of the house, wherein these friendless beings were to find security... During the whole night, the neighbourhood was in complete confusion - the most disorderly scenes were witnessed - men were seen pestering the purlieus of the place. Nor did the Sabbath allow a peaceable moment - on the contrary, during the whole Sunday, a mob, somewhat similar to that seen the day before at the New Jetty, surrounded the house - scarcely could a girl stir herself, but the most obscene language was addressed to her. Those who strolled about Town, shared no better fate, for at every step, and at every turning, knots of blackguards were assembled, whose only pleasure seemed to be, in trying to be more disgusting in their conversation then their companions... Contrast the landing of these free females, with the landing of three hundred and twenty convicts at the same morning. At seven the prisoners were landed - they were in an orderly manner marched up to the prisoners' barracks. They were immediately supplied with rations - their clothing was good. His Excellency arrived and addressed them at considerable length. Sleeping births were provided - they received no insult. We cannot conclude these remarks, without repeating, that the whole affair was improperly managed, and no one can say, what misery and distress may ensue in consequence..."[207]

The very hostile reception given to these female emigrants was rather surprising considering the glowing announcement of their arrival that was also carried in the *Colonial Times*:

"Since our last, the Strathfieldsaye, has arrived with the best of all cargoes, if properly selected - free females. The character of the females by this vessel, are of the best description, and we consider the arrival as a valuable acquisition to the Colony..."[208]

It's interesting to note that there were many in Britain who believed that the children of the first free settlers and the convicts would become criminals. They were after all destined to be abandoned by their parents or raised amongst scenes of debauchery and criminal activity. In fact research into the first-born Australians (of both emigrants and convicts) has shown the opposite to be the case. Words such as: 'sober, law abiding, industrious and honest' have been used by researchers to describe these men and women.[209] Thus life in New South Wales at that time contrasted markedly with life in British society where the factories were exploiting children. It seems that the parents of this first generation (known as Currency children) were interested in having their children acquire some skills and an education. Many of these children moved beyond Sydney to explore and settle in other parts of New South Wales. It's also possible that this was a reason for hostility shown to some of the early emigrants.

The convicts developed in the early years a number of pejorative terms that they used when referring to emigrants. Initially there was use of a rhyming term for emigrants: Jemmy Grants. This was progressively shortened to

---

207. *The Colonial Times.* 19 August, 1834.
208. ibid.
209. Robinson, Potia. The Hatch and Brood Times.

Jemmy and later Jimmy. The new arrivals were also referred to as 'new chums'. This was a derogatory term in use by 1840, meaning the newly arrived free man was ignorant and incompetent compared to the old hand. It's clear that in the first half of the century there was disagreement between the colonists and the authorities in England about the type of immigrant that the colonists wanted and the emigrants being selected and encouraged to emigrate by the Colonial Office and Land Board. Despite several reviews and changes in the processes and selection arrangements the differences were never fully resolved. Even though many emigrants arrived with skills and professional qualifications and extensive experience the colonists frequently felt they were inappropriate and didn't match what was required in the colonies. These disagreements were frequently a topic of discussion in the colonial newspapers, which inevitably took the same viewpoint as the colonists (who often had considerable influence) and criticised those arriving by assisted passage. This is another reason to explain hostility that may have been shown to the new arrivals.

However, it seems that by about the middle of the nineteenth century the feelings of differences between the emancipist and colonists and the emigrants had largely passed. By this time there were other issues more important to the affairs of the colonies and to the future of all people in the colonies. In these matters the two groups found common ground.

The feelings of resentment on the part of the emancipists were largely understandable given the circumstances under which the colonies were conceived and settled. In addition, the free emigrants were only a small minority in the early years of emigration. For example, in 1828 the census found that in a population of 36,598 in New South Wales there were less than 5000 people who had come to the colony voluntarily.[210] However, as the British assisted emigration and colonial immigration schemes took effect the balance began to change and Australia became the country of the emigrants as well as of the prisoners.

For some new arrivals there was a friendly face and a welcome because family or friends were already in the colonies. Even for bounty immigrants brought to the colonies by an employer there was potentially someone interested in their arrival. However, for many there would have

---

210. Madgwick, R B. Immigration into Eastern Australia 1788-1851. Sydney, 1969. p. 65.

been a dreadful feeling of loneliness, intensified by uncertainty about what lay ahead. Ellen Ollard expressed this feeling of being alone rather graphically in her letter to a friend describing her arrival in Melbourne on the **Shannon** on 1 November 1874:

"The voyage was a very pleasant one and I need hardly tell you that I was very sorry when it came to an end, and I found myself for the first time in my life at the mercy of strangers.

We anchored in the Bay on Saturday on 1st of November at about half past one in the afternoon and, never while I live, shall I forget the feeling of despair that took possession of me when I saw everyone on board talking to their friends who had come to meet them. Miss Davis (my cabin companion) came out to be married and her intended husband took her away in a little yacht and Mrs Thompson, the only remaining lady, went away in the Steamer with her husband and, of course, all the gentlemen got away as soon as they could and I was left to indulge my grief and to wonder what would become of me in this strange land ..."[211]

For some emigrants the embarkation process had not been without difficulty because of those who frequented the British emigration ports and made it their business to prey on the unsuspecting emigrant. These practices were not entirely peculiar to the home country for there were some in the colonies that were equally happy to separate the new emigrant from any spare funds. This sometimes occurred on arrival because some vessels did not sail right into harbour, but dropped anchor outside. Dishonest captains were not averse to entering into an arrangement with a local ferryboat operator. The boatman, having a monopoly to ferry the passengers ashore, was able to charge a high price, from which the captain would expect his commission. Because the port facilities were often located some distance from the city there were opportunities to exploit the new arrivals, by charging high prices to transport the emigrants and their belongings.

One young arrival, Richard Harris, wrote to his family in 1853 about his experience on landing:

---

211. Clarke, Patricia. The Governesses Letters From the Colonies 1862-1882. Hawthorn, Victoria, 1985. p. 47.

Arriving

"*Melbourne, February 9th 1853*

My Dear Parents

...Having my boxes all ready to land I was one of the first to come ashore with four Cornish men. We came on shore in the boat belonging to the ship, and landed at Lahardy's beach, a mile and a half from town. The next thing to be considered was, what to do with our luggage. We agreed for a week to erect a tent for 2s 6d, and on Monday I sold the two small boxes and packed all my things, with a few exceptions, in my carpet bag. The large one I was obliged to put in store at 1s 6d per week. Luggage is the worst thing to be encumbered with. Had I again come I would not take more than two carpet bags and what I could take on my back. It cost 10s to take my boxes about a mile, and that was considered cheap. Any coming from England think it a great price ..."[212]

Emigrants Landing at Queen's Wharf Melbourne, 1861 by Frederick Grosse
(National Library of Australia, Bib ID: 422154)

---

212. Grant, Alison. Sailing Ships and Emigrants in Victorian Times. London, 1872. p. 54.

The high cost of transport was not only an example of exploitation of new arrivals but also a reflection of the cost differential between Britain and the colonies. The cost of goods and services in the colonies were higher than at home but wages were also much higher in the colonies. These differences in cost and wage structure were, of course, a disadvantage to the new arrivals, particularly to the majority of steerage passengers who would have arrived with little or no funds in hand.

After the gold rush commenced in the 1850s the newly arrived passenger sought news of the goldfields. The pilots would frequently bring local newspapers on board and passengers eagerly seized them. As the men realised that they would require funds to get to the goldfields they would tumble their belongings out on deck and offer clothes and tools to the highest bidder. Even before the gold rush it was not uncommon to see newly arrived emigrants selling some of their possessions either because they were overloaded or needed the cash.

Despite having city status most of the colonial ports were little more than frontier towns during the first half of the century and into the second half. The new arrivals frequently placed a strain on existing resources. There was, for example, at times insufficient housing and so many had to shelter under canvas. For example in the early 1840s in Melbourne there were as many as 2000 people living in tents at any one time. Even when accommodation was available it was of a poor quality. A Melbourne barrister, Redmond Barry, claimed in July 1842 that large families were "at present crowded into ill-drained, ill-ventilated and unwholesome alleys of Melbourne paying high rents and high prices for fuel and water".[213]

Assistance to the newly arrived emigrant was problematic and at first non-existent. Because of the lack of appropriate and affordable accommodation for many newly arrived emigrants some ports progressively developed special accommodation to house the new arrivals. The *London Times* reported in an article on 'Emigration to Australia' on 16 June 1869:

---

213. Cited in Broome, Richard. The Victorians. Arriving. McMahons Point, N S W, 1984. p. 57.

> "We have here in Melbourne an 'Emigrants' Home', a Government establishment in which new arrivals without means are provided for until they can obtain employment... I have known several hundreds of newly-arrived immigrants engaged from this place in a few hours."

The gender imbalance in the colonies had been of concern to the locals as well as those in Britain from the early part of the century. Special efforts (described elsewhere in this book) were made to correct the imbalance by increasing the number of single women emigrating to the colonies. From the start of free settlement women were in danger of exploitation and abuse on arrival in the colonies. The absence of sound practices for the safe arrival and settlement of women appalled Caroline Chisholm and caused her to intervene to improve these arrangements. She developed the practice of meeting every shipload of emigrants in order to try and protect single women against abuse that was common in the early part of the century.

In 1841 she put forward to Lady Gipps (wife of the Governor of New South Wales) her idea to raise money for a girls' home in which immigrant girls would receive protection in the period between disembarkation and taking up employment. The public responded to her appeals and donated food and money. By the end of that year she had accommodation for ninety in her Immigrants' Home. She also developed a register of employment. Hundreds of single girls were protected by her and placed in situations where they earned good wages and generally got married instead of ending on the street.

In a letter to Lord Stanley (Secretary for War and the Colonies) in August 1842 Caroline Chisholm wrote about the success of the new arrangements to assists women on arrival:

> "...Soon after the opening of the Sydney Home, I received sixty-four girls from ships then in the harbour, and all the money they had amounted to fourteen shillings and three farthings; twenty two had no money; several two pence; others four pence. These

girls I sent into the country. The majority are married, and not one lost her character... "[214]

Organisations also developed in the other colonies to assist passengers on arrival. In South Australia there was a Benevolent and Strangers' Friend Society administering relief to the needy and promoting moral and spiritual welfare to newly arrived immigrants. There was also a Colonial Labour Committee, which assumed the responsibility of finding employment for members of both gender. The female emigrants landing in Melbourne were also assisted by the Ladies' Female Immigration Society, presided over by the head of the Anglican Church.

At certain times, particularly during periods of colonial depression and when large numbers were arriving in the colonies, it was difficult to find employment. As a result of these problems colonial governments were forced to periodically provide work for immigrants. This marked the start of some public works programs. While there was plenty of employment in the rural or country areas many declined to leave the cities, despite their rural backgrounds and agricultural skills. There were instances of colonial governments attempting to force immigrants to leave the cities and move to 'the bush' by ceasing to provide relief. Some declared that they would rather be hanged than move to the less populous country areas of the colonies. It seems that from the earliest times, despite the abundant mythology surrounding bush life, Australians have generally preferred urban living regardless of their background prior to emigration.

It is clear that for some emigrants who arrived in the nineteenth century the period after arrival was difficult. However, if you exclude personal misfortunes and improvident behaviour, the conditions for the majority of those who arrived as steerage passengers, particularly the working class, were considerably better than at home. Many achieved a degree of prosperity that would have been impossible at home.

---

214. Extract from a letter by Caroline Chisholm to Lord Stanley, August 1842. Quoted in Sidney, Samuel. Female Emigration; As it is, as it may be. A letter to his Hon. Sidney Herbert MP. London, 1850. p.41.

Despite setbacks and hardships in a new country these nineteenth-century emigrants, these special people; these pioneers carved out a new life and during the course of the century progressively shaped a new country.

Queens Wharf, Melbourne 1850's, by artist S T Gill
(State Library of Victoria)

It's clear from the diaries and letters of early emigrants that they hoped the new country would look like the place they had left behind. This would seem to be a natural wish as some kind of familiarity would be extremely important after the trauma of leaving home and family and surviving a long and difficult passage to the colonies. There is evidence from the diaries and letters that the first impressions for most emigrants were positive and were reminiscent of the home country. It's possible that this first impression was coloured by a strong desire for it to be that way, or possibly it was the relief of surviving the long sea passage and the sight of any land would appear to be wonderful. However, it is clear from comments made by early explorers and colonists that the land, at least in many parts, had an appearance which resembled the homeland. For example, explorer Charles Sturt commented:

> *"In many places the trees are so sparingly, and I had almost said judiciously distributed as to resemble the park lands attached to a gentleman's residence in England"*[215]

Bill Gammage undertook an enormous amount of research for his book, *The Biggest Estate on Earth*, which involved examining a vast collection of written material by colonists and explorers, and of pictorial material of the colonies at 1788 and in the early years of colonisation. While his work has been directed at describing how the Aboriginal people of Australia "managed their land in 1788" and how "this was possible, what they did and why"[216] his work describes a landscape that in 1788 and in the early years of colonisation would have certainly looked familiar to the early emigrants (complete with rolling hills, open green areas and open woodlands unencumbered by undergrowth). However, this vast continent contained many surprises for the newcomer and progressively changed as English land-management practices spread.

It's difficult to know if the nineteenth-century emigrants came to understand, appreciate and love their new country, particularly its differences. Even with those similarities to the home country, which may have appeared on first sight, there were nonetheless many differences. Some of those differences in climate, geography, fauna and flora were very significant. While the emigrants may have struggles with some of the differences inherent in this new country it is clear that their children readily identified with Australia.

There is plenty of evidence from letters, diaries, newspapers, etc. to indicate that many of the emigrants felt the climate to be superior and healthier than the old country. For example, Watkin Tench, in his writings about the colony of New South Wales, made a number of favourable comments about the climate summarising his views as follows:

> *"To sum up: ... I will venture to assert in a few words that no climate hitherto known is more generally salubrious, or affords more days on which those pleasures which depend on the state of*

---
215. Sturt, C. Narrative of an Expedition into Central Australia 1849. 2 vols. Adelaide, 1965 p.230.
216. Gammage, Bill. The Biggest Estate on Earth. Allen & Unwin, 2012, p.1.

the atmosphere can be enjoyed, than that of New South Wales. The winter season is particularly delightful.

He went further by adding a footnote:

"To this cause, I ascribe the great number of births which happened, considering the age and circumstances of many of the mothers. Women who certainly would never have bred in any other climate here produced as fine children as ever were born."[217]

However while there are many instances of praise for the benefits of the climate found in the colonies there are also records of tragedy and disappointment resulting from the extremes that came with the climate including droughts, floods and bushfires. Many of these events would particularly be experienced by settlers who moved further away from the major cities and into the rural areas. The emigrants would in time also understand the vastness of the country compared with the home country.

In addition to the differences in landscape and climate there were other differences that would have involved the emigrant in making further adjustments. By 1830 England was highly industrialised, with the population concentrated in towns and in closely settled rural communities. At this time the colonies were by comparison primitive, agricultural and pastoral with settlements and towns being rather frontier in nature. Many of the emigrants came with skills and trades that were not suited to the state of development in the colonies and so had to adjust to new employment requirements. These differences, however, offered opportunities, adventures and new experiences that were embraced by many emigrants. Although the colonies often criticised the quality of those who arrived, particularly before 1850, it's clear that the majority of the arrivals came with a willingness to work and contribute. Madgwick concludes that, despite criticism by the colonies of the types of people arriving, there is no doubting their 'economic quality'.[218]

---

217. Tench, Watkin. A Complete Account of the Settlement of Port Jackson in 1788. Flannery, Tim ed. The Text Publishing Company, 1996, p.235.
218. Madgwick, R.B. Immigration into Eastern Australia 1788-1851. Sydney University Press, 1968, p.251.

While those who came after 1850 as part of the gold rush brought a zeal for social, political and economic reform, there is no doubting the substantial contribution made by emigrants in the first half of the century by laying a foundation which could withstand the significant change and development that took place in the second fifty years. The nineteenth-century arrivals had to learn and adapt, often through hard-gained experience, what this new environment demanded. It would seem that conditions for a smooth transition by the emigrants from an advanced industrial society to an agricultural colonial society were not ideal. Many adjustments would have been required on the part of the emigrants. It's clear that those adjustments were made and through hard work hopes and aspirations were fulfilled. Those people prepared to make the changes and work hard under difficult and probably strange conditions were the nineteenth-century pioneers. It's clear that they were the risk-takers compared to their peers who stayed at home. Their letters and diaries show a determination to find a new life, which included attaining the goals they had set for themselves to achieve in this new land.

Dorothea Mackellar's poem, *'Core of My Heart'*, written about 1904, compared English and Australian landscapes. She wrote the poem while homesick in England. First published in the London *Spectator* in 1908, it was reprinted in the *Sydney Mail* as *'My Country'*. Mackellar was a third generation Australian, her grandparents having arrived in Sydney from Scotland in 1839. Although raised as part of a professional urban family her poetry is usually regarded as quintessential bush poetry, inspired by her experience on her brother's farms near Gunnedah, New South Wales. While the poem contained six verses the following two have become the best known and may well depict the country that many of the nineteenth-century emigrants and their children gradually came to know and possibly to love; a country so very different in many ways to the home country.

I love a sunburnt country,
A land of sweeping plains,
Of rugged mountain ranges,
Of droughts and flooding rains.
I love her far horizons,
I love her jewel-sea,

Arriving

Her beauty and her terra -
The wide brown land for me.

An opal-hearted country,
A wilful, lavish land -
All you who have not loved her,
You will not understand.
Though Earth holds many splendours,
Wherever I may die,
I know to that brown country
My loving thoughts will fly.

APPENDIX A

Calendar of Key Nineteenth-Century Events

1787	May 13	First Fleet of 11 ships sailed from Plymouth.
1788	Jan 7	First Fleet sight Tasmania (Van Diemen's Land).
	Jan 18	Captain Arthur Phillip, aboard **HMS Supply**, anchored in Botany Bay (remainder arrived 2 days later).
	Jan 26	First Fleet anchored in Port Jackson.
	Feb 17	Lord Howe Island discovered by Lt. Ball on board HMS Supply.
1789	Jan 4	First blocks of land sold in Sydney.
	Oct 6	First mainland built vessel, the **Rose Hill** Packet, launched in Sydney.
	Nov 21	First convict (James Ruse) granted land at Parramatta.
1790	June 3	First ship of Second Fleet, **Lady Juliana**, arrived at heads.
	June 26	Bulk of ships of Second Fleet moored at Sydney Cove with large cargo of much needed food.

1791	Nov 10	Ship ***Britannia*** returned to Sydney after completing successful whaling and sealing expedition (challenge to East India Co. monopoly).
1792	Nov 1	American brigantine ***Philadelphia*** anchored in Sydney Cove (first trading vessel to arrive).
1795	Sept 11	Captain John Hunter took up office as 2nd Governor of NSW.
1800	Sept 28	Captain Phillip King took over from John Hunter as 3rd Governor of NSW.
1806	Aug 13	Captain William Bligh took office as 4th Governor of New South Wales (NSW).
1810	Jan 1	Major General Lachlan Macquarie took office as 5th Governor of NSW.
1812	Oct 19	Two hundred convicts disembark from the ***Indefatigable*** in Hobart (first convicts to sail direct to Van Diemen's Land).
1813	May 31	Explorers Blaxland, Lawson and Wentworth completed crossing of Blue Mountains.
	Sept 30	The 'holy dollar' and its middle, the 'bump' became Australia's first currency
1814	Feb 22	Sydney to Liverpool road completed.
1816	May 10	*Hobart Town and Southern Reporter* founded.
1817	April 8	Bank of NSW established by group of merchants.
	Dec 21	The name 'Australia' officially adopted by Governor Macquarie and used in despatch to Lord Bathurst.

Appendix A

1818	Nov 13	Macquarie lighthouse (Sydney's South Head) turned on.
1821	Dec 1	Major General Sir Thomas Brisbane assumed office as 6th Governor of NSW.
1824	Feb 3	A penal colony established at Moreton Bay (near Redcliffe).
	May 12	Colonel George Arthur arrived in Hobart Town and took up post as Governor of Van Diemen's Land.
1825	June 14	Van Diemen's Land became a separate colony.
	Sept 10	Name 'Brisbane' used for settlement at Moreton Bay.
	Dec 17	Lt. General Ralph Darling became 7th Governor of NSW.
1826	April 8	Australia's first oil lamps lit in Macquarie Street, Sydney.
1828	March 8	GPO established and first stamps released.
1829	May 2	Captain Charles Fremantle claimed the western third of Australia for Britain when he arrived at the Swan River.
	June 18	Fremantle settled.
	Aug 12	Perth named after the town in Scotland and founded by Captain James Stirling.
1833	Nov 30	Gunpowder in hold of brig **Ann Jamison** exploded during unloading cargo in Sydney (8 died).
1835	April 12	Convict ship, **George III**, wrecked against rocks at D'Entrecasteaux Channel, Tasmania, with loss of 134 lives.

	May 13	Convict ship **Neva** went down in heavy seas after breaking up upon rocks in Navarine Reef off north point of King Island, Bass Strait.
	June 10	Australia's first political party formed when William Wentworth founded the Australian Patriotic Association.
	July 16	The barque **Enchantress** wrecked on rocks in D'Entrecasteaux Channel, Tasmania (50 people died).
1836	Jan 12	Biologist and founder of evolutionary theory, Charles Darwin, arrived in Sydney on the **HMS Beagle**.
	July 27	South Australia's first settlers arrived at Kangaroo Island.
	Sept 9	Governor Bourke announced that Port Phillip district was available for settlement.
	Dec 27	Colonel William Light outlined the plan for Adelaide.
	Dec 28	Captain John Hindmarsh arrived at Holdfast bay, SA, to take up post as first Governor.
1838	Jan 1	Melbourne's *Advertiser* published for the first time.
	Feb 24	Sir George Gipps took office as 9th Governor of NSW.
1840	Nov 18	Two hundred and sixty nine convicts arrived in Sydney Cove on the **Eden** (last group of convicts to NSW).
1841	May 3	New Zealand proclaimed a colony independent of NSW.

	May 15	George Grey began duties as South Australia's 3rd Governor.
	May 24	Streets of Sydney illuminated by gas light for the first time.
1845	Aug 4	Canadian built barque, **Cataraqui** (800 ton), struck rocks off King Island in Bass Strait (406 drowned).
	Oct 25	Lieutenant Colonel Frederick Holt Robe took up duty as 4th Governor of SA.
1846	June 2	*Melbourne Argus* first published.
1848	Aug 2	Sir Henry Young took up office as South Australia's 5th Governor.
1849	Jan 20	Vessel **Fortitude** docked in Moreton Bay, Queensland, with 245 immigrants, sponsored by Rev J D Lang.
	April 13	Melbourne's first postal service began.
	July 21	First clipper ship, **Phoenician**, to arrive in Australia docked at Port Jackson.
1850	Jan 1	Standard postage (Sydney Views) introduced throughout NSW (3d overseas, 2d next State or 1d local).
	Jan 3	Victoria's first stamps issued (featuring Queen Victoria).
	Sept 6	Protest in Sydney over transportation of convicts from UK, attracted 17,000 people who wanted it stopped.

1851	Feb 6	Thousands of square miles of Victorian land set alight from Geelong to South Australian border (10 people die).
	Feb 12	Edmund Hargraves found gold near Bathurst.
	July 1	Victoria formally separated from NSW.
	Oct 24	Sixteen men elected to first elected Legislative Council in Van Diemen's Land.
1852	Aug 3	First mail steamer to arrive in Australia (**Chusan**) docked at Sydney Cove.
1853	May 25	Last convict ship to Van Diemen's Land, **St Vincent**, carrying 207 convicts docked at Hobart Town.
1854	Jan 30	Regular Cobb & Co coach service between Bendigo and Melbourne commenced.
	July 5	First edition of *Hobart Mercury* published.
	Sept 12	Australia's first steam railway line opened, between Flinders Street and Port Melbourne.
	Sept 20	Melbourne to Geelong railway opened.
	Dec 3	Battle of Eureka Stockade took place in Victoria.
1855	Jan 20	William Denison took up office as NSW's 19th Governor.
	May 14	Australia's first mint opened in Macquarie Street, Sydney.
	June 9	Sir Richard MacDonnell assumed office as South Australia's 6th Governor.

	July 21	Queen Victoria signed the Constitution Act, which gave NSW, Victoria, Tasmania and SA self-government (Queensland followed in 1863 and WA remained a crown colony until 1890).
	Sept 26	NSW's first railway opened between Sydney and Parramatta.
1856	Jan 1	Name Tasmania officially adopted (although already in common use), followed by a Grand Tasmanian Regatta the next day to celebrate.
	March 19	Victoria introduced Australia's first secret ballot.
	April 2	South Australia became 2nd colony to adopt secret ballot.
	April 26	South Australia's first steam train made inaugural run between Adelaide and Port Adelaide.
	May 22	First meeting of NSW Parliament held in Parramatta.
	Nov 21	Victorian Parliament sat for first time.
	Dec 2	First Tasmanian Parliament sat.
1857	April 14	Torrens Title of land ownership set up by Robert Torrens in South Australia (made tracing ownership back to original grant unnecessary).
	April 21	South Australia's government sat for first time.
	Aug 20	Fully-rigged vessel ***Dunbar*** struck rocks at Sydney's South Head (one survivor from 59 crew and 63 passengers).
	Oct 24	Clipper ***Catherine Adamson*** smashed against rocks at Sydney's North Head (20 drowned).

	Nov 24	Victoria granted male suffrage.
1858	Oct 29	Telegraph between Sydney and Melbourne completed.
	Nov 24	NSW introduced male suffrage and secret ballot.
1859	Aug 6	The *Amelia*, 395 ton, struck a sunken reef and sank off the SA/Vic border (91 drowned).
	Dec 10	George Ferguson Bowen assumed office as Queensland's first Governor.
1860	May 22	Queensland's first government met at the old convict barracks in Brisbane.
1861	Feb 11	After departing Melbourne in August 1860 Robert Burke and William Wills reached the Gulf of Carpentaria.
	April 13	Queensland's first telegraph service began (Brisbane to Ipswich).
	Nov 7	First Melbourne Cup won by Archer.
	Dec 23	First horse drawn trams appeared in Sydney streets.
1864	June 2	Steamer *Rainbow* lost at sea during a heavy gale near Seal Rocks Bay in NSW (seven drowned).
	Oct 1	First edition of the *Australian* published.
1865	July 31	Queensland's first railway opened between Ipswich and Grandchester.
1866	July 12	Steamship *Cawarra* wrecked on rocks near Newcastle (sixty people lost).

1868	Jan 9	The last convict ship, the ***Hougoumont***, arrived in Fremantle with 279 convicts.
	March 12	His Royal Highness Prince Albert, Duke of Edinborough, was shot in an assassination attempt while attending a gala picnic day in Sydney.
1869	Sept 11	*Weekly Times* first published in Melbourne.
1870	Jan 21	First settlers arrive in Darwin.
1872	May 6	Adelaide's General Post Office opened.
1872	Oct 22	Australia first talked to London by telegraph.
1873	July 30	Sir George Ferguson Bowen assumed office as Victoria's 6th Governor.
1875	Jan 23	William Cairns assumed office as Queensland's 4th Governor.
	Feb 24	Three-masted steamer, ***Gothenburg***, struck the Great Barrier Reef, south of Townsville, Queensland (102 lives lost out of 129 on board).
1876	March 21	Seventeen people drowned when the 86-ton steamship ***Banshee*** was pushed against rocks during a heavy storm at Cape Sandwich, Queensland.
	April 4	Railway line between Sydney and Bathurst completed.
	April 25	Adelaide University opened its doors to students.
1877	March 15	Australia played England in first cricket test, played at Melbourne Cricket Ground (Australia won by 45 runs).
	March 25	Caroline Chisholm died at Liverpool.

	July 19	Sir Arthur Kennedy became Queensland's 5th Governor.
	Oct 2	Sir William Jervois became South Australia's 10th Governor.
1878	Jan 8	First public demonstration of telephone held in warehouse in Elizabeth Street, Melbourne.
	March 20	First shed in Melbourne's Queen Victoria Market opened.
	June 10	Inauguration of Adelaide's horse drawn trams.
	July 22	Three masted iron barque, ***James Service***, struck Murray Reef, south west of Perth (24 drowned).
1879	Feb 19	The Kelly Gang held up Bank of NSW at Jerilderie, NSW.
	Sept 16	Horse drawn trams commenced operation in Sydney.
1880	April 10	Sir William Cleaver Robinson assumed office as WA's 11th Governor.
1880	April 16	Compulsory state schooling for 6 to 14 year olds introduced throughout NSW.
	Oct 20	An Act of Parliament changed the name of Hobart Town to Hobart.
	Nov 11	Bushranger Ned Kelly hanged.
1881	April 3	Australia's first simultaneous census taken (2,250,194 white people living in colonies).
1882	Nov 11	The 5,580 ton coal steamer ***Austral*** sank in Sydney Harbour (5 drowned).

Appendix A

1883	June 2	Sir Frederick Napier Broom took office as WA's 12th Governor.
	June 14	Rail link between Sydney and Melbourne completed at Albury.
	Nov 6	Anthony Musgrave took office as Queensland's 6th Governor.
1885	April 1	Steam train services began between Victor Harbour and Adelaide.
	Aug 10	Horse drawn trams were put into use along Brisbane's Queen Street.
1886	Dec 7	Steamship, **Keilawarra**, sank after colliding with the **Helen Nicol** off North Solitary Island, NSW (43 drowned).
1887	Jan 19	Victoria and South Australia became linked by rail.
	Oct 20	The 1226 ton steamship **Cheviot** came to grief off Phillip Heads, Melbourne (35 drowned).
1888	July 13	Cargo vessel, the **Star of Greece**, smashed against rocks at Lion Point, south of Adelaide (17 died).
1889	April 11	The Earle of Kintore, Algernon Keith-Falconer, assumed office as South Australia's 12th Governor.
	May 1	Sir Henry Wylie Norman assumed office as Queensland's 7th Governor.
	Oct 14	Melbourne's first electric tram service (Box Hill to Doncaster) began operation.
1890	Feb 6	A meeting of colonial delegates began formulation of the Australian Constitution in Adelaide.

1890	Feb 28	Royal merchant ship, **Quetta**, struck uncharted rock off Cape York Peninsula (of 284 on board, 134 drowned).
	April 26	Banjo Patterson's poem "Man from Snowy River" first published in *The Bulletin*.
1891	Sept 6	Barque *Fiji* wrecked near Moonlight Head, Victoria (12 drowned).
	Oct 27	Melbourne to St Kilda tramline opened.
1893	Dec 28	Steamship **Alert** came to grief on rocks off Cape Shanck, Victoria (14 died).
1894	Sept 3	Vessel **Cambus** struck rocks of Stradbroke Island, Queensland (5 died).
	Dec 21	South Australia first state to give women the right to vote and to stand for parliament.
1895	Oct 29	Sir Thomas Buxton assumed office as South Australia's 13th Governor.
1896	April 9	Lord Lamington took office as Queensland's 8th Governor.
1897	March 22	A convention headed by Edmund Barton in Adelaide formulated what would be moulded into the Australian Constitution.
	June 21	Electric tram service began in Brisbane.
1899	April 10	Baron Tennyson began four year term as South Australia's 14th Governor.

Appendix A

NOTE: The following sources were drawn upon to compile this calendar of key events in Australian history to the end of the nineteenth century:

- Barker, Anthony. What Happened When. A Chronology of Australia from 1788. North Sydney 1992.

- Brown, Robin. Milestones in Australian History, 1788 to the Present. Sydney 1986.

- Fraser, Bryce Ed. The Macquarie Book of Events. McMahon's Point, NSW 1984.

- Perno, Richard. The Diary of Australia. Kenthurst, NSW 1987.

APPENDIX B

Glossary of Terms

In order to assist the reader, who might be unfamiliar with the nautical terms that will be encountered in this book a list of the more common nautical and other unusual terms are provided in this appendix.

Able-bodied	Refers to an experienced seaman, as distinct from a less experienced ordinary seaman.
Abeam	At or from a point level with the centre of the hull of a vessel.
Amidships	A point midway along the centre-line of a hull, but commonly used for the centre part of a vessel.
Ballast	Heavy substances (including water, if tanks are fitted) carried, low down in the hull, to stabilise an empty vessel.
Barquentine	Vessel of three or more masts; square rigged on the fore, fore and aft rigged on the others.
Beam	Width of a hull at its widest point.
Beam ends	A vessel is said to be 'on her beam ends' when forced completely over on her side.

Appendix B

Beam wind	A wind blowing at or close to right angles to the length of the vessel.
Bear up	To turn a vessel's head away from the wind.
Beat	To advance towards the wind by a series of alternate tacks.
Bowspit	Spar projecting from the bows, and setting the head-sails.
Brig	Vessel of two masts, square rigged on each.
Broach-to	Describes a vessel unable to be controlled by her helm and lying broadside to high sea, in danger of capsizing or being dismasted.
Catwalk	A railed foot bridge connecting the superstructures on a vessels main-deck.
Clew	Generally refers to the bottom corner of a sail to which sheets are attached to work the sail.
Companion	A stairway leading below from the deck
Dead-reckoning	Navigation based purely on course and distance, without aid of celestial observation.
Doldrums	Sections of calm, with fickle winds and often heavy rain-squalls, lying between the Trade-wind regions.
Draught	The depth of water required to float a vessel.
Easting	An open areas of sea where strong westerly winds prevail (for ships coming to Australia via the Cape of Good Hope these occur below latitude 45 S). These conditions enable fast and continuous

eastward sailing. This was referred to as 'running the Easting down'.

Feedin the fishes	Term used to describe sea sick passengers hanging over the side of a vessel.
Forward	Pronounced 'forrard', is towards the bow of a vessel.
Full-rigged	A sailing vessel with three or more masts, all of which are square-rigged.
Galley	Kitchen on a vessel.
Harpie	A person who preyed on travellers waiting to embark ship.
Heave-to	To put a vessel (during bad weather) with her weather bow facing wind and sea, with the sails trimmed so that she rides in that position. May also involve setting her sails aback in order to check forward progress.
Jib	A triangular sail set between foremast and bowsprit.
Ketch	Two-masted, fore and aft rigged vessel, the mizzen being stepped forward on the stern post.
Lee	The side of the vessel away from the wind; opposite to the weather.
Nautical mile	A mile at sea; equal to 1852 metres.
Packet	A passenger vessel engaged in regular mail-carrying service.
Passage	A journey between two ports.
Plain-sail	Full, normal orthodox sail.

Port	The left-hand side of a vessel (facing forward).
Port tack	A vessel sailing with the wind blowing on her port side.
Reefing	To decrease the area of sail by using only the upper section (or reef).
Scuppers	Gully or open drain running around the outer edge of a deck
Sheets	Ropes, wires or tackles, attached to clews of sails or ends of booms, for purpose of working them when sail is set.
Square-rigger	A sailing vessel whose masts carry yards from which square sail is set.
Tack	To put a vessel about by bringing her head across the wind; a series of tacks producing a zigzag course towards the wind.
'Tween decks	Area between decks used to accommodate steerage passengers.
Veer	To let out a line or cable.
Windlass	A large capstan (drum) employed to raise the anchor.
Windward	The weather side of a vessel; opposite to leeward.
Yards	Spars that cross the masts of a square-rigged vessel. They are attached to the mast at their centre point.
Yard-arm	These are the outer extremity of a vessel's yards.

Bibliography

Adamson, Margaret. Australian Women Through 200 Years. Kangaroo Press, 1988.
Alison, Grant. Sailing Ships and Emigrants in Victorian Times. London, 1872.
Aspin, James. Emigration Who Should Emigrate How to Emigrate and Where to Emigrate. Howden, 1884.
Ball, Adrian. Is Yours An SS Great Britain Family? Hampshire Mason, 1988.
Bassett, Jan ed. The Oxford Illustrated Dictionary of Australian History. Oxford University Press, Melbourne, 1993.
Bassett, J, Bomford, J, & Abrahams, O. Voices From the Past Australian History to Federation. Jacaranda Press, 1994.
Berzins, Baiba. The Coming of the Strangers. Life in Australia 1788-1822. Collins, 1988.
Bowen, Farnk, C. The Golden Age of Sail. London, 1825.
Boyce, James. Van Diemen's Land. Black Inc., 2008.
Brophy, Patrick. Sailing Ships. Middlesex, England, 1974.
Broen, Bruce & Morrissey, Sylvia. Old Dreams and New Australia to 1901. Edward Arnold (Australia) Pty. Ltd., 1989.
Broome, Richard. The Victorians Arriving. Fairfax, Syme & Weldon Associates, 1984.
Cannon, Michael. Who's Master? Who's Man? Penguin Books Australia, 1988.
Carrothers, W.A. Emigration From the British Isles. Orchard House, 1929.
Carter, William E. & Carter, Merri, S. The Age of Sail: A Time When the Fortunes of Nations & Lives of Seamen Literally Turned with the Winds Their Ships Encountered at Sea. The Journal of Navigation, 2010, No. 63, pp. 717-731.

Castleton, Phillip. Last Voyage of a Jinxed Ship. Geo, Australasia's Geographical Magazine, Volume 14, Number 2, May-July 1992, pp.75-85.
Charlwood, Don. The Long Farewell. Settlers Under Sail. Allen Lane, 1981.
Charlwood, Don. Wrecks & Reputations. Angus & Robertson, 1977.
Chuck, Florence. The Somerset Years. Pennard Hill Publications, 1987.
Clark, C.M.H. A History of Australia III. The Beginning of An Australian Civilization 1824-1851. Melbourne University Press, 1979.
Clarke, Patricia. The Governesses Letters From The Colonies 1862-1882. Hutchinson Publishing, 1985.
Coleman, Peter & Tanner, Les. Cartoons of Australian History. Nelson, 1967.
Collett, David and Pocock, Celmara. Assessment of the Indigenous National Heritage Values for Wurrwurrwuy Stone Picture Site. A Report to the Department of the Environment and Heritage. University of Southern Queensland July 2012.
Cornwell, E.L. ed. The Illustrated History of Ships. Octopus Books Limited, 1979.
Crowley, Frank. A New History of Australia. William Heinemann, 1974.
Day, David. Claiming a Continent: A New History of Australia. Harper Collins, 2001.
Day, David. Coming South Australia's Days of Sail. Australia Post, 1998.
Dean, Phillis. The First Industrial Revolution. Cambridge University Press, 1967.
Derby, W. L. A. The Tall Ships Pass. David & Charles Ltd., 1970.
Dugan, Michael & Szware, Josef. Australia's Migrant Experience. Edward Arnold (Australia) Pty. Ltd., 1987.
Fitzpatrick, David, ed. Home or Away? Immigrants in Colonial Australia. Australian National University, 1992.
Flannery, Tim ed. The Explorers. Text Publishing, 1998.
Flannery, Tim ed. Watkin Tench 1788. The Text Publishing Company, 1996.
Gammage, Bill. The Biggest Estate on Earth. Allen & Unwin, 2012.

Giggal, Kenneth. Great Classic Sailing Ships. Chancellor Press, 1994.

Greenhill, Basil & Giffard, Ann. Travelling by Sea in the Nineteenth Century. London, 1972.

Greenhill, Basil & Giffard, Ann. Women Under Sail. David & Charles, Newton Abbott, 1970.

Gross, Alan. Charles Joseph La Trobe. Melbourne University Press, 1956.

Haines, Robin. Emigration and the Labouring Poor: Australian Recruitment in Britain and Ireland 1831-60. Macmillan, 1997.

Haines, Robin. Doctors at Sea: Emigrant Voyages to Colonial Australia. Palgrave Macmillan, 2005.

Haines, Robin. Life and Death in the Age of Sail: the Passage to Australia. University of New South Wales Press, 2003.

Haines, Robin & Schomowitz, Ralph. Nineteenth Century Immigration from the United Kingdom to Australia: an Estimate of the Percentage Who Were Government Assisted. Flinders University, South Australia, 1990.

Hamilton, Pauline. The Irish. Thomas Nelson (Australia) Ltd., 1978.

Handy, Amy. The Golden Age of Sail. Robert M. Tod, 1996.

Hasluck, Alexandra. Unwilling Emigrants. Oxford University Press, 1959.

Hassam, Andrew. Sailing to Australia. Shipboard Diaries By Nineteenth-Century British Emigrants. Manchester University Press, 1994.

Hawkins, David T. Bound For Australia. The History Press, 2012.

Hodgson, Arthur. Emigration to the Australian Settlements. Second edition. Trelawney Saunders, London, 1849.

Horden, Marsden. King of the Australian Coast. The Work of Phillip Parker King in the Mermaid and Bathurst 1817-1822. Melbourne University Press, 2002.

Horne, Donald. The Story of Australian People. Readers Digest, 1985.

Hughes, Robert. The Fatal Shore. Vintage, 2003.

Inglis, K.S. Australian Colonists. An Exploration of Social History 1788-1870. Melbourne University Press, 1993.

Isaacs, Jennifer. Australian Dreaming 40,000 Years of Aboriginal History. Lansdowne Press, 1982.

Jones, W.H.S. All Hands Aloft! London, 1969.

Joyce, Alfred. A Homestead History. Oxford University Press, 1969.

Keneally, Tom. The Commonwealth of Thieves. Random House, 2006.
Kociumbas, Jan. The Oxford History of Australia, Volume 2 1770-1860. Oxford University Press, 1992.
Koskie, Jack L. Ships That Shaped Australia. Angus & Robertson, 1987.
Laird Clowes, G.S. Sailing Ships Their History and Development, Part I. London, 1930.
Lane, Peter. The Victorian Age 1830-1914. B.T.Batsford Ltd, 1972.
Little, Norman. Australia's Foundations. Longman Cheshire, 1972.
Lubbock, Basil. The Blackwall Frigates. Glasgow, 1922.
Lubbock, Basil. The Colonial Clippers. Glasgow, 1924.
MacDougall, P.L. Emigration. It's Advantages to Great Britain and Her Colonies. T&W Boone, London, 1848.
MacKenzie, J.M. Sealing, Sailing and Settling in South-Western Victoria. Lowden Publishing Co., Kilmore, 1976.
Maconochie, K.H. Emigration With Advice to Emigrants. Olliver, London, 1848.
Madgwick, R.B. Immigration Into Eastern Australia 1788-1851. Sydney University Press, 1969.
Malthus, Thomas. An essay on the Principle of Population. London, 1798.
Martin, Terry. Maritime Paintings of Early Australia 1788-1900. Melbourne University Press, 1998.
McConville, Chris. Croppies, Celts & Catholics. The Irish in Australia. Edward Arnold (Australia) Pty. Ltd., 1987.
Meredith, Louisa Anne (Mrs. Charles). Notes and Sketches of New South Wales. Ure Smith, 1973.
Mills, Richard Charles. The Colonization of Australia (1829-42). The Wakefield Experiment in Empire Building. Sydney University Press, 1974.
Morgan, Dalma & Poole, Harry. Voyage of a Lifetime. Adelaide, 1978.
Morsely, Clifford. News From The English Countryside 1750-1850. Harrap, London, 1979.
National Library of Australia. Mapping Our World Terra Incognita To Australia. NLA, 2014.
Noble, John. The Golden Age of Sail of Australia and New Zealand. Currey O'Neil Ross Pty. Ltd., 1985.

Northrup, David. Indentured Labour in the Age of Imperialism 1834-1922. Cambridge University Press, 1995.
O'Farrell, Patrick. The Irish in Australia. New South Wales University Press, 1987.
O"Neill, Judith. Transported to Van Diemen's Land. Cambridge University Press, 1977.
Parsons, Ronald. Migrant Ships for South Australia 1836-1850. Parsons, 1983.
Parsons, Ronald. Sailing in the South. Rigby Limited, 1975.
Pook, Henry. A Worker's Paradise? A History of Working People in Australia, 1788-1901. Oxford University Press, 1981.
Priestley, Susan. The Victorians Making Their Mark. Fairfax, Syme & Weldon Associates, 1984.
Richards, Eric ed. Poor Australian Immigrants in the Nineteenth Century. Australian National University, Research School of Social Sciences, 1991.
Richards, Eric, Reid, Richard & Fitzpatrick, David. Visible Immigration. Australian National University, 1989.
Rickard, John. Australia A Cultural History. Longman, 1988.
Robinson, Tony. History of Australia. Viking, 2011.
Roe, J. Marvelous Melbourne, The Emergence of an Australian City. Hicks, Smith & Sons, Sydney, 1974.
Shaw, A.G.L. Modern World History 1780-1950, Books 1 and 2. F.W. Cheshire, 1959.
Sherington, Geoffrey. Australia's Immigrants 1788-1988. Allen & Unwin, 1980.
Sidney, Samuel. The Three Colonies of Australia: New South Wales, Victoria and South Australia. London, 1852.
Smith, James Montague. Send the Boy to Sea. The Five Mile Press, 2001.
Smyth, Dacre. Immigrant Ships to Australia. 1992.
Snodin, David. A Mighty Ferment. Britain in the Age of Revolution 1750-1850. The Seabury Press, 1978.
Sutherland, Alexander. Victoria and its Metropolis, Past & Present, Volume 1. McCarron, Bird & Co. Melbourne, 1888.
Sweny, Christopher. Transported In Place of Death Convicts In Australia. MacMillan, 1981.

Terry, Martin. Maritime Paintings of Early Australia 1788-1900. Melbourne University Press, 1998.
Townsley, W.A. Tasmania From Colony To Statehood 1803-1945. St. David's Park Publishing, 1991.
Tudball, Libby. Australians Our Lives Through Time. Rigby, 1988.
Villiers, Alan. Men Ships and the Sea. National Geographic Society, Washington, 1963.
Villiers, Alan. The Way of a Ship. Hodder & Stoughton, 1954.
Villiers, Alan. Vanished Fleets. Sea Stories From Old Van Diemen's Land. Cambridge, 1974.
Walker, Mary Howitt. Come Wind, Come Weather. Melbourne University Press, 1971.
Wilson, Charles. Australia 1788-1988, The Creation of A Nation. Weidenfeld & Nicholson, London, 1987.

INDEX

Aberdeen, 114, 122
Aboriginal people, 2–3, 5, 11, 13, 243
Aborigines, see Aboriginal people
Adamant, 67
Adelaide, 13, 45, 53, 68–70, 128, 135, 153, 162, 171, 180, 198, 216, 227, 251, 254, 256–259
agriculture, 9, 26–27, 30–31, 43, 62, 74, 101
agricultural/farm labourers, 27, 34, 38–39, 41–42, 44, 46, 48, 57, 60, 62, 65, 72–75, 90–91, 98–99, 101–102, 160, 241
agricultural servants, *see* farm servants gricultural workers, *see* agricultural/farm labourers
Albert William, 135
Alert, 259
Amelia, 255
America, 74, 79, 110–111, 199
 and ship-building, 126, 128, 249
 colonies, 8, 17
 emigration to, 1, 11, 46–47, 53, 55, 80, 82, 85, 89–90, 153–154
 plantations, 7
 War of Independence, 10, 32
Amity, 12
Ann Jamison, 250
Arab, 163, 224–225
Arnhem Land, 2–4, 6
artisans, 48, 91, 99, 233
assisted emigration, 9, 23, 26, 40, 46–67, 69–70, 72, 82, 84–86, 90, 94–96, 98–99, 101–102, 128, 131, 144, 153–154, 159–160, 166, 233, 236
 and skilled labour, 9, 58, 101
 Bounty Scheme(s), 51, 59–66, 90
 for females, 48–51, 54–56, 95–96, 101
 from Scotland, 37, 57, 89, 98, 233
 from Ireland, 54, 57, 89, 98
 government assistance, 46–58, 94
 Government Scheme, 51–53, 59
 indenture, 66–67, 92
 Irish Orphan Scheme, 53
 land sales, 48
 mechanics, 48
 private schemes, 66–67
assisted passage, *see* assisted emigration
Austral, 257
Banks, Joseph, 17
Banshee, 256
barques, 6, 106–107, 132, 135, 174–175, 203, 251–252, 257, 259
Bass, George, 6
Bateman, John, 13
Baudin, Nicolas, 6
Beejapore, 131
Benevolent and Strangers' Friend Society, 241
Bentham, Jeremy, 8

Birt, Louisa, 79
births at sea, 130, 135, 207–208, 244
Black, Captain Thomas, 134, 249
Bligh, Governor William, 10, 249
Blue Mountains, crossing of, 18, 101, 249
Botany Bay, 6, 8, 248
bounty schemes, 46, 51, 59–66, 77, 90–91, 96, 100, 152, 162, 178, 201, 222
    and children, 77, 100
    and shipowners, 60–66
    and the Colonial Office, 64, 90
    and the Land Board, 63–65
    bounty immigrants, 60–65, 77, 90, 96, 178, 222, 236
    bounty rates, 61, 63
Bourke, Governor, 13, 60, 251
Bourneuf, 128–129
Boyle, Captain Thomas H, 129–130
Boyter, Dr, 90
Brightman, 203, 231
Brilliant, 61
Brisbane, 12–13, 250, 255, 258–259
Brisbane, Sir Thomas, 94, 250
Britannia, 249
British Government, *see also* Colonial Land and Emigration Commission
    and assisted emigration, 47
    and Bounty Schemes, 51, 57, 59, 64–65
    and expenditure on the colonies, 66
    and the Emigrations Advances Act, 57
British King, 91

Buffalo, 225
Caledonia, 225–226
Cambus, 259
Cape York Peninsula, 4, 259
Carriage of Passengers in Merchant Vessels Act, 205
Caroline, 67
Caroline Chisholm, 176
Cataraqui, 222, 252
Catherine Adamson, 254
Cawarra, 255
Cheviot, 258
childbirth, see births at sea
children, 1, 9, 12, 14, 23, 55–56, 60–61, 75, 77, 79, 100, 131, 142, 155–156, 200, 206–208, 243–244
    deaths of, 35–36, 123, 128, 131, 196–197, 208, 222
    on vessels (numbers and conditions), 15–16, 50, 96, 100, 123, 131, 157, 162, 170, 177–178, 201, 2 07–208, 212
    health, welfare and education of, 39, 43, 77, 79, 160, 197, 235
China, 17
    and the gold rush, 92–93
    Chinese traders, 3–4
    emigration from, 87, 91–92
Chisholm, Caroline, 76–77, 97, 176–177, 240
cholera, 33, 35–36, 49, 134, 189
Chusan, 253
CLEC, *see* Colonial Land and Emigration Commission
Clements, William, 69–70
Clifton, 176, 194, 206, 211

clippers, 110–114, 117, 119, 124–127, 133, 169, 252, 254
Colonial Land and Emigration Commission, 53–54, 56, 150, 161
Colonial Office, 49, 64, 77, 90, 99, 128, 236
Commissioners for Emigration, 19, 48–49, 55, 128, 130–131, 144, 150, 153, 161–162, 169, 189–190, 201–202
Comus, 134
Constance, 184, 187–190
convicts, 7–13, 15, 25, 47, 63, 77, 84–85, 89, 92, 94–95, 233–235, 248–253, 255–256
    convict ships, 109, 167–168, 170, 199, 204
    deaths at sea, 224
    from Ireland, 85, 89
Cook, Captain James, 2, 5–6, 219
Corn Laws, 28
Coromandel, 135
Crofters, 36–38, 213
    and assisted immigration, 89–90
Croesus, 121–122
Cutty Sark, 112–113
Dampier, William, 5–6
Darwin, settlement of, 14, 256
deaths at sea, 128–131, 134–135, 179, 189, 193–194, 196–197, 200, 207–208, 219–224, 250–259
diarrhoea, 128–130, 189, 197
Dickens, Charles, 77, 100
disease and sickness
    cholera, 33, 35–36, 49, 134, 189
    diarrhoea, 128–130, 189, 197
    measles, 123, 128, 131, 160, 196–197
    scarlet fever, 128, 130, 160, 196–197
    seasickness, 138, 146–147, 178, 185, 189, 197, 199–200, 205–206, 208, 214
    smallpox, 34, 56, 160
    typhus, 35, 130, 179
    whooping cough, 160, 197
Dover Castle, 137–139
Dunbar, 220–221, 254
Duyfken, 5
Dutch East India Company, 3, 5, 11, 109, 249
East India Company, *see* Dutch East India Company
East Indiamen, 109–110, 167–169
Eden, 251
Eendracht, 5
Elliot, Thomas Frederick, 51–53
Ellora, 177
Emigration Advances Act, 57
Emigration Commissioners, See Commissioners for Emigration
Emigration Committee, 95, 158–159
Enchantress, 251
enclosure, of land in Britain, 27
Family Colonisation Loan Society, 77, 176, *see also* Chisholm, Caroline
farm labourers, *see* agricultural/ farm labourers
farm servants, 52, 60, 65
farmers, as immigrants, 9–10, 66, 94, 101
Faulkner, John, 13

Female Middle Class Emigration Society, 78, 155
females, 77–78, 157
    and gender imbalance, 48, 52, 95–97, 240
    and assisted emigration, 48–51, 54–56, 95–97, 101
    emigration of, 65, 85, 130–131, 233–235, 240–241
Flinders, Matthew, 3–4, 6
Forbes, James 'Bully', 124
Fortitude, 161, 252
free emigrants, See free settlers
free settlers, 8–10, 15–18, 47, 55, 84–85, 232–236, 240
Gag Acts, 31
Game Laws, 27
gender imbalance, 48, 52, 95–97, 240
Godfrey, Captain, 184, 187 gold
    and Chinese immigrants, 91
    and impact on emigration, 23, 176, 184
    discovery of, 13, 57, 79–82, 88–89, 102, 110, 122–123, 183
    goldfields, 13, 65, 80, 92, 118, 239
    gold rushes, 47, 65, 79–80, 91–93, 98–99, 102, 128, 153, 176, 183, 239, 245
    shipments of, 123, 125, 132
Gothenburg, 256
Great Britain, 117–120, 140
Guthrey, Thomas, 223
Hargraves, Edward, 80

Harriott, 67
Harrison, John, 192
Hartog, Dirk, 5
Havering, 180, 229
Helen Nicol, 258
Henning, Rachel, 164
Hesperus, 187
highland clearances, 36, 38, 91
Hindmarsh, Captain John, 225–226, 251
Hobart Town, 11–12, 14, 17, 63, 97, 162, 178, 233, 249–250, 253, 257
HMS Beagle, 251
HMS Endeavour, 6
HMS Roebuck, 5
HMS Supply, 248
Hougoumont, 256
Howitt, William, 214–215
Hunter, Captain John, 10, 249
illiteracy, *see* literacy
Indefatigable, 249
India, emigration from, 92
indenture system, 67, 91–92
Ireland, 23, 26, 34–36, 48, 54, 73, 76, 84, 87–88, 158, 188–189, 213
    Commission on the Poor in Ireland, 34–36
    conditions in, 6, 34–36, 53–54, 57–58, 88–89, 99, 212
    emigration from, 57, 67, 73, 88, 99
    Irish convicts, 85
    Irish Orphan Scheme, 53
Fiji, 259
James Service, 257
Janszoon, Willem, 5

Jay, Charles, 74
Jennison, Joseph, 206
John, 174
John Barry, 195
Johnson, Dr Samuel, 193
Johnson, James, 221
Johnstone, William, 163, 224
Kangaroo Island, 13, 217–218, 227
Keilawarra, 258
Kent, 167, 214
King, Captain Philip Parker, 3
Labour, skilled, see skilled labour
Lady Ebrington, 106
Lady Juliana, 248
Lady McNaghten, 167–168, 195
Land Board, 236
    and Bounty Schemes, 63–65, 77
land grants, 8–9, 16, 59, 66–67
land sales, and assisted emigration, 47–48
Lang, J Dunmore, 78–79, 176
    and mechanics, 79
Larpent, 176
Layton, 96, 196
letters from the colonies, 45, 70, 73, 146, 164, 242–243, 245
Light, Colonel William, 13, 251
Lightning, 124–127
literacy, 25, 46, 72–73, 76, 93, 98, 212
Loch Ard, 221–222
London Emigration Commission, 49, 51
Lusitania, 136
Lysander, 130
Macassans, 2–3
Maitland, 196

Mackellar, Dorothea, 245
Malthus, Thomas, 16, 40
Marco Polo, 123–124, 212–213
Marmion, 206
McArthur, John, 18
McNeill, Sir John, 37
MacPherson, Annie, 79
measles, 123, 128, 131, 160, 196–197
mechanics, 48, 52, 60, 79, 94, 99
Melbourne, 13, 45, 94, 219, 221, 224, 226, 228, 232, 237, 239–242, 252–259
Merchant Shipping Act, 111, 219
Mermaid, 3
Midge, 224
Mona, 109, 196, 226
National Agricultural Labourers Union, 74–75
Neva, 251
New Guinea, see Papua New Guinea
New Holland, 5–6
New South Wales, 6, 8–11, 13, 15–18, 23, 52–55, 75, 80, 90, 92, 94, 99, 218, 235–236, 243–244, 249
    and Scottish emigration, 61
    assisted female emigration to, 48–51, 56
    and Bounty Schemes, 62–64, 85
    convict population, 15–16, 85
    labour shortages, 47, 65–66, 101
New Zealand, 8, 77–79, 91, 99, 121, 132, 135, 137, 153–154, 162, 181, 187, 219, 251
Newman, Charles, 229

Index

North America, See America
Northern Territory, 2, 14
Nugget, 228
occupations, see also skilled labour
    agricultural/farm labourers/ worker, 27, 34, 38–39, 41–42, 44, 46, 48, 57, 60, 62, 65, 72–75, 90–91, 98–99, 101–102, 160, 241
    agricultural/farm servants, 52, 60, 65
    artisans, 48, 91, 99, 233
    boot makers, 98
    carpenters, 44, 60, 98
    domestic servants, 9, 48–49, 60, 65, 78, 87, 97
    herdsmen, 65
    professionals (e.g. lawyers), 66, 98–100, 102
    masons, 60, 100
    mechanics, 48, 52, 60, 79, 94, 99
    shepherds, 44, 60, 65, 69, 91, 99, 160
    shopkeepers, 78, 92, 94, 102, 147
    smiths, 9, 60, 98
    wrights, 9, 60
Ollard, Ellen, 237
pamphlets, 18, 25, 40, 45, 72, 76, 145–146, 152
Pacific Islands, emigration from, 93
Palimira, 196
Papua New Guinea, 2, 4, 6
Passenger Acts, 167, 202, 208
pastoralists, see squatters
paupers, 49, 58, 84, 86
    and the emigration debate, 18–22
    and the Poor Laws, 39–42
Peel, Sir Robert, 28
Peel, Thomas, 66–67
Philadelphia, 249
Phillip, Governor Arthur, 6, 8–10, 248
Phoenician, 252
Plimsoll, Samuel, 219
poachers, 27–28
Poor Law(s), 31, 37, 43, 47, 54, 99, 103, 159
    and pauperism, 39–42
    Irish Poor Law Extension Act, 54
Poor Law Amendment Act, 43, 54
Port Jackson, 6, 131, 229, 248, 52
Port Phillip, 13, 44, 53, 62–63, 65–66, 90, 121, 129, 135, 167, 222–223, 251
potato famines and crop failures, 34–35, 37
Preussen, 132
Prince of Wales, 168–169
Queen, 117
Queensland, 12–13, 56, 70, 74–75, 89, 91, 93, 131, 252, 254–259
Queiros, Pedro Fernandex, 4
Quetta, 259
Rainbow, 255
Red Jacket, 78, 125–126
Roberts, Tom, 136
Robinson, Mary, 88
Rose Hill, 248
Rye, Maria, 77–79, 156
sailing ships, 104–105, 109–111, 121–122, 127, 132, 135, 167, 181, 192–193, 200, 218

278

sailing vessels
    Aberdeen, 122
    Adamant, 67
    Albert William, 135
    Alert, 259
    Amelia, 255
    Amity, 12
    Ann Jamison, 250
    Arab, 224–225
    Austral, 257
    Banshee, 256
    barque, 6, 106-107, 132, 135, 174–175, 203, 251–252, 257, 259
    Beejapore, 131
    Bourneuf, 128–129
    Brightman, 203, 231
    Brilliant, 61
    Britannia, 249
    British King, 91
    Buffalo, 225
    Caledonia, 225–226
    Cambus, 259
    Caroline, 121–122
    Caroline Chisholm, 176
    Cataraqui, 222, 252
    Catherine Adamson, 254
    Cawarra, 255
    Chusan, 255
    Cheviot, 258
    Clifton, 176, 193, 206, 211
    clippers, 110–114, 117, 119, 124–127, 133, 169, 252, 254
    Comus, 134
    Constance, 184, 187–190
    Coromandel, 135
    Croesus, 121–122
    Cutty Sark, 112–113
    David Scott, 5
    Dover Castle, 137–139
    Dunbar, 220–221, 254
    Duyfken, 5
    East Indiamen, 109–110, 167–169
    Eden, 251
    Eendracht, 5
    Ellora, 177
    Enchantress, 251
    Fiji, 259
    Fortitude, 161, 252
    George III, 250
    Gothenburg, 256
    Great Britain, 117–120, 140
    Harriott, 67
    Havering, 180, 229
    Helen Nichol, 258
    Hesperus, 187
    HMS Adventure, 219
    HMS Beagle, 251
    HMS Endeavour, 5
    HMS Roebuck, 106
    HMS Supply, 248
    Hougoumont, 256
    Indefatigable, 249
    James Service, 257
    John, 174, 195
    Keilawarra, 258
    Kent, 167, 214
    Lady Ebrington, 124
    Lady Juliana, 248
    Lady McNaghten, 167–168, 195
    Larpent, 176
    Layton, 196
    Lightning, 124–127

Loch Ard, 221–222
Lusitania, 136
Lysander, 130
Maitland, 196
Marco Polo, 123–124, 212–213
Marmion, 206
Mermaid, 96
Mona, 196, 226
Neva, 251
Nugget, 228
Palimira, 196
Philadelphia, 249
Phonecian, 252
Preussen, 132
Prince of Wales, 168–169
Queen, 117
Quetta, 259
Rainbow, 255
Red Jacket, 125–126
Rose Hill, 248
sailing ships, 104–105, 109–111, 121–122, 127, 132, 135, 167, 181, 192–193, 200, 218
Sarah, 57
Schomberg, 114–117, 124, 221
Shannon, 237
Slains Castle, 176
Skelton, 67
St James, 75
St Vincent, 253
Stag, 153, 171, 180, 204, 216
Star of Greece, 258
steamships, 110, 119–122, 131–132, 144, 255–256, 258–259
Strathfieldsaye, 96, 233–235
Superb, 208
Supply, 248
Thermopylae, 112–113
Ticonderoga, 129–130
Trade Wind, 178
Travancore, 176
William Rogers, 196
Sanger, Dr J C, 129
scarlet fever, 128, 130, 160, 196–197
Schomberg, 114–117, 124, 221
Scotland, 26, 36–38, 61–62, 66, 73, 76, 88–91, 103, 110, 148, 156, 233, 245, 250
    assisted emigration, 56–57, 61–62
    Scottish deaths during passage, 128–129
seasickness, 138, 146–147, 178, 185, 189, 197, 199–200, 205–206, 208, 214
sheep, *see* wool industry
ship builders, 108, 110
ship owners, 49, 106, 133, 219
ship owners, and Bounty Schemes, 60–66
shopkeepers, 78, 92, 94, 102, 147
sickness, *see* disease and sickness
Sidmouth, Lord, 30–31
Sidney, John, 21, 86
Sidney, Samuel, 45, 72, 87
Skelton, 67
skilled labour, shortage of/demand for, 43, 47, 58, 65, 86, 98–99, 101–102, 128, 244 *see also* occupations
Skirving, Dr R, 177
Slains Castle, 176

smallpox, 34, 56, 160
Superb, 209
South Australia, 13–14, 21, 37, 53, 55–56, 63, 72, 91, 99, 109, 130, 204, 225, 230–231, 241, 251–259
squatters, 13, 92–94, 99
St James, 75
St Vincent, 165, 253
Stag, 153, 171, 180, 197–198, 204, 216
Star of Greece, 258
Steam Navigation Act, 111
steamship, 110, 119–122, 131–132, 144, 255–256, 258–259
steerage passage, conditions, 128, 144–145, 153, 162, 165, 167–171, 176–179,195–197, 199, 204, 208, 213, 215
steerage passage, cost of, 46–47
steerage passengers, 46, 98, 126, 136, 144, 204, 239, 241
Strathfieldsaye, 96, 233–235
Sturt, Charles, 242–243
Sutherland, Alexander, 45
Swan River, 13, 66–67, 79, 250,
systematic colonisation, 21, 64, 94
Sydney, 11–14, 17, 49, 60, 65, 68, 76, 92, 96, 128, 131, 134, 177, 180, 182, 218, 220, 227, 233, 235, 245, 248–258
Tasmania, 6, 178, 209, 219, 248, 250–251, 254
Taylor, Francis, 153, 180, 197, 204, 216
Tench, Watkin, 243–244
Terra Australis, 4
Thermopylae, 112–113
Thompson, William, 204

Ticonderoga, 129–130
tonnage, 108–110, 171
Torres Strait, 4, 6
Trade Wind, 178
trade union movement, 74–75
transportation, 7–8, 13, 27–28, 85, 92, 224, 252
Travancore, 176
trepang, 2–3
typhus, 35, 130, 179
urbanisation, impact of, 26, 38
Van Diemen's Land, 13, 15, 89, 101, 253
    and Bounty Schemes, 62–64
    and indentured workers, 67
    assisted female migration to, 48
    convict population, 85
Veitch, Dr James William Henry, 129
Victoria, 13, 45, 53, 55–57, 66, 72, 80, 89, 91–92, 99, 117–118, 206, 219, 221, 252–259
Wakefield, Edward Gibbon, 21, 48, 59, 64
West Indies, 11, 17
Western Australia, 13, 55, 66, 79, 218
whooping cough, 160, 197
William Rogers, 196
wool industry, 14, 18, 23, 27, 67, 101, 113
workhouses, 26, 39, 41–43, 49, 53, 54, 58, 75, 77–78, 101, 153,
Wurrwurrwuy, 2

www.ingramcontent.com/pod-product-compliance
Lightning Source LLC
Chambersburg PA
CBHW040302170426
43194CB00021B/2863